STUDIES IN BAPTIST HISTORY AND THOUGHT
VOLUME 17

Edification and Beauty

The Practical Ecclesiology of the English Particular Baptists, 1675-1705

STUDIES IN BAPTIST HISTORY AND THOUGHT

STUDIES IN BAPTIST HISTORY AND THOUGHT
VOLUME 17

Edification and Beauty

The Practical Ecclesiology of the English Particular Baptists, 1675-1705

James M. Renihan

Foreword by Robert W. Oliver

WIPF & STOCK · Eugene, Oregon

Wipf and Stock Publishers
199 W 8th Ave, Suite 3
Eugene, OR 97401

Edification and Beauty
The Practical Ecclesiology of the English Particular Baptists, 1675–1705
By Renihan, James M.
Copyright©2008 Paternoster
ISBN 13: 9781498253031
Publication date 2/17/2009
Previously published by Paternoster, 2008

"This Edition Published by Wipf and Stock Publishers
by arrangement with Paternoster".

Series Preface

Baptists form one of the largest Christian communities in the world, and while they hold the historic faith in common with other mainstream Christian traditions, they nevertheless have important insights which they can offer to the worldwide church. Studies in Baptist History and Thought will be one means towards this end. It is an international series of academic studies which includes original monographs, revised dissertations, collections of essays and conference papers, and aims to cover any aspect of Baptist history and thought. While not all the authors are themselves Baptists, they nevertheless share an interest in relating Baptist history and thought to the other branches of the Christian church and to the wider life of the world.

The series includes studies in various aspects of Baptist history from the seventeenth century down to the present day, including biographical works, and Baptist thought is understood as covering the subject-matter of theology (including interdisciplinary studies embracing biblical studies, philosophy, sociology, practical theology, liturgy and women's studies). The diverse streams of Baptist life throughout the world are all within the scope of these volumes.

The series editors and consultants believe that the academic disciplines of history and theology are of vital importance to the spiritual vitality of the churches of the Baptist faith and order. The series sets out to discuss, examine and explore the many dimensions of their tradition and so to contribute to their on-going intellectual vigour.

A brief word of explanation is due for the series identifier on the front cover. The fountains, taken from heraldry, represent the Baptist distinctive of believer's baptism and, at the same time, the source of the water of life. There are three of them because they symbolize the Trinitarian basis of Baptist life and faith. Those who are redeemed by the Lamb, the book of Revelation reminds us, will be led to 'fountains of living waters' (Rev. 7.17).

Contents

FOREWORD

It is a real joy to me that Professor James Renihan's doctoral dissertation is now being made available to a wider public. It has too long remained the preserve of an academic community. It has an important message for all who are concerned about the nature and quality of modern Baptist church life.

The republication of the *Second London Baptist Confession* in 1959 was for many of us the discovery of a treasure that we never knew that we possessed. Since that time it has been the object of careful study and analysis. It demonstrated that the theological roots of Particular Baptists push deeply into the soil of Puritanism and Reformation theology. Professor Renihan's work underlines this, making it clear that these seventeenth century Baptists were catholic in inheritance and in vision. They shared so much theology with their paedobaptist brethren and were not too proud to learn from them.

The distinctive contribution of these men of the *Confession* was a Baptist ecclesiology and this is the theme of this study. Even here they believed that their testimony was "the final application of the Reformation principle of *sola scriptura*". It is in the area of church life that Renihan's work is so valuable. As a true historian he does not study the *Confession* in isolation from the life of the men who compiled and the churches that received it. He brings to it careful attention to the writings of the Particular Baptists of that generation and most importantly a study of their church minute books, association records and assembly documents. We are presented with a graphic picture of the way in which the *Confession* worked in the life of the churches. The men of that generation were confessionalists, high churchmen in the best sense, and unashamedly primitivist. They were loyal to each other because they confessed a common faith and above all loyal to the Lord whose glory was the object of their *Confession*. They did not unchurch their paedobaptist brethren, although they longed to share the full riches of their heritage with them. This book is not a blue print to be slavishly followed. It is however a work from which we can learn important lessons.

Robert W. Oliver
Bradford on Avon,
Wiltshire
March 2008

Acknowledgements

I wish to thank the many people who have helped to make the research and writing of this book possible. I am deeply indebted for their assistance to the staffs of the Rolfing Library at Trinity Evangelical Divinity School, the Dinand Library of the College of the Holy Cross, Worcester, Massachusetts, the Worcester Public Library, Worcester, Massachusetts, the Roberts Library of Southwestern Baptist Theological Seminary, Fort Worth, Texas, and the Bodleian Library, Oxford. In addition, much help was received at the specialized libraries of the American Baptist Historical Society in Rochester, New York, The Guildhall Library, London, The Public Record Office, London, and the Warwickshire County Record Office, Warwick, England. Special thanks must be made to Mrs. Susan Mills, former Archivist and Librarian at the Angus Library, Regent's Park College, Oxford. Her knowledge of Baptist literature was a tremendous aid to me during my time there. My work would have been immensely more difficult without her kind and cheerful expertise.

Prof. Paul Fiddes, former Principal of Regent's Park College, Oxford, extended to me an invitation to be a Visiting Member of the Senior Common Room during the Michaelmas Term, 1994. Dr. B. R. White kindly consented to an interview, and I have benefited greatly from his advice. I have very fond memories of my stay at Regent's Park College. Mr. and Mrs. Ray Trainer of Warwick made extra efforts to make a visiting American feel welcome, as did Pastor and Mrs. David Campbell of Darlington, County Durham, and Pastor and Mrs. Austin Walker of Crawley, West Sussex.

In my pursuit of primary source materials, several individuals gave special aid. Dr. Michael A. G. Haykin of Ontario, Canada has been exceedingly generous in allowing me to borrow hard-to-find material, and in sharing copies of old books. Pastor Achille Blaize of East London, and Pastor Austin Walker of West Sussex obtained material in the United Kingdom that I was not able to find here in the United States. Pastor Len Byerly of Salisbury Center, New York loaned me a large number of books.

Many individuals provided financial support for my studies, particularly for my stay in England. Special thanks go to Pastor Dale Smith and the members of Grace Reformed Baptist Church of Rockford, Illinois for their deep and abiding love for me and my family. They gave sacrificially to help us, and organized an effort to raise funds for my journey. Many churches and individuals contributed to that project, and I once again thank them for their assistance. Two ladies, one from the Midwest and the other from Florida gave sacrificially to my support. I cannot adequately express my appreciation to them for all that they have done for my family. Mr. Harry Maples of Worcester, Massachusetts has been an enthusiastic supporter of this project for several years. I hope that he understands how much I appreciate his help and friendship.

Dr. Tom Nettles, my mentor and first reader has been an enthusiastic, and patient, teacher. I appreciate the opportunity to have served as his teaching assistant and research fellow while at Trinity Evangelical Divinity School. His love for Baptist history has kindled my own interests and desires to bring these things to light. His colleague, Dr. John Woodbridge has also been a great encouragement to me. I am very happy to have had the privilege of studying under these two Christian scholars.

My brother, Rev. Dr. Michael Renihan has also been a great help. While I was first writing this work, he was engaged in the pursuit of an advanced degree as well, writing a thesis on the great antipaedobaptist John Tombes. His expertise in seventeenth century sacramental literature has given me much assistance.

How can I fully express my thanks to my family? They have endured much throughout my period of study. Beth, Nathan, Micah, Sam and Susannah all deserve a thank you from Dad for their love and support, and their cheerful perseverance through some trying family circumstances. My mother, Lillian Renihan has encouraged me a thousand times.

Finally, and most importantly, my wife Lynne deserves the greatest appreciation. More than anyone else, she has endured the hardships associated with this project. I could not have completed my work without her. She has been at my side in every difficult circumstance, and has been through several difficulties on her own. Thanks to God for such a wonderful wife.

James M. Renihan
Escondido, California
March 2008

Abbreviations

ARPB   *Association Records of the Particular Baptists*

BDBR   *Biographical Dictionary of British Radicals*

BHH   *Baptist History and Heritage*

BQ   *The Baptist Quarterly*

CB   Church Book

CHEB   Crosby, *History of the English Baptists*

CMB   Church Minute Book

DNB   *Dictionary of National Biography*

HEB   Ivimey, *History of the English Baptists*

TBHS   *Transactions of the Baptist Historical Society*

Introduction

This book is a study in Historical Theology. It is an attempt to describe in detail the implementation of confessional ecclesiological principles among a large group of churches which subscribed the Second London Baptist Confession in the final quarter of the seventeenth century. First seeing the light of day in December 1997 as my Ph.D. Dissertation at Trinity Evangelical Divinity School, Deerfield, Illinois, it is at last ready for publication. Sadly, due to heavy academic demands in my current post, I have been unable to update its contents in any significant sense.

In 1968, the British Baptist historian B. R. White suggested that there was a need for "microscopic study of Baptist history, if only to serve as a check upon the too fluent pens of those who advocate and practice the inaccuracies and inadequacies of the telescopic approach."[1] Baptist history has frequently suffered at the hands of ideologues and controversialists, who have approached their work with conscious *a priori* prejudices, forcing the product of their efforts to reflect those biases. Most nineteenth century Baptist histories were polemic attempts at demonstrating the antiquity, continuity, and at times direct succession of Baptist principles through the ages. When William Heth Whitsitt proposed an alternate historiography in 1896, tracing believer's baptism by immersion only as far back as the 1640s, the hue and cry was so great that he was forced from the presidency of the Southern Baptist Theological Seminary in Louisville, Kentucky. The prejudices of a theologically driven historiography could not be overcome by careful historical research. In the twentieth century, some ground has been gained, but not much.[2] The popular notions of the so-called Landmark movement, with its commitment to Baptist exclusivism and an attendant denial of any kind of Universal Church, as well as an insistence on Baptist continuity and succession, are persistently disseminated in many Baptist circles.[3] The present work provides some insight

---

[1] B. R. White, "The Baptists of Reading 1652-1715," *The Baptist Quarterly* 22, no. 5 (Jan. 1968): 263.

[2] J. F. McGregor and Barry Reay speak of the seventeenth-century Baptists as "a group curiously neglected by historians." The reason for this may be because "there was always an inner tension in the Baptist movement between the desire for involvement in the turmoil of the period and the Baptist obsession with the minutiae of organization. In the end obsession won." J. F. McGregor and Barry Reay, *Radical Religion in the English Revolution* (Oxford: Oxford University Press, 1984), vii.

[3] An effective study of some of these matters has recently been published by James McGoldrick under the title *Baptist Successionism: A Crucial Question in Baptist History*, ATLA Monograph Series, No. 32 (Metuchen, N.J.: The American Theological Library Association and the Scarecrow Press, 1994).

into these claims. The evidence cited here demonstrates that the early Calvinistic Baptists cannot be enlisted as precursors of the Landmark notions. Genuine catholicity marked the lives of the Particular Baptists. On a different level, some noted Baptist historians have argued that the central theme in Baptist life has been the notion of soul liberty.[4] Freedom of individual belief and expression has been championed as a means to oppose any attempt to bring creedal or confessional standards to bear on modern Baptist life. This study gives substantial evidence that the self-identification of the largest group of early Baptists was closely tied to detailed confessional theology. By placing one *locus* of theology under the microscope, and considering its place in the midst of a definable group of churches, correctives to these approaches may be found. Telescopic treatments of Baptist history must be based on more narrow and detailed studies.

Another motive for taking up this study is more pastoral. It arises from a particular interest on my part, developed out of several observations over a number of years. As a pastor of a modern church that subscribed this Confession, I came to the realization that there was little available information on the implementation of the ecclesiological material contained in it by the original churches responsible for its publication. The second half of the twentieth century has witnessed the abundant republication of Puritan works from a variety of publishing houses. In many cases, these works shed much light on the theological views of the English Particular Baptists. The *Second London Confession* is a recension of the two major paedobaptist confessions of the seventeenth century, the Independent *Savoy Declaration*, and the Presbyterian *Westminster Confession of Faith*. The Baptists state that they used these works because there was explicit agreement among them on the fundamental doctrines of Christianity. For this reason, Puritan treatises on most theological subjects provide great insight into the doctrinal convictions of the Baptists.

Ecclesiology, however, was the distinguishing tenet of the Baptists, and cannot be treated in the same fashion. It is a mistake to draw a straight line from the paedobaptist Puritan ecclesiological writings to the beliefs and practices of the Baptists. Reprints of specifically Baptist material from the

---

[4]Most notable is H. Leon McBeth's *The Baptist Heritage: Four Centuries of Baptist Witness* (Nashville: Broadman Press, 1987). This massive work (822 pages of text) is an extended polemic for the centrality of soul liberty in the lives of Baptists. The author seeks to demonstrate that freedom is at the very core of Baptist faith and practice. In doing so, he supports the notion that Baptists have been reluctant to define themselves in precise theological terms. They have rather placed liberty to dissent, even within the community of faith, as a core value. This motif becomes the basis of modern resistance to theological authority. Appeals to external authority, even that of Scripture, become, according to this historiography, intrusions on the central theme of the heritage of Baptists.

seventeenth century have been very few, and the extant books from the era are rare and expensive when available on the market. The average pastor has little opportunity to examine the ecclesiological writings of the early Baptists, and thus may lack important insights into the doctrines contained in their Confession of Faith.

As I considered the Confessional statements and their implementation in contemporary churches, I came to realize that this lack of information created a vacuum of historical and confessional perspective. Assumptions that did not seem to be entirely warranted were made about the teaching of the Confession and its practice in the churches. A study needed to be undertaken, using primary source material, to attempt to delineate the specific understanding of the ecclesiological principles placed in the Confession by its editors and enacted in the original churches. This is not because I believe that modern subscribers must follow the practices of their predecessors in every detail, but rather that confessional subscription should be informed not simply by modern interpretation, but by a full-fledged understanding of the historical and theological implementation of the document.

This study was conceived in order to accomplish this purpose. It is an attempt to investigate the "practical ecclesiology" of the churches that subscribed the *Second London Confession*. This phrase is intended to refer to the outworking of ecclesiological principles in the ongoing life of the churches.

The method used to pursue this matter may be likened to a set of three concentric circles. The innermost ring is the *Second London Baptist Confession* itself.[5] This document contains technical theological statements on ecclesiology, and was solemnly adopted by over 100 churches in the era under consideration. The middle ring contains the ecclesiological writings of the Particular Baptists. These flesh out the doctrines of the Confession, and provide a more detailed theoretical and theological framework by which to understand the positions adopted in the churches. The outermost circle contains manuscript Church Books. These were the chronicles of the churches, kept as official records of the life and deeds that took place. They are a fascinating example of church history brought to life. In these Church Books, the real-life mechanisms of ecclesiology are evidenced. They demonstrate the specific means used by the churches to put the theory of ecclesiology into practice.

Chapter 1 is an historical overview of the emergence and development of the Particular Baptist churches. It sets the stage for the ecclesiological analyses contained in Chapters 2 through 6. In those chapters, the relevant Confessional statements have been examined, the ecclesiological writings have been consulted, and the Church Books have been used to illustrate the doctrinal principles advocated in written form.

The three decades represented in the title to the work, 1675-1705, were

---

[5]Spelling and punctuation of primary source material has been left as in the original throughout this work.

chosen for their specific relation to the Confession. By 1675, all of the major leaders in London and the Countryside were in the pastoral positions that they would hold throughout these decades. By 1705, nearly all of these men were dead, and the leadership of the movement was passing into new hands.

The Confession was first published anonymously in 1677, during a time of persecution, as a statement of the faith of "many churches in London and the Country." It was publicly adopted twelve years later in a period of toleration, by more than 100 churches, and provided the framework for a theology of the church in these congregations. In these three decades, it was an important marker for all observers. It squarely placed the Baptists among the reformed dissenters, while giving evidence of their unique perspectives, especially on ecclesiological matters.

It has been necessary at many points to make reference to the earlier writings and practices of the Particular Baptists. Some of the leaders in 1689 had been part of the movement from its beginning, and contributed to the development of thought. There is no bifurcation between the earlier men and churches and the later, rather there is continuity. As a movement that only emerged self-consciously in the 1640s, there is a natural progression without significant differences. The decades under consideration marked the first settled period after the initial stage of development,[6] and provide a fair sample of the ecclesiological practices of the subscribing churches. As the original adherents to the Confession, their practices shed much light on the explicit understanding of its implementation. The vast majority of illustrations have been taken from the period under examination, and from the churches known to have adopted the document.

I have attempted to concentrate on the most salient features of the implementation of ecclesiology. Some subjects, such as the theological nature of believer's baptism in contradistinction to paedobaptism have, of necessity, received only summary treatment. Likewise, apparently idiosyncratic practices, found in isolated circumstances have not been included. Given the limitations necessary for this work, it has been impossible to identify and investigate every possible nuance of each church's practice.

At the root of Particular Baptist ecclesiology was a keen primitivistic impulse. T. L. Underwood has identified this as "the emphasis in faith and practice on the first, earliest form or pattern as described in the New Testament

---

[6]White argues that in the earlier period of the 1650s, the issues discussed at the Association meetings were attempts "to think all the old questions out afresh in the light of their understanding of the Bible and in an attempt to provide virtually a new framework of *Baptist* casuistical divinity. By trial and error they were seeking to build up a pattern of inter-church relations, of the duties of members to each other and to their churches." White, "The Baptists of Reading," 256, emphasis his. By the 1670s, many of the questions had been answered, with a generally settled ecclesiology as the result. The inherent progression of principles is evident in the primary sources.

that entailed efforts to re-create or imitate such a form in the present."[7]
Throughout this investigation, it will be evident that the Baptists sought
relentlessly to apply this principle to their doctrine and practice. It was the
impetus behind the development of believer's baptism, the practice of
immersion, the order and government of the church, the roles of officers, the
various aspects of worship and the outworking of inter-church relationships.
Richard Baxter's use of Tertullian's phrase "*Quod primum id optimum*"[8] suits
well the Baptist approach to the theory and application of ecclesiology. A high
view of Scripture, combined with a belief in the present activity of God in
Christ in the gathered assembly drove the Baptists to define and develop their
doctrine of the church with caution and care. The pattern was found in the New
Testament, and the responsibility to replicate it was paramount in the
congregations of saints. In the words of one of their leaders,

> The Edification and Beauty of the Church is much concerned in her
> *Order* , not such an Order as Superstition will dictate, or litigious
> Nicety contend for, but such as we have ... described; which sets her
> in a conformity to Christ's Will.[9]

As a whole, the Particular Baptists provide a picture of lively ecclesiology
informed by a primitivist urge to ground their ways in Scripture and consistent
with the teaching of their Confession. Their methods may help their theological
heirs to think more carefully through their own practice of church life, and
better inform modern subscription to the Confession of Faith.

---

[7]T. L. Underwood, *Primitivism, Radicalism, and the Lamb's War: The Baptist-Quaker
Conflict in Seventeenth-Century England*, Oxford Studies in Historical Theology (New
York: Oxford University Press, 1997), 4. Underwood provides helpful background for
the presence of primitivism in Puritanism as a whole, and more specifically among the
Baptists and Quakers.

[8]Cited in Underwood, *Primitivism*, 6.

[9]N[ehemiah] C[oxe], *A Sermon Preached at the Ordination of an Elder and Deacons in
a Baptized Congregation in London* (London: Tho. Fabian, 1681), 5.

CHAPTER 1

'Christ ... ever shall have a kingdome in this world': The Emergence and Development of the Particular Baptist Churches

Two[1] strands of English Baptists are generally recognized to have developed in the seventeenth century. The earliest group, which came to be known as General Baptists, was the result of the return from exile in the Netherlands, in 1611, of a church formerly associated with John Smyth, but by then led by Thomas Helwys. This group defined itself by, among other theological convictions, its rejection of the prevailing Calvinism of much of English Church life.

The Emergence of the Particular Baptist Churches

A second Baptist movement developed three decades later, out of the matrix of one of the London Separatist churches. These Baptists came to be called Particular Baptists, because of their adherence to the tenets of Calvinism.

The Genesis of the English Particular Baptists

While it is clear that the two Baptist groups had different origins, their genesis has not been regarded with unanimity. Different theories of relationships, especially to the Continental Anabaptists, have been advanced.

SEPARATISM AND SEMI-SEPARATISM: THE JACOB/LATHROP/JESSEY CHURCH

In the nineteenth century, the prevailing theory seems to have been that there were direct organic links between the Continental Anabaptists and both sets of English Baptists.[2] Towards the end of that century, however, a new set of ideas

---

[1]Some portions of this chapter have been published under the title 'An Examination of the Possible Influence of Menno Simons' *Foundation Book* upon the Particular Baptist Confession of 1644', *American Baptist Quarterly* 15, no.3 (Sept. 1966): 191-95.

[2]For examples of this type of historiography see, Thomas Armitage, *A History of the Baptists* (New York: Bryan, Taylor and Co., 1890; Watertown, Wis.: Baptist Heritage Press, 1988 reprint); William Cathcart, *The Baptist Encyclopedia* (Philadelphia: Louis

began to be advanced. Finding their impetus in the controversy over William Whitsitt's book *A Question in Baptist History*,[3] a different set of historians argued that at least the Particular Baptists must be regarded as a movement springing from the English Separatists, without any organic link either to the Continental Anabaptists or to the earlier General Baptists. It has been asserted that they developed especially out of one church in London, founded in 1616 under the ministry of Henry Jacob, as an Independent Congregational church with semi-separatist views. While it claimed its right to independent existence as a church, it did not denounce the National Church as apostate, and maintained cordial relationships with the puritan ministers still in the Establishment. Jacob was succeeded in the pastorate by John Lathrop, who was followed by Henry Jessey. In the 1630s, events transpired leading to the secession of at least one group (who were apparently more radical in their objections to the validity of the National Church), and this ultimately led to the formation of the first Particular Baptist church.

Everts, 1881; Paris, Ark.: The Baptist Standard Bearer, 1988 reprint); and J. M. Cramp, *Baptist History: From the Foundation of the Christian Church to the Present Time* (London: Elliot Stock, 1871; Watertown, Wis.: Baptist Heritage Press, 1987 reprint).

[3]William H. Whitsitt, *A Question in Baptist History* (Louisville, Ken.: Charles Dearing, 1896). He argued that baptism by immersion was not practiced before 1641, and thus Baptist history proper must be dated from this year, making it impossible to demonstrate any kind of lineal succession. His work caused such a stir that he was forced to resign from his position as professor at Southern Baptist Theological Seminary, Louisville, Ky. See Ian Sellers, 'Edwardians, Anabaptists and the Problem of Origins', *The Baptist Quarterly* 29 (July 1981): 97-112. The list of articles, which followed over the next seventy-five years is very lengthy. Some agree with Whitsitt, others accept parts of his theory, others reject it outright. A sample of the literature would include the following, in alphabetical order (inclusion in this list does not imply that they directly addressed the issues presented by Whitsitt): William R. Estep, 'Anabaptists and the Rise of the English Baptists', *The Quarterly Review* 28, no. 4 (Oct. 1968): 43-53; idem, 29, no. 1 (Jan. 1969): 50-62; A. J. D. Farrer, 'The Relation between English Baptists and the Anabaptists of the Continent', *BQ* 2 (1924): 30-36; James Leo Garrett, Jr., 'Restitution and Dissent Among Early English Baptists: Part 1', *Baptist History and Heritage* 12 (Oct. 1977): 198-210; Winthrop Hudson, 'Who Were the Baptists?' *BQ* 16 (July 1956): 303-312; Hudson, 'Baptists were not Anabaptists', *The Chronicle* 16 (1953): 171-179, (These two articles are almost identical in content); James D. Mosteller, 'Baptists and Anabaptists', *The Chronicle* 20 (1957): 3-27; Ernest A. Payne, 'Who were the Baptists?' *BQ* 16 (Oct. 1956): 339-342; W. Morgan Patterson, 'The Development of the Baptist Successionist Formula', *Foundations* 5 (Oct. 1962): 331-345; Gunnar Westin, 'Who were the Baptists?' *BQ* 17 (Sept. 1957): 55-60; W. T. Whitley, 'Continental Anabaptists and Early English Baptists', *BQ* 2 (1924): 24-30.

THE CONTINUING REFORMATION: THE ADOPTION OF BELIEVER'S BAPTISM AND
THE RECOVERY OF IMMERSION

The most important source of information for Particular Baptist origins is the
so-called Kiffin Manuscript.[4] While the original apparently no longer exists, a
copy from the early eighteenth century, most likely transcribed by Benjamin
Stinton, is deposited in the Angus Library of Regent's Park College, Oxford.
Stinton may have received the original from Richard Adams, a Particular
Baptist minister from the second half of the seventeenth century who had been
an associate of William Kiffin in the Devonshire Square Church in London.[5]
This manuscript details the events in the Jacob/Lathrop/Jessey church which
led to one group's adoption of Baptist practices.[6] The section of the Kiffin
Manuscript most relevant for this study is as follows:

> 1640 3d. Mo. The Church became two by Mutall consent just half being
> with Mr. P. Barebone & ye other halfe with Mr H Iessey Mr Richard Blunt
> wth him being convinced of Baptism, yt also it ought to be by diping ye
> Body into ye Water, resembling Burial & riseing again. 2 Col: 2.12. Rom.
> 6.4 had sober Conferance about it in ye Church, & then wth some of the
> forenamed, who also ware so convinced: And after Prayer & conferance
> about their so enjoying it; none haveing then so so [sic] practised in England
> to professed Believers & hearing that some in ye Nether Lands had so
> practised they agreed & sent over Mr Rich Blunt (who understood Dutch)
> wth Letters of Comendation, who was kindly accepted there & Returned wth
> Letters from them, Jo Batte a Teacher there & from that Church to such as
> sent him.

> 1641 They proceed on therein viz. Those Persons yt ware perswaded
> Baptism should be by dipping ye Body had mett in two Companies & did
> intend so to meet after this: all these Agreed to proceed alike togeather: And
> then Manifesting (not by any formal Words a Covenant) wch Word was
> Scrupled by some of them, but by mutual desires & agreement each
> Testified: These two Companyes did set apart one to Baptize the rest, so it
> was solemnly performed by them Mr Blunt Baptized Mr Blacklock yt was a
> Teacher amongst them, & Mr Blunt being Baptized, he & Mr Blacklock
> Baptized ye rest of their friends that ware so minded, & many being added
> to them they increased much.[7]

---

[4]The Kiffin Manuscript may be found transcribed in Barrie R. White, 'Baptist
Beginnings and the Kiffin Manuscript', *BHH* 2 (Jan. 1967): 29-34; and Champlin
Burrage, *Early English Dissenters in the Light of Recent Research* (1550-1641) 2 Vols.
(New York: Russell & Russell, 1967 reprint), 2:292-305.

[5]The details of the history of the Kiffin Manuscript may be found in Barrie R. White,
'Who Really Wrote the Kiffin Manuscript?' *BHH* 1 (Oct. 1966): 3-10, 14. White
concludes that Kiffin may have been the author of the original.

[6]See White, 'Baptist Beginnings', 31-32.

[7]White, 'Baptist Beginnings', 31-32.

There follows a list of forty-one names, apparently of those who participated in
this baptism. According to the old calendar still used in England, the '3d. mo.'
would have been May, 1640. The baptisms were said to have taken place '11
Mo. Ianu,' which seems to be January 1641/42. Among those listed are three
whose names were also affixed to the 1644 Confession: Tho. Kilcop, Tho.
Munden and Tho. Shepard.[8]

This portion of the Kiffin manuscript makes one issue very clear: there was
some contact with Dutch Anabaptists,[9] as Richard Blunt was sent to the 'Nether
Lands' in order to receive instruction concerning baptism.

The most disputed issue with regard to the Kiffin Manuscript revolves
around Blunt's actions while in the Netherlands. Was he baptized there, or was
his baptism part of the mass baptism in London? The text is somewhat
ambiguous, and it is probably impossible to say for certain at this point. There
is, however, some evidence to believe that he may not have been baptized
during his mission, but rather during the ceremony in January 1641/42. One of
the leaders of the two churches which separated, Praisegod Barbone, wrote a
treatise in 1642 entitled *A Discourse Tending to Prove the Baptisme in, or
under the Defection of Antichrist to be the Ordinance of Jesus Christ.*[10] Since
he was so close to the group that became Baptists, and since this work was
specifically directed towards them (he called some of them 'my loving friends
and acquaintance'),[11] his statements carry much weight in the historical
situation. In several places, he said things such as

> there is no ground for this practice of raising Baptisme, by men Baptizing
> themselves .... It must needs be answered of Men, for no Commission can
> any shew to raise Baptisme thus fallen out of the world; nor to Baptize
> themselves, or others, being themselves unbaptized .... What warrant hath
> any Unbaptized person to Baptise himself? ... for a man to Baptise himselfe,
> and so to begin Baptisme ... discovereth it selfe to be erroneous and not of
> God .... But now very lately some are mightily taken, as having found out a

---

[8]White, 'Baptist Beginnings', 31-32.

[9]The Dutch Anabaptists with whom Blunt appears to have made contact were the
Collegiants or Rijnsburgers. They were apparently a lay movement, formed to promote
spiritual causes with no formal organization, buildings or officers, although their
societies (Collegia) met at many places throughout the Netherlands. They practiced
baptism by immersion, not as a church ordinance, but in order that it might be provided
for those who desired it. Close ties were established with the Dutch Mennonites, as well
as with the Polish (Socinian) Brethren. See N. van der Zijpp, 'Collegiants', in *The
Mennonite Encyclopedia* (Hillsboro, Kan.: Mennonite Brethren Publishing House,
1955), 1:639-40.

[10]Praisegod Barbone, *A Discourse Tending to Prove the Baptisme in, or under the
Defection of Antichrist to be the Ordinance of Jesus Christ* (London: R. Oulson & G.
Dexter, 1642). (The author's name is found with at least four different spellings:
Barbone, Barebone, Barebones, and Barbon).

[11]Barebone, *Discourse*, unnumbered p. 2 of the 'Epistle'.

new defect in the Baptisme under the defection ... concerning the manner of
Baptizing .... The particular of their opinion and practise is to Dip.[12]

Two possibilities seem to arise from Barbone's expressions, (1) Richard Blunt
baptized himself, as had John Smyth years before, or (2) Blunt and Blacklock
baptized each other ('themselves') and then proceeded to baptize the rest. In
either case, Barbone's objection rests on the lack of a qualified administrator.
This would tend to undermine the view that Blunt was baptized in the
Netherlands.

There are indications in the writings of some Particular Baptist authors
which seem to confirm this interpretation. While seeking to defend the validity
of Believer's Baptism as practiced by the young churches against Barbone's
criticism that it was spurious because of the lack of a proper administrator in
succession from the Apostles, John Spilsbery wrote,

> By vertue of this union they [i.e. the local church] have with their head
> Christ, the body thus joyntly considered, hath the power & authoritie of
> Christ within her selfe, to chuse and make use of any one, or more of her
> members, as occasion offers, and authorises him or them to administer
> baptisme upon the whole body, and so upon themselves in the first place, as
> a part of the same.... Where a thing is wanting, there must be of necessitie a
> beginning to reduce that thing againe into beeing.[13]

Spilsbery argued that the church had a right to appoint its own administrator(s)
of baptism, who were thus authorized to restore the ordinance without prior
baptism. In the second edition of the book (1652), he expanded the defense by
arguing that approved preachers, though themselves at first unbaptized, may
administer the ordinance to others. Their warrant for doing so does not depend
on succession from the Apostles, but from Scripture:

> If any object, How can such receive others into the Gospel order, that never
> were in it themselves?
>
> The answer is, where there is a beginning, some must be first, and our
> obedience to God depends only upon his word, that gives being to all order
> of worship, and the Gospel order once instituted stands firm for ever
> unalterable, for all that believe to obey and submit themselves thereunto, by
> a practical profession of the same, 2 Tim. 3.15,16,17. Rev. 22.18,19. Mat.
> 28.19,20.[14]

---

[12]Barebone, *Discourse*, 4, 6, 8, 12.
[13]J[ohn] S[pilsbery], *A Treatise Concerning the Lawful Subject of Baptisme* (London:
n.p., 1643), 38.
[14]John Spilsbery, *A Treatise Concerning the Lawfull Subject of Baptism* the second
Edition corrected and enlarged by the Author (London: Henry Hills, 1652), 63.

For Spilsbery, the lack of an administrator in succession from the apostles was no difficulty. Scripture provides the warrant for the recovery of the lost ordinance.

Another author, John Gosnold, writing in a work entitled *Of the Doctrine of Baptisms, or, A Discourse of the Baptism of Water and of the Spirit* said

> If any shall object, that at first amongst us in this Nation an unbaptiz'd person did Baptize, and so could be no lawful Administrator .... We conceive the answer is ready and at hand, that the first Baptizer must of necessity be unbaptiz'd, even John the Baptist himself, and yet judged a fit Administrator of so excellent a subject as our Lord himself was.[15]

Gosnold's words imply that the first administrator of baptism among the Particular Baptists was in fact unbaptized, and thus could not have been baptized in the Netherlands. Lest it be thought that Gosnold was referring to John Smyth, the words of another Particular Baptist leader need to be heard. In his 1691 work *Believers Baptism From Heaven and of Divine Institution*, Hercules Collins wrote with some vehemence in response to the charges of one John Wall,

> Could not the Ordinance of Christ, which was lost in the Apostacy, be revived, (as the Feast of Tabernacles was, tho lost a great while) unless in such a filthy way as you falsly assert, viz. that the English Baptists received their Baptism from Mr. John Smith? It is absolutely untrue, it being well known, by some yet alive, how false this Assertion is.[16]

For Collins, association with John Smith was completely undesireable. The oral testimony of still living eye witnesses (William Kiffin was alive and active among the London Particular Baptists at this time) was sufficient to refute such a notion. It therefore seems best to conclude that baptism among the Particular Baptists was restored from within their own circle, and was not received from anyone else.

THE DISAVOWAL OF THE CONTINENTAL ANABAPTISTS

By the time that they published their Confession of Faith in 1644, the Particular Baptists sought to disavow any ties with the Continental Anabaptists. This is evident by a glance at the title page which says, 'The Confession of Faith, of

---

[15]John Gosnold, *Of the Doctrine of Baptisms, or, A Discourse of the Baptism of Water and of the Spirit* (London: Printed by J. S. for the Author, 1657), 7.

[16]Hercules Collins, *Believers Baptism From Heaven and of Divine Institution* (London: J. Hancock, 1691), 115. Benjamin Keach also argues that the recovery of baptism by immersion is analogous to the reinstitution of the Feast of tabernacles among the Old Testament Jews. Benjamin Keach, *Gold Refin'd; or Baptism in its Primitive Purity* (London: Nathaniel Crouch, 1689), 23-24.

those Churches which are commonly (though falsly [sic]) called Anabaptists'.[17] The epistle at the beginning of the Confession identifies the problem:

> Wee question not but that it will seeme strange to many men, that such as wee are frequently termed to be, lying under that calumny and black brand of Heretickes and sowers of division as wee doo, should presume to appear publickly as now wee have done: ... it is no sad thing to any observing man, what sad charges are laid, not only by the world, that know not God, but also by those that thinke themselves much wronged, if they be not looked upon as the chiefe Worthies of the Church of God, and Watchmen of the Citie: ... charging us with holding Free-will, Falling away from grace, denying Originall sinne, disclaiming of Magistracy, denying to assist them either in persons or purse in any of their lawfull Commands, doing acts unseemly in the dispensing the Ordinance of Baptism, not to be named among Christians.[18]

It is evident that in this list of charges there are several that were relevant, either in reality or fancy, to the Anabaptists of the Continent. All that an opponent of the Baptists had to do was say the name 'Münster', and all of the supposed horrors of that sad city would be imputed to their English 'counterparts'.[19] Evidently, the Particular Baptists felt the pressure of these charges, and desired to remove as many of them as possible. They therefore openly asserted that the name 'Anabaptist' was falsely given, and did not reflect their own convictions.

Nevertheless, in spite of this denial, the pertinent question remains: is there evidence for Anabaptist influence? The best resource is in the previously mentioned Kiffin Manuscript. Evidently, these Particular Baptists had some knowledge of the practices of the Dutch Anabaptists, and esteemed them enough to seek advice, at the least, and perhaps more, from them. Richard Blunt spoke Dutch, and so could have been the source for their contact with these Anabaptists. While these things are true, nothing more can be established at this point. The Kiffin Manuscript seems to imply that the growing convictions about Believer's Baptism developed within the Jacob/Lathrop/Jessey church, and that a considerable period of time (a minimum of 7, and a maximum of 19 months, depending on the reckoning) passed between the adoption of baptist convictions and the actual institution of baptism. This would certainly leave enough time for theological ferment, and for the development of doctrinal convictions based on a study of Scriptural passages.

---

[17]William L. Lumpkin, *Baptist Confessions of Faith*, rev. ed. (Valley Forge: Judson Press, 1969), 153.

[18]Lumpkin, *BCF*, 154-55.

[19]Lumpkin mentions two books which may have been especially obnoxious in their charges against the Baptists: *A Short History of the Anabaptists of High and Low Germany* (1642), and *A Warning for England especially for London* (1642), *BCF*, 145.

Two of the men who signed the Confession in 1644, William Kiffin and Samuel Richardson, are known to have had commercial dealings with the Dutch. In 1643, Kiffin made a business trip to Holland which was financially successful. In 1645, he enlisted one of the members of his church in his business, and this individual made another trip to the Dutch provinces. This journey was even more successful than the first, and seems to have placed Kiffin in a comfortable financial situation for the rest of his life.[20] Nothing more can be said about Kiffin's relationship to the Dutch. It is not known if he had any contact with any Anabaptist groups while there.

Samuel Richardson also had business dealings in Holland, but according to Paul Gritz, the source of his wealth must be traced to trade with North America. Gritz indicates that Richardson did not travel to the Netherlands until 1656.[21] This would obviously preclude him as the source for an organic connection with the Anabaptists.

It will be seen, then, that evidence is somewhat scanty for a direct connection beyond Blunt's mission to the Anabaptists of the European mainland. This does not undermine the possibility of Anabaptist influence. It simply makes such influence more difficult to demonstrate.

THE SEPARATIST/INDEPENDENT MILIEU

One might presume that the literary lineage of the Second London Confession provides a direct backdrop against which its ecclesiology may be understood.[22] In reality, the situation is much more complex than a first glance might imply. The question of influence is always difficult. Does it refer simply to literary dependence, or are other less obvious avenues of influence to be recognized? An analysis of the Particular Baptist writings does provide some help. The sources named in their ecclesiological treatises[23] provide direct links to other theologians, but these cannot be regarded as the only avenues by which their thinking was molded and shaped. In the tumultuous era during which they emerged, full of pamphlets, books and preachers advocating a wide variety of options for theological thought and practice, there may have been many

---

[20]Details of Kiffin's business dealings may be found in Barrie R. White, 'William Kiffin—Baptist Pioneer and Citizen of London', *BHH* 2 (July 1967): 91-103, 126.
[21]Paul Gritz, 'Samuel Richardson and the Religious and Political Controversies Confronting the London Particular Baptists, 1643 to 1658' (Ph.D. diss., Southwestern Baptist Theological Seminary, 1987), 118-21.
[22]I refer to the Westminster Confession/Savoy Declaration/Second London lineage of the Confession. Especially pertinent is the material found in the Savoy Platform of Polity, much of which was taken directly over into the body of Chapter 26 of the Second London Confession. See below.
[23]It is impossible to give an exhaustive list of even the cited sources. Among those noted in various works are John Owen, Thomas Goodwin, John Cotton, Jeremiah Burroughs, William Ames, and Isaac Chauncy.

discussions over the issues which contributed to the development of ecclesiological practices. Presbyterians, Episcopalians, Independents, Seekers, Quakers and a host of other sects must have crossed the paths of the Particular Baptists. Some of the more fringe groups may have been easily dismissed, but not so others. The literary remains of the Particular Baptist thinkers are full of critiques of various sectarian writers.

When they first appeared in the 1640s, the Particular Baptists faced challenges on several sides. One of the leaders of the separatist Jacob/Lathrop/Jessey Church in London, Praise God Barbone, responded almost immediately in print to their newly recovered practice of Believer's Baptism by immersion.[24] The Episcopalian Daniel Featley wrote against their 1644 Confession,[25] while the Presbyterians Robert Baylie[26] and John Bastwick,[27] the Seeker William Erbery,[28] and the enigmatic John Saltmarsh[29] all went into print against them. Each of these, and in all likelihood others, may have contributed to the shape taken by the practices of the Particular Baptists.

---

[24]Barbone, *A Discourse*. For an analysis of the relationship between this work and the 1644 Confession, see Renihan, 'An Examination', 200-203.

[25]See his *The Dippers dipt. Or, The Anabaptists Duck'd and Plung'd over Head and Eares, at a Disputation in Southwark,* 6th ed. (London: Printed by Richard Cotes for N. B., 1651), especially pages 177-186.

[26]Robert Baylie, *A Dissuasive from the Errours of the Time* (London: Printed for Samuel Gillibrand, 1646). Baylie's attacks are primarily against the Independents, or Brownists, but he views the 'Anabaptists' as the logical extension of the principles of Independency. Baylie was a Scottish Commissioner to the Westminster Assembly, and wrote in the midst of the ecclesiological debates made famous there. His perceived line of descent is made clear when he states, 'The principall by-paths, wherein most among us this day do tread, who divert from the high, open, and straight way of the Reformed Churches, may be reduced to ten generall Heads: The *Brownists*, or rigid Separatists, are the first to break off to the side: the *Independents*, their children, go on with them for a time; but, wearied with the wideness of their Parents wandring, professe to come in againe towards the rode way, yet not so closely, but still they keep a path of their own. How much nearer these men professe to draw towards us then their Fathers, so much the farther their other Brethren run from us: for the *Anabaptists* go beyond the *Brownists* in wandring; the *Antinomians* are beyond the *Anabaptists*, and the *Seekers* beyond them all', 6.

[27]John Bastwick, *Independency Not God's Ordinance* (London: John Macock, 1645). Hanserd Knollys responded to this work with, *A Moderate Answer unto Dr. Bastwick's Book Called, Independency not God's Ordinance* (London: Jane Coe, 1645).

[28]William Erbery, *The Testimony of William Erbery, Left upon Record for the Saints of the Succeeding Ages* (London: Calvert, 1658). For this information on Erbery, I am indebted to Michael A. G. Haykin, 'Hanserd Knollys (ca. 1599-1691) on the Gifts of the Spirit' *Westminster Theological Journal* 54 (1992): 107.

[29]John Saltmarsh, *The Smoke in the Temple* (London: Ruth Raworth, 1642). Knollys responded to this with *The Shining of a Flaming fire in Zion* (London: Jane Coe, 1646).

It is clear, nevertheless, that the most significant sources for their practices are to be found in the Independents, and the more radical Separatists preceding them.[30] Both of the general Confessions issued in London were to a large degree based on existing Separatist or Independent documents. The First London Confession is primarily drawn from the True Confession of 1596, and the Second London Confession is closely dependent on the 1658 Savoy Declaration of Faith and its Platform of Polity. The Baptists adopted the documents of the orthodox Paedobaptists around them, intending to demonstrate to their critics their own complete orthodoxy through the use of these existing declarations of faith.

The Separatist/Independent theological matrix from which the Particular Baptists emerged provides a helpful grid against which their polity must be understood. Rejecting the nation-oriented definition of the church common to both the Episcopalian and Presbyterian parties, the Independents argued for an understanding of ecclesiology centered primarily on the local assembly.

The debate over church polity at the Westminster Assembly is famous, and rightly so. The Presbyterian majority argued for the *jure divino* of a presbyterial/national form of government, with ascending church courts providing something of a centralized church controlled not by Bishops, but by Presbyters. The Independent minority argued against this system and for a form of church government in which local rule was vested in the presbyters of each individual church and not over churches, but they were unable to carry the argument and convince the majority of their views.[31] The Westminster Standards have been Presbyterian documents from the beginning.

The Independent 'Dissenting Brethren' at the Assembly were Thomas Goodwin, Philip Nye, Jeremiah Burroughs, William Bridge and Sidrach Simpson. Their *Apologeticall Narration*[32] is a clear description of their own congregational polity. In 1644, Goodwin and Nye published John Cotton's *The*

---

[30]Prior to the Act of Uniformity in 1662, there was a clear distinction between Separatists and Independents. The Separatists were not willing to have *formal* relationships with the National Church, while the Independents did. After August 1662 the distinction is moot, as all of those outside the national church were considered to be non-conformists.

[31]The history of the debate has been recounted in several places. For a Presbyterian interpretation of the events, see William M. Heatherington, *History of the Westminster Assembly of Divines* (Edmonton: Still Waters Revival Books, 1993 reprint of 1856 edition), 157-226. A different view is presented in Daniel Neal, *The History of the Puritans* (Minneapolis, Minn.: Klock & Klock Christian Publishers, 1979 reprint of 1837 ed.), 2:264-277. See also Wiliston Walker, *The Creeds and Platforms of Congregationalism* (New York: Pilgrim Press, 1991 reprint), 341-345.

[32]*An Apologeticall Narration, Humbly Submitted to the Honourable Houses of Parliament* (London: Robert Dawlman, 1643).

Keys of the Kingdom of Heaven[33] stating that it fleshed out the principles of the 'middle way' between Brownism and Presbyterianism which they had advocated in the *Apologeticall Narration*.[34]

These Independent apologists were in close relationship with the early Particular Baptist leaders. During the era of the appearance of distinct Calvinistic Baptist churches, men such as Hanserd Knollys and William Kiffin were in contact with Goodwin, Burroughs, Nye and their circle of associates.[35] In 1640, an anonymous sermon (though undoubtedly from within this circle of fellowship)[36] entitled *A Glimpse of Sion's Glory*, was published with a brief preface signed by 'W. K.' In all likelihood, the W. K. was William Kiffin.[37] The preface stated, among other things,

> It is a sad thing of consequence to consider how we have been kept under blindness and darkness, although not totally, yet in a great measure, in regard of such truths as do immediately strike at antichrist and his false power: as namely this great truth, CHRIST THE KING OF HIS CHURCH; and that Christ hath given this power to his church, not to a hierarchy,

---

[33]This text may be found in Larzer Ziff, ed. *John Cotton on the Churches of New England* (Cambridge, Mass.: The Belknap Press, 1968), 69-164.

[34]Ziff, *John Cotton*, 77.

[35]The details of these relationships are well stated in Murray Tolmie, *The Triumph of the Saints* (Cambridge: Cambridge University Press, 1977), 42-45.

[36]There is a long debate over the identity of the author of the sermon itself. One copy was apparently published with the initials 'T. G.' attached, thus leading some interpreters to assert that Thomas Goodwin was the author. The sermon is published in vol. 12 of the Works of Goodwin, with this note from the editor: 'There can be no doubt that the Sermon is an authentic production of Dr. Goodwin.' *The Works of Thomas Goodwin, D.D.*, ed. Thomas Smith, vol. 12, *A Glimpse of Zion's Glory* (Edinburgh: James Nichol, 1866), 61. William Haller argues against Goodwin's authorship, and attributes the sermon to Hanserd Knollys, cf. William Haller, *The Rise of Puritanism* (New York: Columbia University Press, 1938) 270, 396. I am indebted to Iain Murray, *The Puritan Hope* (Edinburgh: The Banner of Truth Trust, 1971), 272, for this information. Murray likewise considers the suggestion of Goodwin's authorship to be unlikely. John F. Wilson, 'A Glimpse of Syon's Glory' *Church History* 31, no. 1 (March 1962): 66-73, argues for Goodwin's authorship, and is supported by Tolmie, *Triumph*, 45. Pope A. Duncan, in his monograph *Hanserd Knollys: Seventeenth Century Baptist* (Nashville: Broadman Press, 1965), 53-4, argues against both Goodwin's and Knollys' authorship. Relying primarily on H.M. Dexter, *The Congregationalism of the Last Three Hundred Years* (New York: Harper & Brothers, 1880), 40, he suggests Jeremiah Burroughs as the leading candidate for authorship. In any case, all of the proposed authors can be found in the same circle of Independent acquaintance in the 1630s and 1640s.

[37]Geoffrey Nuttall, *Visible Saints* (Oxford: Basil Blackwell, 1957), 8. Tolmie, *Triumph*, 45, likewise accepts this identification.

neither to a national presbytery, but to a company of saints in a congregational way.[38]

Nuttall indicates that this is the first published use of the phrase 'congregational way'.[39] The close relationship between Kiffin and the Independent divines is demonstrated by the presence of this preface.

Much more evidence supports this consideration. Kiffin states in his autobiography that he had been much helped by the ministry of Jose Glover, an Independent minister who died *en route* to New England, and Jeremiah Burroughs.[40] Hanserd Knollys entered Katherine Hall, Cambridge in 1629, while Richard Sibbes was Master and Thomas Goodwin one of its Fellows.[41] Around 1638, Knollys fled the Laudian persecutions and arrived in Boston, New England. After a conflict with the Reverend Elders there, he returned to England around 1641[42] and became involved with the Jacob/Lathrop/Jessey circle of churches. The story of his adoption of Baptist views is especially telling.[43] In January 1643/44, he was unsatisfied in conscience with the propriety of baptizing his child, and requested a conference on the issue. Discussions on the question lasted for several months, with an increasing number of members of Jessey's church convinced of the impropriety of infant baptism, and finally withdrawing under the leadership of William Kiffin. At this point, Jessey's church was divided over the necessity and propriety of censuring those who had separated. It was decided that the advice of several elders in the city should be sought, and a meeting was convened. Tolmie's comments are helpful:

> The attendance is revealing of the inner structure of puritan radicalism at this time, and of the Particular Baptist relationship with it. The most important men there were four of the authors of the *Apologeticall Narration*, Thomas Goodwin, Philip Nye, Jeremiah Burroughes, and Sidrach Simpson, the unofficial leaders of Independency in England. Representatives of three of the leading separatist Independent congregations, Praise-God Barbone, Sabine Staresmore, and Edmund Rosier, were there. So were William Erbury—at some undetermined stage of his radical career—and two prominent Independent laymen, Dr. Parker and the lawyer John Cook. These men, representing the whole spectrum of organized radicalism in London at this date apart from the General Baptists, decided that Kiffin and his

---

[38]Goodwin, *Works*, 12:63, emphasis his.

[39]Nuttall, *Saints*, 8.

[40]William Orme, ed. *Remarkable Passages in the Life of William Kiffin* (London: Burton and Smith, 1823), 14; Joseph Ivimey, ed. *The Life of Mr. William Kiffin* (London: Printed for the Author, 1833), 15.

[41]James Culross, *Hanserd Knollys* (London: Alexander and Shepheard, 1895), 13.

[42]Duncan, *Knollys*, 10.

[43]The primary source material for this incident has been reprinted as 'Debate on Infant Baptism, 1643' *Transactions of the Baptist Historical Society* 1 (1908-09): 237-245.

associates were motivated by 'tender conscience and holiness' rather than obstinacy, and that they should not be excommunicated or admonished. They also advised that the Jessey church should regard the dissidents still as members and 'desire conversing together so far as their principles permit them,' unless they grow 'giddy and scandalous.' William Kiffin's Particular Baptist congregation thus came into existence with the blessings of separatist and Independent leaders alike.[44]

The implications of this are patent. The Particular Baptists developed directly out of the climate of separatist and Independent ecclesiology, and in their early days continued to maintain cordial relationships with these ministers and churches.

Throughout the 1640s and 1650s, these groups found opportunities to cooperate with each other. E. B. Underhill,[45] reprints an anonymous document from 1647 which was published in order to respond to several false charges made against Congregational and 'Anabaptist' churches in London. A Second declaration was published in 1651 by the same group, only with names appended.[46] Among those given are the Independents William Greenhill, Thomas Brooks, and Christopher Feake, and Baptists Hanserd Knollys, William Kiffin, and Thomas Harrison.

Contemporary authors seem to have considered the Baptists to be closely akin to the Independents. According to Michael Watts, Thomas Edwards 'defined Anabaptism as "the highest form of Independency"' and

John Winthrop, the Governor of Massachusetts, acknowledged that in England not only the 'godly and orthodox ... Mr. Goodwin, Mr. Nye, and Mr. Burroughes', but even Anabaptists, Antinomians, and Seekers 'went under the name of Independents.'[47]

---

[44]Tolmie, *Triumph*, 56.

[45]E. B. Underhill, ed., *Confessions of Faith, and Other Public Documents, Illustrative of the Baptist Churches of England in the 17th Century* (London: The Hanserd Knollys Society, 1854), '*A Declaration by Congregationall Societes in, and about the City of LONDON; as well of those commonly called Anabaptists, as others. In way of Vindication of themselves. Touching, 1. Liberty. 2. Magistracy. 3. Propriety. 4. Polygamie. Wherein their Judgments, concerning the particulars mentioned are tendred to consideration, to prevent mis-understanding.*' (London: M. Simmons, 1647), 273-287.

[46]Underhill, *Confessions*, 287.

[47]Michael Watts, *The Dissenters* (Oxford: The Clarendon Press, 1978), 97-98. The inclusion of Antinomians and Seekers in Winthrop's list should strike a note of caution. These groups, further out on the left wing of seventeenth century radical religion would not have been recognized as churches by the Congregational and Particular Baptist men. They may have claimed the name for themselves, but it is not so certain that others who welcomed the name would have been willing to share it with them.

Nuttall points out that Richard Baxter, writing in 1652, noted that the definable variations among English Protestants could be classified into "'4 differing partyes (Episcopall, Presbyterian, Indep^{d}ent and Erastian)" and thought of "Anabaptists"as differing solely "in pt of Worshipp"'.[48]

B. R. White argues that the Jacob/Lathrop/Jessey Church 'over the years ... took care to nourish a tradition of consultation and concern for other congregations and other leaders'.[49] That church was noted for its 'semi-separatist' relationship to the National Church, being unwilling to condemn the Church outright, and maintaining cordial relations, while still remaining without its boundaries.[50] This catholicity was similarly expressed towards the more rigorous groups which seceded from them at various points during the 1630s and 1640s. There was a deep respect for the tender consciences exhibited by others. It may well have provided the climate for the close relations between the Particular Baptists and their Independent Paedobaptist acquaintances during the first two decades of the Baptists' existence. Having said this, it is nevertheless important to remember that the Particular Baptists did not themselves maintain ambivalent opinions toward the National Church. White is correct in asserting

> They were ... not 'Semi'-Separatists. The convictions about believer's baptism which they held helped them towards wholehearted, no-compromise, separatism from the established Church of England, from their beginnings.[51]

In many of their writings and documents, the term 'Babylon' is used to refer to the National Church.[52] They could maintain cordial relations with Godly men,

---

[48]Nuttall, *Visible Saints*, 120. The material from Baxter is found 'in letters of May 7th and November 20th, 1652, to John Durie, in Dr. William's Library, MSS. 59.6.90 and 88'.

[49]B. R. White, 'The Doctrine of the Church in the Particular Baptist Confession of 1644', *Journal of Theological Studies*, n.s., 19, pt. 2, (October 1968): 586.

[50]Watts, *Dissenters*, 50-53 describes these ecclesiological relationships in detail. Watts prefers not to use the term 'semi-separatist' as he argues that it would not have been recognized by those whom it is intended to describe, and urges the use of 'Jacobite' instead. For the purposes of the present study, 'semi-separatist' is more descriptive of the nature of the practices of the Church than is 'Jacobite'

[51]B. R. White, 'The Origins and Convictions of the First Calvinistic Baptists', *BHH* 25, no. 4, (October, 1990): 41-42.

[52]See the extended discussion of the propriety of paying tithes to ministers of the Established Church in B. R. White, ed. *Association Records of the Particular Baptists of England, Wales and Ireland to 1660* (*ARPB*) (London: The Baptist Historical Society, 1974), 151-52. The records say, 'the paying of tithes to the nationall ministrie is likewise an owning and supporting of it and of their nationall service and worship which yet we know to be Babilonish and antichristian'. Similarly, Edward Terrill, the author of the Broadmead, Bristol records concludes his twelve stage description of how the reformed

but could not countenance the practices in the Church. In this sense, the Particular Baptists must be understood to be strict Separatists.

THE WEDDING OF CALVINISTIC THEOLOGY WITH BAPTIST POLITY: SELF-CONSCIOUSLY REFORMED CHURCHES

As these churches emerged, they adopted a self-conscious identity placing themselves among the reformed churches. So far as they were concerned, their views were thoroughly orthodox, in agreement with the best of churches in all things except baptism. The authors of the First London Confession made this explicit in its preface,[53] as did the editors of the Second Confession.[54] Daniel Featley understood the purpose of the 1644 Confession, stating

> if we give credit to this Confession and the Preface thereof, those who among us are branded with that title [i.e. Anabaptist], are neither Hereticks, nor Schismatics, but tender hearted Christians: upon whom, through false suggestions, the hand of authority fell heavy, whilst the Hierarchy stood: for, they neither teach free-will; nor falling away from grace with the *Arminians*, nor deny originall sinne with the *Pelagians* ... and to this purpose they have published this confession of Faith, subscribed by sixteen persons, in the name of seven Churches in *London*.[55]

John Tombes, writing in 1645 in response to Stephen Marshall appealed to the statements in the Confession in defense of the orthodoxy of the Baptists.[56] He was not part of these churches, though he shared a common commitment to Believer's Baptism by immersion.

A fascinating description of the Particular Baptist self-identity is found in the Records of the Broadmead, Bristol, church. The author, Edward Terrill, one of the elders of the church, begins his account with a lengthy history of the origins of his own assembly. Using a twelve point summary, he describes how 'ye Lord led them by Degrees, and brought them out of Popish Darknesse into

---

doctrines and practices came to Bristol by stating 'They were holpen by ye Lord to cast off this alsoe, and to step this further in their Reformation, That at last they would not hear those men that did read Common prayer, that therby did declare themselves to owne or partake in any parte Consentingly to ye Worship of ye Beast.' Roger Hayden, ed., *The Records of a Church of Christ in Bristol, 1640-1687* (Bristol: The Bristol Record Society, 1974), 95-96.

[53]Lumpkin, *BCF*, 155.

[54]*A Confession of Faith*, unnumbered pages 4-5 of 'To the Judicious and Impartial Reader'.

[55]Featley, *The Dippers Dip't*, 177-78. He did not accept the Baptist claims to orthodoxy.

[56]John Tombes, *Two Treatises and an Appendix to them Concerning Infant Baptisme* (London: George Whittington, 1645), 31, 34. The statements are in the second treatise, entitled 'An Examen of the Sermon of Mr. Stephen Marshal, about Infant Baptism, in a Letter sent to him'.

his Marvellous light of ye Gospel'.[57] The first degree refers to the global reformation under Luther and Calvin. This is followed by the gradual reformation of the Church of England and the adoption of further reforms leading to the formation of the church in Bristol. He says, 'Thus I have briefly recited Twelve steps that doth compleate a demonstration that they, this Church, in their beginning, were truly reformed in a greate measure, in turning from ye Worship of Antichrist.'[58]

This self-conscious identity grew out of the high view of Scripture held by the Particular Baptists. They considered it to be a fully authoritative document,[59] and understood their doctrine of baptism to be the logical (and theological) conclusion to the principles of the Reformation. Hanserd Knollys expressed the fundamental authority of Scripture:

> Christ is the Legislator, the Law-giver, the Bible is his and the Churches Statute Book, and all the Churches, Ministers and Saints of God are to be governed by his Royal Law of Liberty, in obeying and keeping.[60]

Benjamin Keach applied this principle to his contemporaries:

> Why will not our Brethren keep to the great Institution, and exact rule of the Primitive church? Must we content our selves with the Light which the Church had in respect of this and other Gospel-Truths at the beginning of the Reformation, —since God hath brought forth greater (to the praise of his own rich Grace) in our Days?[61]

In 1690, five London elders expounded this theme in a preface to Philip Cary's *A Solemn Call*. The 'Blessed Reformers, Luther, Calvin, &c.' restored the doctrine of justification by faith to the church. Afterwards, 'Dr. Ames, Mr. Ainsworth, and Dr. Owen, with others' gave proper scriptural definition to the church. But they did not complete the work, so that 'now of latter Years the Lord hath been pleased to raise up some worthy and learned Men to detect the vanity of Infant Baptism'. This was, for them, the explicit fulfillment of the

---

[57]Hayden, *Broadmead Records*, 93.

[58]Hayden, *Broadmead Records*, 96. More than three decades later, Isaac Marlow also spoke of the Baptist churches as 'Reformed Churches'. See Isaac Marlow, *The Purity of Gospel-Communion, or, Grounds and Reasons For Separation* (London: J. Astwood, 1694), 39.

[59]L. Russ Bush and Tom J. Nettles, *Baptists and the Bible* (Chicago: Moody Press, 1980), 47-99.

[60]Hanserd Knollys, *The Parable of the Kingdom of Heaven Expounded* (London: Benjamin Harris, 1674), 13.

[61]Keach, *Gold Refin'd*, unnumbered page 5 of the Epistle.

promise of Daniel 12.4, 'Many shall run to and fro, and Knowledg shall be increased.' 'Antichristian' darkness was being overcome in stages by light.[62]

Knollys, Keach and the others are typical of the convictions held among the Particular Baptists. They believed that they had taken the principles of the Reformation to their proper conclusion. The recovery of the Gospel and all of the related truths was finalized in the ordering of the church according to the Scriptural pattern. In this sense, they were self-consciously more reformed than the paedobaptist reformed churches.

The Second London Baptist Confession of Faith
in its Historical and Theological Context

The Second London Baptist Confession of Faith of 1677/89, and its predecessor of 1644/46, are perhaps the two most influential Baptist Confessions in existence.[63] In many ways, the more recent Confession eclipses the earlier in importance, for by 1689 the First London Confession had become scarce, so much so that one of the key subscribers to the Second Confession stated that he had not previously seen the earlier document.[64] It was the latter

---

[62]'To the Reader', in Philip Cary, *A Solemn Call Unto all that would be owned as Christ's Faithful Witnesses, speedily, and seriously, to attend unto the Primitive Purity of the Gospel Doctrine and Worship: Or, a Discourse concerning Baptism* (London: John Harris, 1690), unnumbered page 1. The five elders were William Kiffin, John Harris, Richard Adams, Robert Steed and Benjamin Keach.

[63]Lumpkin, *BCF*, 239.

[64]When the 1677 Confession was published, the editors paid tribute to the earlier Confession in their epistle 'To the Judicious and Impartial Reader'. They assert that the new Confession contains the same doctrine as the earlier one, which 'is not now commonly to be had'. *A Confession of Faith put Forth by the Elders and Brethren of Many Congregations of Christians (baptized upon Profession of their Faith) in London and the Country* (London: n.p., 1677), unnumbered page 2 of 'To the Reader ....' This scarcity was confirmed several years later by an unfortunate incident in the controversy over hymn singing. Benjamin Keach, in one of his printed writings on the subject (apparently *A Reply to Mr. Steed's Epistle Concerning Singing*) stated that the early Particular Baptist churches did not 'unanimously conclude and declare' that minister's should receive financial support from their churches (cited in William Kiffin, Robert Steed, George Barrett, and Edward Man *A Serious Answer to a Late Book, Stiled, A Reply to Mr. Robert Steed's Epistle Concerning Singing* (London: n.p., 1696), 18). They immediately criticize Keach for this blunder, demonstrating that the 1644 Confession explicitly advocated such ministerial 'maintenance'. Keach issued a retraction stating, 'Nor do I think it grievous to me to retract any Fault of Error this way; but contrariwise, since I have seen a Confession of Faith, put forth by several Brethren in Behalf of themselves and seven of the first baptized Churches in London, published in the Year 1644, I am glad to have this to say for the clearing of the said baptized Churches in this great Case; though I declare to you that I knew nothing of that Confession till I was informed of it by the offended Brethren ....' Benjamin Keach, *To all the Baptized*

document which quickly became the standard of Calvinistic Baptist orthodoxy in England, North America, and today, in many parts of the world.

This Confession, influential as it is, may perhaps best be understood against its historical and theological backgrounds. It did not appear *de novo*, the product of a sudden burst of theological insight on the part of an author or authors, but in the tradition of good Confession making, it is largely dependent on the statements of earlier Reformed Confessions. The First London Confession, published prior to the Westminster Standards, relied heavily on the 1596 True Confession, and on the writings of William Ames.[65] A quick glance will demonstrate that the Second Confession follows the same methodology, being based, to a large degree, on that most Puritan of documents, the Westminster Confession of Faith of 1647. A closer inspection will reveal that it is even more intimately related to the revision of the Westminster Confession made by John Owen and others in 1658, popularly known as the Savoy Declaration and Platform of Polity. In almost every case the editors of the Baptist Confession follow the revisions of the Savoy editors when they differ from the Westminster document.[66] In addition, the Baptists make occasional

---

Churches and faithful Brethren in England and Wales, Christian Salutations (London: n.p., 1692), 4.

[65]The literature on the sources of the 1644 Confession is growing. B. R. White states that it was William Whitley, in his *A History of British Baptists* Rev. Ed. (London: n.p., 1932), 94, who first identified the connection between the First London Confession and the True Confession. See White, 'The Doctrine of the Church in the Particular Baptist Confession of 1644', *Journal of Theological Studies* n.s., 19, no. 2 (Oct., 1968): 575-582. A second source has been identified by Glen H. Stassen in his article 'Anabaptist Influence in the Origin of the Particular Baptists,' *The Mennonite Quarterly Review* 36, no. 4 (Oct. 1962): 322-348. He demonstrates that the Particular Baptists drew from William Ames' *The Marrow of Theology* for some of their material. Stassen's suggestion of the use of Ames' work has been supplemented by Stanley A. Nelson, 'Reflecting on Baptist Origins: The London Confession of Faith of 1644', *BHH* 29 (April 1994): 33-46. W. J. McGlothlin points to a third source in the 1603 'Points of Difference', a brief statement of fourteen points of difference between the Amsterdam Separatists and King James; see W. J. McGlothlin, 'The Sources of the First Calvinistic Baptist Confession of Faith' *Review and Expositor* 13, no. 4 (Oct. 1916): 502-505, cited in Richard Belcher and Anthony Mattia, *A Discussion of the Seventeenth Century Particular Baptist Confessions of Faith,* (Southbridge, Mass.: Crown Publications, 1990), 2. The text of the 'Points of Difference' may be consulted in Walker, *The Creeds & Platforms of Congregationalism,* 77-80. A fourth source has been suggested in Renihan, 'An Examination', 200-202. In that work, the possible influence of Menno Simons is rejected, while the writings of Praise God Barbone are analyzed as a potential source or paradigm for some of the Baptists' expressions.

[66]Samuel Waldron, *A Modern Exposition of the 1689 Baptist Confession of Faith* (Darlington: Evangelical Press, 1989), 425-432. Waldron demonstrates that the Savoy Documents provide the vast majority of materials for the Second London Confession, occasionally supplemented by the First London and other as yet unidentified sources.

use of phraseology from the First London Confession. When all of this material is accounted for, there is very little that is new and original to the 1677/89 Confession.

This heavy dependence on previous sources was very much part of the purpose of the composition of the Confession. In the epistle 'To the Judicious and Impartial Reader' attached to the first edition of the Confession, the editors state:

> And forasmuch as our method, and manner of expressing our sentiments, in this, doth vary from the former [i.e. the First London Confession] (although the substance of the matter is the same) we shall freely impart to you the reason and occasion thereof. One thing that greatly prevailed with us to undertake this work, was (not only to give a full account of ourselves, to those Christians that differ from us about the subject of Baptism, but also) the profit that might from thence arise, unto those that have any account of our labors, in their instruction, and establishment in the great truths of the Gospel; in the clear understanding, and steady belief of which, our comfortable walking with God, and fruitfulness before him, in all our ways, is most neerly concerned; and therefore we did conclude it necessary to expresse our selves the more fully, and distinctly; and also to fix on such a method as might be most comprehensive of those things which we designed to explain our sense, and belief of; and finding no defect, in this regard, in that fixed on by the assembly [i.e. the Westminster Assembly], and after them by those of the Congregational way [i.e. the Savoy Synod], we did readily conclude it best to retain the same *order* in our present confession: and also, when we observed that those last mentioned, did in their confession (for reasons which seemed of weight both to themselves and others) choose not only to express their mind in words concurrent with the former in sense, concerning all those articles wherein they were agreed, but also for the most part without any variation of the terms we did in like manner conclude it best to follow their example in making use of the very same words with them both, in these articles (which are very many) wherein our faith and doctrine is the same with theirs, and this we did, the more abundantly, to manifest our consent with both, in all fundamental articles of the Christian Religion, as also with many others, whose orthodox confessions have been published to the world; on the behalf of the Protestants in divers Nations and Cities: and also to convince all, that we have no itch to clogge Religion with new words, but do readily acquiesce in that form of sound words, which hath been, in consent with the holy Scriptures, used by others before us, hereby declaring before God, Angels, & Men, our hearty agreement with them, in that wholesome Protestant Doctrine, which with so clear evidence of Scriptures they have asserted: some things indeed, are in some places added, some terms omitted, and

---

The English Baptist historian Robert Oliver corroborates Waldron's views. Dr. Oliver says, '*The Second London Confession* tends to follow the *Savoy Declaration* where that differs from *Westminster*', Robert Oliver, 'Baptist Confession Making 1644 and 1689', unpublished paper delivered to the Strict Baptist Historical Society, March 1989, 20.

some few changed, but these alterations are of that nature, as that we need
not doubt, any charge or suspition of unsoundness in the faith, from any of
our brethren upon account of them.[67]

The Baptists were concerned to demonstrate to all that their doctrinal
convictions had been, from the very start, orthodox and in most ways identical
with the convictions of the Puritans around them. In both of their general
Confessions, the Baptists purposely used existing documents in order to
demonstrate their concurrence with much of current theological thinking. In the
quote above, they argue that the doctrines expressed in both Baptist
Confessions are the same, but they have chosen to base the newer Confession
upon the more recent and widely available documents of Westminster and
Savoy. In doing this, they were declaring with some vigor their own desire to
be placed in the broad stream of English Reformed Confessional Christianity.

This methodology provides us with some insight into understanding the
Confession and its teaching. When it concurs with these other documents, it can
be read as an endorsement of the views espoused by those Presbyterians and
Independents who subscribed those documents, and of the theological works
they published in defense of the Confessional statements. Thus, if one wonders
how the Baptists understood the doctrine of the Decree of God, or Justification,
or the application of the Law to people's consciences, or how they worked out
the implications of the teaching on the Perseverance of the Saints, one may
consult the writings of paedobaptist Puritans with much profit. Since both the
Westminster Confession and the Savoy Declaration are readily available, it is
relatively easy to compare the documents in order to determine agreement. Of
course, not every word of every author is necessarily a fair representation of
their views, but in general, their method implies substantial theological
agreement with the writings of their orthodox contemporaries.

There is one significant instance in which the Baptists differ in methodology
from the Independents, and this has to do with the major portion under
consideration in this study, the statements of Chapter 26 of the Second London
Confession. The Savoy Divines explained their own method of compiling and
asserting their views in the preface to their publication. Their documents were
originally published in two parts: the Declaration, which is a Confession of
Faith, and the Platform of Polity, or as it is entitled, *Of the Institution of
Churches, and the Order Appointed in them by Jesus Christ.* They are very
plain in their reasons for separating these documents:

> We have endeavored throughout, to hold to such Truths in this our
> Confession, as are more properly termed *matters of Faith*; and what is of
> *Church-order*, we dispose in certain Propositions by it self. To this course
> we are led by the Example of the Honorable *Houses of Parliament,*

---

[67]*A Confession of Faith*, unnumbered pages 2-5 of 'To the Judicious and Impartial
Reader'.

observing what was established, and what omitted by them in that *Confession* the Assembly presented to them. Who thought it not convenient to have matters of *Discipline* and *Church-Government* put into a *Confession of Faith*, especially such particulars thereof, as then were, and still are controverted and under dispute by men Orthodox and sound in Faith.... There being nothing that tends more to heighten dissentings among Brethren, then to determine and adopt the matter of their difference, under so high a title, as to be an Article of our Faith.[68]

The Independent methodology is clear. Many doctrines, held in common with the Presbyterians as expressed in the Westminster Confession, deserve to be regarded as matters of faith, and so to be included in the Confession. But matters of ecclesiological polity, since they are to some degree debatable, are placed in a separate document so that no one will be offended by thinking that the Independents treat these things on the same level as the matters contained in the Declaration itself.

The Baptists did not follow this method when they published their Confession in 1677. In Chapter 26, they used an editorial method different from that used in the rest of the Confession. The redactors took some of the material placed by the Savoy divines in the Platform of Polity, incorporated it into their chapter on the Church, and in so doing, elevated these matters to Articles of Faith. By this action, they consciously invested the statements of Chapter 26 with a greater authority than did the Independents who placed this material in a distinct Platform. In this way, the statements of Chapter 26 which are taken from the Savoy Platform may, in some cases, be understood in a peculiarly Baptist fashion even though the language may be identical to that of the Savoy Platform. No contemporaries would have missed this significant alteration in methodology. Caution must be exercised in evaluating this material in the light of the ecclesiology of the Independents.

The use of earlier confessional material explains the reason why certain subjects are addressed in the Confession. In the troubled times of the second half of the seventeenth century, topics such as the relationship between church and state, the role of the magistrate, and even the Christian doctrine of marriage were important contemporary issues. The Independents, like the Baptists were very much concerned for liberty of conscience. The Presbyterian party, with an ecclesiology more conducive to a national church, had some within its ranks who argued strongly against toleration for any dissenters. After the Restoration of 1660, and the enforcement of the Clarendon Code, non-conformists were subject to severe penal acts. It must also be remembered that the Protestants of England feared a return to Roman Catholicism throughout most of the century. Charles I and Charles II both married Roman Catholics, and James II was a

---

[68]From the Preface to the Savoy Declaration, Walker, *The Creeds and Platforms of Congregationalism*, 363.

professing Romanist. The old doctrines of the Reformation needed to be asserted in the face of this royal departure and its potential implications for church and society. From this mix came the pressing need to address these contemporary issues in a Confession, and accounts for the presence of the topics included there.

The Origins of the Baptist Confession of Faith

Based on the available information, it is impossible to determine precisely the origins of the Second London Confession. There are, however, some indications which help to narrow the field.

The first known reference to the document is found in the manuscript minute book of the Petty France Church in London. On 26 August, 1677, this note was entered: 'It was agreed that a Confession of faith, wth the Appendix thereto having bene read & considered by the Bre: should be published.'[69] Joseph Ivimey, the English Baptist historian of the early nineteenth century took this to imply that the Confession originated in the Petty France Church,[70] very likely an accurate supposition. In E. B. Underhill's *Confessions of Faith and Other Public Documents Illustrative of the Baptist Churches of England in the 17th Century*, a noteworthy 'advertisement' is prefaced to the reprint of the Second London Confession. It says,

> This Confession of our Faith, together with the brief Instructions of the Principles of Christian Religion, or the Catechisms, both with the proofs in the margin, and also that with the words of the scriptures at length; with this Confession, put forth by the ministers, elders, and brethren of above one hundred congregations of Christians, baptized on profession of their faith in England and Wales, denying Arminianism, owning the doctrine of personal election and final perseverance: having sold the property, right and title of the printing thereof, to John Marshall, bookseller, at the Bible in Gracechurch Street, by us, William Collins and Benjamin Keach, it is desired that all persons desirous to promote such useful books, do apply themselves to him.[71]

This 'advertisement' is said to have been prefaced 'To the fifth edition, 1720'. It indicates that William Collins, one of the elders at London's Petty France

---

[69]Petty France Church Minute Book 1675-1727, The Guildhall Library, London, 5.

[70]Joseph Ivimey, *A History of the English Baptists* (*HEB*) (London: B. J. Holdsworth, 1823), 3:332. Ivimey writes, 'It should seem ... that this confession was prepared for the purpose of expressing the faith of that particular church, but was adopted by upwards of one hundred churches at the General Assembly in 1689.'

[71]E. B. Underhill, *Confessions of Faith and Other Public Documents Illustrative of the Baptist Churches of England in the 17th Century* (London: The Hanserd Knollys Society, 1854), 172.

Church from 1675 to 1702,[72] and Benjamin Keach, from 1668-1704[73] an elder of the Southwark, Horselydown Church owned the proprietary rights to these two documents, the Confession and the Catechism. This would tend to indicate that they had some stake, as holders of the 'property, right and title' to them, in the authorship, or editing of the two. Keach could not have been the original editor of the Confession. It incorporates several statements from the 1644 London Baptist Confession, and Keach stated in 1692 that he had not seen that document until just prior to the General Assembly held in London during that year.[74] Although he could not have been responsible for the appearance of the Confession, he has been frequently identified with the Catechism.[75] It is possible that he owned the 'property, right and title' to it, and that Collins owned the 'property, right and title' to the Confession as its original editor. Both Collins and Keach died by 1704, thus the advertisement must have been appended to an earlier edition of the Confession.

Another factor contributing to the view that the Confession originated with the Petty France church and its elders is based upon the status of the church and its two pastors. The Petty France church was one of the original seven London churches. In 1675, Nehemiah Coxe and William Collins were ordained as co-pastors on the same day.[76]

Nehemiah Coxe was the son of the early Particular Baptist leader Benjamin Coxe.[77] In 1669, he joined the Bedford Independent church made famous by John Bunyan, and in 1673 was called to serve as pastor of the church's sub-congregation at Hitchin. In 1674, he was censured by the Bedford church for certain miscarriages. His acknowledgment has been recorded in the church book:

---

[72]Petty France *CMB*, 1; John Piggott, 'A Funeral Sermon Occasioned by the Death of the reverend Mr. William Collins, Late Minister of the Gospel in London, Who died the 30th of October, 1702,' in *Eleven Sermons Preach'd upon Several Occasions, by the Late Reverend Mr. John Piggott, Minister of the Gospel* (London: John Darby, 1714), 241-286.

[73]Thomas Crosby, *The History of the English Baptists (CHEB)* (London: Printed for the author, 1740) 4:272. Crosby's text has the date '1688', but this is evidently a misprint for '1668' as he immediately states that Keach was 28 years old at his ordination to this church. He was born in 1640.

[74]Benjamin Keach, *To all the Baptized Churches*, 4.

[75]It is popularly known as 'Keach's Catechism', and has been published in a modern edition under that title. See *The Philadelphia Confession of Faith being the London Confession of Faith Adopted by the Baptist Association 1742, with Scripture References and Keach's Catechism* (Sterling, Va.: Grace Abounding Ministries, 1977). See below for a discussion of Collins' relationship to the Catechism.

[76]Petty France *CMB*, 1, entry for 'ye 21th of ye 7th M' (Aug. 21, 1675).

[77]W. T. Whitley, 'Benjamin Cox' *TBHS* 6 (1918-19): 58.

> Whereas several words and practices have been uttered and performed by
> me, that might justly be censured to have a tendency to make rents and
> divisions in the congregation, I do declare myself unfeignedly sorry and
> repentant for the same.[78]

It may be that Coxe's words and practices were related to the issue of open or
closed membership, so hotly debated at the time.[79] Benjamin Coxe clearly
advocates a closed membership position in his published writings,[80] while the
Bedford church, and especially Bunyan, resisted such a notion with great
vigor.[81] Could Nehemiah have been advocating such views, which the Bedford
people would view as having 'a tendency to make rents and divisions in the
congregation'? His appearance at the closed membership Petty France church
so soon after this could help to explain the situation.

Coxe was a qualified physician,[82] skilled in Latin, Greek and Hebrew,[83] and
a discerning theologian. When the West Country evangelist Thomas Collier
began to deviate from the Calvinistic Orthodoxy of the London Churches, the
elders in London asked Coxe to reply in print to Collier's views. He did this in
his 1677 work *Vindiciae Veritatis, or a Confutation of the Heresies and Gross
Errours Asserted by Thomas Collier*. In a brief epistle at the beginning of the
work, they address the issue of Coxe's 'inferiority in years', stating that he did
not write the book out of a sense of personal ability, but at their request,
because 'we did judge him meet and of ability for the work' and because his
responsibilities at the time provided him with the opportunity to answer
Collier's errors. They say of this work,

> we hope, we may truly say, without particular respect to his Person, he hath
> behaved himself with that modesty of Spirit, joined with that fulness and

---

[78]*The Church Book of Bunyan Meeting 1650-1821* (London: J. M. Dent & Sons, 1928
facsimile reprint), 27, 54.

[79]I am indebted for this suggestion to T. E. Dowley, 'A London Congregation during the
Great Persecution: Petty France Particular Baptist Church, 1641-1688,' *BQ* 27, no. 5
(Jan. 1978): 238. Dowley says 'It has been suggested that his error lay in his advocacy
of closed-membership—a principle rejected by both Hitchin and Bedford.' He does not
identify the source of the suggestion.

[80]Benjamin Cox 'An Appendix to a Confession of Faith' reprinted with *A Confession of
Faith of Seven Congregations of Churches in London, Which are Commonly (but
unjustly) Called Anabaptists* (Rochester, New York: Backus Book Publishers, 1981),
32-33.

[81]John Bunyan, 'A Confession of My Faith, and a Reason of My Practice' in *The Works
of the Eminent Servant of Christ, John Bunyan* (Philadelphia: J. W. Bradley, 1860),
2:203. Bunyan published two other works on the subject, 'Differences in Judgment
about Water Baptism no Bar to Communion' and 'Peaceable Principles and True'.

[82]Dowley, 'A London Congregation', 234.

[83]Ivimey, *HEB*, 2:404.

clearness of answer and strength of argument, that we comfortably conceive (by God's blessing) it may prove a good and sovraign Antidote against the poison.[84]

The book is a solid exposition of Reformed doctrine. The esteem expressed for such a man, in a very important circumstance,[85] would suit one responsible for the editing of the Confession of Faith which appeared in the same year. His reputation was such that his contemporary C. M. du Veil spoke, in his 1685 *Commentary on Acts*, of 'that great divine, eminent for all manner of learning, Nehemiah Cox'.[86]

Nehemiah Coxe was held in high regard by his peers, and would thus have been well equipped to serve as an editor of the Confession of Faith. He died in 1688, prior to the General Assembly of 1689, leaving behind one son.

Coxe's co-elder William Collins received a thorough education, graduating B.D. and touring Europe prior to his call to serve at Petty France. In a funeral sermon preached by John Piggott, a fortnight after Collins' death on 30 October, 1702, mention is made of 'the encouraging Offers he had to join the National Church, which he judiciously refus'd; for "twas Conscience, not Humour, that made him a Dissenter"'.[87] Collins, according to Piggott, was a studious elder and a good pastor, noted for his peaceable spirit.

> The Subjects he ordinarily insisted on in the Course of his Ministry, were the great and important Truths of the Gospel, which he handled with great Judgment and Clearness. How would he open the Miseries of the Fall! And in how moving a manner would he discourse of the Excellency of Christ, and the Virtues of his Blood, and his willingness to save poor awaken'd burdned [sic.] Sinners! ... His sermons were useful under the Influence of Divine Grace, to convert and edify, to enlighten and establish, being drawn from the Fountain of Truth, the Sacred Scriptures, with which he constantly convers'd in their Original Languages, having read the best Criticks, Antient and Modern; so that Men of the greatest Penetration might learn from his Pulpit-Discourses, as well as those of the meanest Capacity.[88]

---

[84]Nehemiah Coxe, *Vindiciae Veritatis, or a Confutation of the Heresies and Gross Errours asserted By Thomas Collier in his Additional Word to his Body of Divinity* (London: Nath. Ponder: 1677), unnumbered pages 1 and 2. The letter is signed by William Kiffin, Daniel Dyke, Joseph Maisters, James Fitton, Henry Forty and William Collins.

[85]Michael Haykin speaks of Collier's defection as 'perhaps the most pressing reason for a new confession'. Michael Haykin, *Kiffin, Knollys and Keach: Rediscovering Our English Baptist Heritage* (Leeds: Reformation Today Trust, 1996), 68.

[86]C. M. du Veil, *A Commentary on the Acts of the Apostles* (London: The Hanserd Knollys Society, 1851 reprint), 70.

[87]Piggott, 'Funeral Sermon', 279.

[88]Piggott, 'Funeral Sermon', 280-81.

Such a testimony of his character and abilities well suits one thought to be co-editor of the Confession of Faith.

The esteem in which he was held by his brethren may be noted in the fact that he was requested by the 1693 General Assembly to draw up a Catechism,[89] and on the strength of this Ivimey asserts 'It is probable that the Baptist Catechism was compiled by Mr. Collins, though it has by some means or other been called Keach's Catechism.'[90] A few pages later, Ivimey transcribes a letter from Collins to Andrew Gifford, pastor of the Pithay Church in Bristol, and arguably the most important Particular Baptist outside of London. In the letter, Collins refers to the latest impression of the Catechism, and states that there are 'some thousands left'.[91] These facts seem to point to significant involvement, on the part of Collins, in the editing of the Catechism as well.[92] It would make sense to ask the man who had proven his ability to edit a Confession to do the same with a catechism.[93]

Though it cannot be stated with certainty, much circumstantial evidence points to Coxe and Collins as the originators of the Confession. They were both qualified and respected men, and the first mention of the document is found in their church book, approving publication. Each one of them was requested to take the lead in theological writing, a fact that would be expected of such men. Until other evidence is found, this seems to be the most likely scenario for the origin of the Confession.

The Acceptance of the Confession

When the Second London Confession was initially published in 1677, its title page indicated that it contained the views of 'many congregations of Christians ... in London and the Country'.[94] Some have read this statement as an indication of a general meeting held to endorse the document in 1677, but there is no external evidence to corroborate such a notion.[95] It is probably impossible to determine the number of, or even the identity of, most of the 'many

---

[89]Ivimey, *HEB*, 1:533.

[90]Ivimey, *HEB*, 2:397.

[91]Ivimey, *HEB*, 2:414. The letter is dated 5 July 1698.

[92]The *A Brief Instruction in Principles of Christian Religion* 5th ed.(London, 1695), used the same principle method as in editing the Second London Confession. The Westminster Shorter Catechism is the basis for the Baptist work.

[93]What then of the involvement of Benjamin Keach? The traditional identification of Keach as the author is strong, and the presence of the advertisement linking his name with Collins is weighty. It may be that Collins and Keach collaborated on the Catechism. There is reason to believe that Collins was slow to produce a Catechism, as the Bristol Association wrote to Kiffin and Collins in 1694, urging them, among other things, to press ahead with the Catechism. See Ivimey, *HEB*, 1:534-35.

[94]*A Confession of Faith*, title page.

[95]Waldron, *Modern Exposition*, 428; Oliver, 'Baptist Confession Making', 15.

congregations' willing to confess their faith by means of this document in 1677. But there are some indications of its acceptance in the 1680s.

In 1681, Hanserd Knollys makes direct reference to the Confession in his book *The World that Now is; and the World that is to Come*. In the midst of a section explaining the procedure of church discipline, Knollys incorporates phrases from Chapter 26, paragraphs 3 and 13.[96] Nehemiah Coxe, in a sermon preached and published in 1681, similarly incorporates phrases from Chapter 26, paragraphs 8 and 10 into his expressions.[97] In both of these cases, the confessional statements are woven into the argument of the writer without attribution.

The propaedeutic nature of the Confession is demonstrated by an incident from the life of the Broadmead, Bristol church. In April 1682, they required Thomas Whinnell, a member of a General Baptist church who was attempting to join their assembly, to subscribe the Confession, in order to ensure that his views were consonant with their own.[98] The serious differences in the convictions of these theologically diverse groups were settled paradigmatically by means of this personal affirmation. Whinnell went on to become pastor of the Taunton, Somersetshire Particular Baptist church.

Benjamin Keach used the Confession as an apologetic tool in 1694. He was engaged in a debate over the validity of infant baptism, responding to a question on the status of infants. Asserting that 'all infants are under the Guilt and stain of original sin ... and that no infant can be saved but through the Blood and Imputation of Christs righteousness'. He refers to the 'Article of our Faith', and bluntly says 'See our confession of Faith'. For Keach, the doctrine contained in the Confession was a handy means by which to refute the notion of 'habitual [infant] faith' held by his opponent.[99]

---

[96]Hanserd Knollys, *The World that Now is; and the World that is to Come* (London: Tho. Snowden, 1681), 96, 99.

[97]Nehemiah Coxe, *A Sermon Preached at the Ordination of an Elder and Deacons in a Baptized Congregation in London* (London: Tho. Fabian, 1681), 15, 36-38.

[98]Hayden, *The Records of A Church of Christ*, 241. The records actually state that he 'professed to believe ye principles contained in ye Baptist Confession of Faith, 1667'. The modern editor states 'No Confession of Faith of this date is known. It is likely that Terrill [the author of the *Records*] is referring to the Particular Baptist Confession of Faith for 1677, which was a standard test of orthodoxy among Particular Baptist Churches of the time.'

[99]Benjamin Keach, *A Counter Antidote to purge out the Malignant Effects of a Late Counterfiet, Prepared by Mr. Gyles Shute, an Unskilful Person in Polemical Cures* (London: H. Bernard, 1694), 12. Habitual faith is 'The God-given spiritual capacity of fallen human beings to have faith'. See Richard A. Muller, *Dictionary of Latin and Greek Theological Terms* (Grand Rapids: Baker Book House, 1985), 134. Shute seems to have argued that this habit of faith, apart from the actual act of faith, was sufficient to save infants, and was thus a basis for their baptism.

At the 1689 General Assembly, the importance of the Confession was manifest. As many as 108 churches were represented or sent communications to the Assembly, and the Confession was endorsed in famous terms:

> We the Ministers and Messengers of, and concerned for, upwards of one hundred Baptized Congregations in *England* and *Wales* (denying *Arminianism*) being met together in *London* from the 3*d* of the 7*th* Month to the 11*th* of the same, 1689, to consider of some things that might be for the Glory of God, and the good of these Congregations; have thought meet (for the satisfaction of all other Christians that differ from us in the point of Baptism) to recommend to their perusal the Confession of our Faith, Printed for, and sold by, Mr. *John Harris* at the *Harrow* in the *Poultrey*; Which Confession we own, as containing the Doctrine of our Faith and Practice; and do desire that the Members of our Churches respectively do furnish themselves therewith.[100]

They 'own' the Confession, and insist that it is a plain statement of their belief and practice. For them, the Confession was an apologetic tool. Outsiders would be able to read its declarations and recognize that these churches were doctrinally orthodox. The seriousness of this statement is exemplified in the words of the host Broken Wharf church, whose pastor in 1691 was Hanserd Knollys. In 1706, when an attempt was being made to revive the defunct London Association, they refused to join in

> Because the solemn owning & ratifying of our so well attested & generall approved Confession of Faith, as transmitted to us in ye full evidence of yt word by our late pastors &c in ye general assembly seems to us as it did also to them a thing absolutely nessesary to ye just & regular constitution of all associations: but ye admitting of the above sd churches into Association renders this altogether impracticable.[101]

They published these words in a public letter explaining their reasons for remaining aloof,

---

[100]*A Narrative of the Proceedings of the General Assembly Of divers Pastors, Messengers and Ministring Brethren of the Baptized Churches, met together in London, from Septemb. 3. to 12. 1689, from divers parts of England and Wales: Owning the Doctrine of Personal Election, and final Perseverance* (London: Printed in the Year, 1689) 18. It is curious that though the document is commonly known as the 1689 Confession, I can find no bibliographic evidence that it was printed in that year. It was published in 1677, 1688, and 1699. See Donald Wing, *Short-Title Catalogue of Books Printed in England, Scotland, Ireland, Wales, and British America and of English Books Printed in Other Countries 1641-1700*, 2d ed., (New York: The Index Committee of the Modern Language Association of America, 1972), 1:369.
[101]Bagnio/Cripplegate Church Minute Book 1695-1723, Angus Library, Regent's Park College, Oxford, unnumbered page facing page 27.

> Humbly offered to ye consideration of all those Baptized Churches wch
> have or can sign the confession of our Faith printed in ye year 1688 and
> recommended to ye churches by ye Generall Assembly that met at Broken
> Wharf in London 1689.[102]

Confessional subscription was considered to be a serious matter among many
churches.[103] It was 'solemn owning and ratifying', a commitment to a definitive
theological system. So strongly were these men committed to the words
contained in their Confession that they considered anyone 'the grossest sort of
Hypocrite, in professing the contrary by their Profession of Faith, and yet
believing and practicing quite otherwise to what they solemnly professed as
their Faith in that matter'.[104] Throughout the period under consideration, the
Second London Confession was accepted as the defining standard of
theological orthodoxy and orthopraxy within a large circle of churches.

The Demographics of the Particular Baptists

There is no certain means by which to determine precisely the number of
Particular Baptist churches in England, or the total number that subscribed the
Second London Confession. Several factors contribute to this difficulty. Most
obvious is the lacunae in the historical record. Beyond the known churches,
there may have been others that have escaped attention. B. R. White
acknowledges the difficulty of identification in several cases.[105] Some of the
churches that participated in the regional associations were not represented at
the General Assemblies.[106] In some cases, churches failed, others were born,
and splits were not unknown.[107] Further confusing the matter, the historian must
recognize that a neat taxonomy of churches is not always possible. At least five
different kinds of 'Baptist' assemblies may be identified in the last decade of

---

[102]Bagnio/Cripplegate CMB, 26. Broken Wharf was the location of this same church
when Knollys' was pastor.

[103]When the Maze Pond church was constituted in Feb., 1694, it explicitly adopted the
Confession in the first article of the church covenant. Maze Pond Church Book 1691-
1708, The Angus Library, Regent's Park College, Oxford, 1.

[104]William Kiffin, Robert Steed, George Barrett and Edward Man, *A Serious Answer to
a Late Book, Stiled, A Reply to Mr. Robert Steed's Epistle concerning Singing* (London:
Printed in the Year, 1692), 18.

[105]White, *ARPB*, 42, 210.

[106]This is true of both the earlier and latter associations. See White, *ARPB*, 106-107;
Copson, *Northern Association*, 9.

[107]W. T. Whitley, *The Baptists of London 1612-1928* (London: The Kingsgate Press,
n.d.). This book is of great value in tracing the history of the London churches. Whitley
indicates that by 1699, 41 Baptist churches (both Particular and General) had been
known in London alone, 126.

the seventeenth century:[108] General Baptist, Closed-Membership Particular Baptist, Open-Membership Particular Baptist,[109] Seventh Day Baptist and non-Calvinist, non-Arminian Baptist.[110] Occasionally, Churches moved between these positions.[111]

W. T. Whitley, in a 1910 article, summarized and supplemented the Baptist presence contained in the so-called 'Evans Manuscript'.[112] By his count, in 1715 there were 220 Particular Baptist churches in existence in England and Wales, and about half as many General Baptist churches.[113] Included in many of Whitley's entries is a figure of approximate attendance. After extensive comparisons with other extant records, Michael Watts concludes that the figures are generally accurate for the period.[114] According to him, the Particular Baptist strength in England in 1715-18 was 206 churches with 40,520 'hearers', or about 0.74% of the English population, and in Wales, 14 churches with 4,050 'hearers', or 1.31% of the Welsh population.[115] Their presence was greatest 'in the same counties as the Independents from whom they had originally sprung', namely Monmouthshire, Bedfordshire, Hertfordshire,

---

[108]B. R. White, 'Open and Closed Membership among the English and Welsh Baptists', *BQ* 24, no. 7 (July 1972): 330-34, 341. White deals with the first three categories.

[109]The Open-Membership Churches may be further categorized in terms of their relationship to the Closed-Membership churches. Some, such as Broadmead, Bristol, maintained intimate relations with the closed-membership churches, even to the point of participating in the General Assemblies. Others, such as John Bunyan's Bedford church were more closely akin to the Paedobaptist Independent churches, and maintained cool, and sometimes antagonistic relations with the closed-membership Particular Baptists. See Harry Poe, 'John Bunyan's Controversy with the Baptists', *BHH* 23, no. 2 (April 1988): 25-26.

[110]The Paul's Alley, Barbican church sought to maintain a theological position apart from either view of sovereignty and responsibility. See W. T. Whitley, 'Paul's Alley, Barbican, 1695-1768', *TBHS* 4 (1914-15): 50-51; Whitley, *The Baptists of London,* 112.

[111]The Stevington, Bedfordshire church endured a split when it moved from an open-membership to closed-membership position in 1691. See H. G. Tibbutt, ed., *Some Early Nonconformist Church Books* (Bedford: The Bedfordshire Historical Record Society, 1972), 37, 39, 47, 59. The splinter group formed the Carlton, Beds. Independent Church.

[112]W. T. Whitley, 'The Baptist Interest under George I', *TBHS* 2 (1910-11): 95-109. Whitley supplemented the Evans Manuscript at several points. The Evans Manuscript is held at Dr. William's Library in London. It was an attempt to list 'every Presbyterian, Independent, and Baptist congregation in England and Wales' in the period 1715-18. A detailed analysis of its statistics is found in Michael Watts, *The Dissenters* (Oxford: The Clarendon Press, 1978), 267-89, and in the Appendix, 491-510. The quote is from Watts, 268.

[113]Whitley, 'Baptist Interest', 108.

[114]Watts, *Dissenters*, 504.

[115]Watts, *Dissenters*, 509-10.

Somerset, Cardiganshire and Radnorshire.[116] Watts indicates that the Particular Baptist churches were almost evenly divided between urban and rural areas. He says, 'on the basis of the Evans list it is possible to calculate that in England ... 58.0 per cent of Particular Baptists ... worshipped in cities, boroughs, or market towns'. 105 churches were located in cities, boroughs or towns, and 115 were located in rural areas.[117] One might expect that the urban churches would have larger attendance than the more rural churches.

While these figures are for a period a decade later than the current study, they give an approximate sense of the relative strength of the Particular Baptists. There is no reason to believe that they would be significantly different if compiled ten or twenty years earlier. Figures for several churches over a twenty year period indicate little change in total membership.[118]

The 1689 and 1692 *Narratives* of the General Assemblies list the names of the churches which sent representatives 'or otherwise communicated their state' to the Assemblies.[119] The 1690 and 1691 *Narratives* list the churches according to regional associations, though they do not specifically indicate attendance at the London meetings. The numbered totals for 1689 and 1692 are both 107, but there are slight differences in the complexion of the lists. The 1689 register includes three churches not mentioned in the 1692 *Narrative*, most notably Richard Adams' Shad Thames church, which was actually General Baptist. Adams could not persuade them to change their position, and he left the next year to become co-pastor with William Kiffin at the Particular Baptist Devonshire Square church.[120] The 1692 *Narrative* incorporates two new assemblies, Colchester, Essex, and Winchester House, 'Surry' [sic].[121] These numbers account for only about half of the probable number of churches in

---

[116]Watts, *Dissenters*, 282, 509-10. J. F. McGregor states, 'There is no general explanation of the relative distribution of the two wings of the Baptists or the movement's particular strength in some parts but not others. Much depended on the successful qualities of local evangelists.' J. F. McGregor, 'The Baptists: Fount of All Heresy', in *Radical Religion in the English Revolution*, ed. J. F. McGregor and Barry Reay (Oxford: Oxford University Press, 1984), 35. Watts' sugesstion supplements McGregor's.

[117]Watts, *Dissenters*, 285-86.

[118]See below.

[119]1689 *Narrative*, 19.

[120]Murdina MacDonald, 'London Calvinistic Baptists 1689-1727: Tensions Within a Dissenting Community Under Toleration', (D.Phil. Thesis, Regent's Park College, Oxford, 1982), 35.

[121]A discrepancy between the lists is found under the heading for 'Surry'. In the 1689 list, the name 'Southwark' is placed at the head of the churches, and is configured in the same fashion as other churches that did not send a representative, but is not given a number. In the 1692 list, the entry is the same except for the addition of the number '88'. This would seem to indicate that there were actually 108 churches communicating with the 1689 Assembly.

England and Wales. It is presumed that difficulty of travel[122] and the relative weakness of smaller churches may have contributed to their absence from the Assemblies. According to Stephen Copson, the Assembly 'was national in the sense that messengers from different areas attended, but not every church was represented.... Nearly a third came from London and the Home Counties and nearly half from the West of England.'[123] Only two of the churches in the Northern Association were represented at or communicated with the General Assemblies.[124] This pattern may have been repeated in other outlying areas as well.

Indications of the relative strength of certain churches may be drawn from a variety of documents. The records from London's Petty France congregation contain a register of the members beginning on 31 July 1676.[125] In the manuscript, 538 names are listed, 345 women, and 193 men. Sixty-seven married couples are noted. From 21 December 1690 through 7 June 1702, the church received 88 new members by profession of faith and baptism, 28 men and 60 women.[126] These figures indicate membership. It may be assumed that regular attendance was greater than recorded. In 1682, a 'spy' compiled a report on the dissenters in and near London and, according to this document, there were 600 in attendance at Petty France at that time.[127]

---

[122]Joan Parkes, *Travel in England in the Seventeenth Century* (Oxford: Oxford University Press, 1925, reprint, Westport, Conn.: Greenwood Press, 1970), 185-224.

[123]Copson, *Northern Association*, 7.

[124]1689 *Narrative*, 20; 1692 *Narrative*, 15. The 1690 and 1691 *Narratives* list five churches in their suggested ordering of the Northern Association.

[125]Petty France Church Minute Book 1675-1727, The Guildhall Library, London, 1-23 of the 'Catalogue' at the front of the book. The catalogue lists some as 'deceased', but neither Nehemiah Coxe nor William Collins are marked in this way. Some are marked 'cast out' or 'cut off'. Others are noted with place names, apparently either received from or going to, such as Ireland, Bristol, Theobalds, Porton, Steventon, and Morton Hinmarsh, all locations of known Particular Baptist churches. Some of the women are noted with name changes, evidently indicating marriage. The great majority of the names are in the same hand, matching the text of the church book through page 23, 20 January, 1688. This is approximately the time of Nehemiah Coxe's death, and leads me to suppose that it was kept by him to this point. The names mentioned in the Church Book proper stop being added to the membership list at about the same time. The list probably reflects those in membership between 1675-1688/89, with many comings and goings.

[126]Petty France CMB, 30-42 (the pagination in the manuscript is confused. Page 30 is marked 28, and many of the succeeding pages are unnumbered).

[127]W. T. Whitley, 'London Churches in 1682', *BQ* 1 (1922): 82-87. The original is transcribed from the Calendar of State Papers Domestic, Volume 419, Document 55.

The Devonshire Square 'Members Book' contains three lengthy lists of members.[128] It records approximately 216 members, 156 women and 60 men. Thirty married couples may be identified. Among the few 'occupations' given are elder, baker, nursekeeper, weaver, 'a burlers wife', 'A dyers wife', and 'a shoomaker's wife'.[129] Kiffin himself was fabulously successful at his trading business. The famous story of Kiffin's monetary encounter with Charles II is worth repeating. The King sent word to Kiffin that he desired a loan of £40,000. The minister responded that while he could not provide the King with such a large amount in loan at that time, he would be more than happy to provide the King with £10,000 as a gift. Charles accepted, and Kiffin reckoned that he saved himself £30,000![130]

The Assembly meeting at Old Gravel Lane, Wapping, under the ministry of Hercules Collins recorded 387 members in 1686. Six years later, their church book states, 'about 290 person Removed from our church in the course of less than 18 years. about [*sic*] 216 by death the other Rent withdrawn from and excommunicated'.[131] So strong was this church that in 1687, after the issuance of the Declaration of Indulgence, they began plans to build a meeting house, raised the necessary funds, and moved into the building on 7 August. According to Ernest Kevan, 'this is one of the first nonconformist chapels built for this object' in the country.[132]

Hanserd Knollys' church had 134 members in the early 1690s. Of these, 92 were women and 42 were men.[133] The 1682 'spy' had reported that about 200 were then in attendance at this church.[134] They were said to be 'poor': Knollys supported himself through much of his ministry by teaching school.[135]

---

[128]Devonshire Square Church Members Book, The Guildhall Library, London. The first list has an undetermined date, circa 1660. At least one, and probably more, early pages have been torn out. The second list is dated 3 August 1670. The third was made 6 October 1690. It has 4 columns to a page: (1) 'The Names of ye Brothers & Sisters'; (2) 'The place of ther habitation'; (3) 'Their Callings and Relations'; (4) 'Ther Condition whether in Communion or not'. The first pair of names in this list is 'Br. Wm Kiffin Sr Sarah his wife' and it is later noted with regard to her: 'excluded from communion'. The list has received obvious additions and emendations, and it is probably impossible to determine the exact extent of the membership in 1690. There is, however, a change of handwriting at one point. I have treated this as the end of the original list.

[129]Devonshire Square Church Members Book, *passim*.

[130]Thomas Crosby, *The History of the English Baptists, from the Reformation to the Beginning of the Reign of King George I* (*CHEB*) (London: John Robinson, 1740), 3:4.

[131]Ernest F. Kevan, *London's Oldest Baptist Church* (London: The Kingsgate Press,1933), 38-39.

[132]Kevan, *Church*, 46-47.

[133]H. Wheeler Robinson, 'Baptist Church Discipline 1689-1699', *BQ* 1 (1922): 113-16.

[134]Whitley, 'London Churches in 1682', 82.

[135]Hanserd Knollys, *The Life and Death of that Old Disciple of Jesus Christ, and Eminent Minister of the Gospel, Mr. Hanserd Knollys, who Dyed in the Ninety Third*

The larger churches were not restricted to London. The transcript of the Kensworth, Bedfordshire church records lists 395 people, 144 men and 251 women in membership between 1675 and 1694.[136] They were scattered throughout 31 different villages in Bedfordshire and Hertfordshire. Stevington had 170 members, 110 women, 58 men[137] between 1673 and 1700, and in 1679, Broadmead, Bristol had 151 members, 108 'sisters', and 43 'brethren'.[138]

Other churches were not so large as these. Between 1657 and 1684, the Broughton, Hampshire congregation recorded 84 members living in 15 different villages.[139] Bromsgrove, Worcestershire, had 97 members, 41 men and 56 women, in 1670, 80 members, 38 men and 42 women, in 1690, and 96 members, 43 men and 53 women, in 1694.[140] The Plymouth assembly in 1690 had 52 members, 42 women and 10 men,[141] and the Warwick church had 15 male members in the mid 1690s[142]

In Norwich, Norfolk, 51 members were recorded around 1689, 28 men and 23 women, one of the few churches where men outnumbered women in membership. According to C. B. Jewson, 10 male members appear on the city's roll of freemen, with such occupations as worstead weaver, tanner, dyer, tailor, clothworker, tallow chandler, grocer, cordwainer and baker. The pastor of the church, Henry Austine, was a dyer.[143] In 1698, a church was formed in

---

Year of his Age (London: John Harris, 1692), unnumbered page 3 of 'To the Reader'. This autobiography was published posthumously and completed by William Kiffin.

[136]Tibbutt, *Some Early Nonconformist Church Books*, 10-14. It must not be thought that this figure reflects the membership at any one time. This is the total recorded for the two decades. There were many comings and goings during those years. Nonetheless, this was a large church.

[137]Tibbutt, *Nonconformist Church Books*, 23-26. Two of the names were obscured in the original and not reproduced in the transcript, making it impossible to determine the sex of these individuals.

[138]Hayden, *The Records of a Church of Christ*, 273-75. Fifteen other members were 'removed by distance of habitation' or were under discipline, E. B. Underhill, ed., *The Records of A Church of Christ, meeting in Broadmead, Bristol. 1640-1687* (London: The Hanserd Knollys Society, 1847), 419.

[139]Broughton Church Book 1, 1657-1684, The Angus Library, Regent's Park College, Oxford, 108-111.

[140]Bromsgrove Baptist Church Record Book Volume 1 1670-1715, Peter Wortley, Transcriber, (Bromsgrove, Worcs.: Bromsgrove Baptist Church and the Baptist Historical Society, 1974), 13 (86), 25 (98), 31 (104), 49 (121), 51 (122). The typescript has no pagination. Numbers refer to the pages of the original book as recorded in the typescript.

[141]Plymouth (George St.) Church, Manuscript Copy Extracts from Church Book 1648-1776, The Angus Library, Regent's Park College, Oxford, 26.

[142]Warwick Baptist Church Book 1698-1760, Warwickshire County Record Office, 22b. No mention is made of the number of female members.

[143]C. B. Jewson, *The Baptists in Norfolk* (London: The Carey Kingsgate Press, 1957), 38-39.

Bridlington, East Yorkshire by 22 members, 13 women and 9 men.[144] According to Stephen Copson, 'forty-two further were baptized', apparently in the next years. This church became a part of the Northern Association.[145]

A criticism leveled against the Particular Baptists and their ministers was based on the perception that they were without theological training and sophistication. They were 'mechanick preachers'[146] and thus ill-suited for pastoral responsibility. Among their leaders, Kiffin was a merchant, Knollys a school teacher, and Keach a tailor and a book seller. J. Barry Vaughn argues that the anonymous publication of *The Gospel Minister's Maintenance Vindicated* was an attempt to remove this criticism.[147] In several cases (for example Keach, Knollys and Kiffin), ministers were not supported by their churches at a level sufficient to provide for the needs of everyday life. When the Plymouth church was in negotiations over a pastoral call with a 'Mr. Warner' in 1688, they offered him £40 per year, but he requested £50.[148] He did not come as pastor to Plymouth. The Broadmead church in 1671 provided its pastor with a stipend of £80 per year, but this appears to be unusually generous.[149] The more common lot, even among the larger London churches, seems to have been a small salary supplemented by some kind of secular employment. With some notable exceptions, the Particular Baptists seem to have been drawn from the lower classes of English life.[150]

---

[144]Bridlington Church Book, Public Record Office Microfilm R64-3019, London, 1.

[145]Copson, *Northern Association*, 21.

[146]Watts, *The Dissenters*, 82.

[147]J. Barry Vaughn, 'Benjamin Keach's The Gospel Minister's Maintenance Vindicated and the Status of Minister's among Seventeenth Century Baptists', *The Baptist Review of Theology* 3, no. 1 (Spring 1993): 53-60. Vaughn details Keach's occupations on page 56.

[148]Plymouth Manuscript, 17.

[149]H. Foreman, 'Baptist Provision for Ministerial Education in the 18th Century', *BQ* 27 (Oct. 1978): 359. He draws this information from Hayden, *Records of A Church of Christ*, 134-6, 204-5.

[150]Raymond Brown, *The English Baptists of the 18th Century* (London: The Baptist Historical Society, 1986), 10. Kiffin the merchant and Isaac Marlow the jeweler (he was a member of the Mile End Green, London, church, and a messenger at the General Assembly) exemplify the exceptions. Lawrence Stone has identified six different 'status' groups in seventeenth-century England: (1) Dependents on charity, apprentices and servants (15-25% of the population); (2) Laborers (agricultural and urban); (3) Husbandmen and lesser yeomen (tenants, freeholders, artisans, shopkeepers and small traders); (4) Lesser (parish) gentry; (5) Country elite (Squires, knights, baronets); (6) Peers of the realm. Four 'semi-independent occupational hierarchies' should also be noted: (A) Merchants, large scale exporters and wholesalers; (B) Lawyers; (C) Clergy (of the established church); and (D) Administrators (officers of state, Army and Navy, and office holders in the royal household). Lawrence Stone, 'Social Mobility in England, 1500-1700', in *17th Century England: A Changing Culture*, vol. 2, Modern Studies, ed. W. R. Owens (Totowa, N.J.: Barnes & Noble Books, 1980), 8-9. Most of

Though it may be impossible to determine precise statistics on the numerical strength of the Particular Baptists or their churches across the county,[151] it is possible to gain insights from these snapshots. Some of the churches were large, others small. With one or two exceptions, they were relatively poor and were not able to support their pastors at a level sufficient for full time ministry. In all but one church, women outnumbered men, sometimes by a significant margin.[152] The regional distribution of the churches reflected the relative strengths of the Independents with whom the Particular Baptists had so much in common. In any case, they were a relatively small portion of the population of their country.

Conclusion

From inauspicious beginnings during a period of persecution and trouble, the Particular Baptists experienced rapid growth. In 1644, seven churches existed in London. By the end of the century, twenty five times that number were spread across the countryside. They set down the practical foundations for Baptists in England, North America, and through missionaries, to many parts of the world. As a tiny minority of the population of England, they had little political impact. But their theological heritage continues to this day. It was rooted in the soil of the Reformation, nurtured by the radical Biblicism of the Separatists and Independents, and came to fruition in spite of fierce persecution, as an important participant in the development of Baptist theology and practice.

---

the Baptist church members would have come from the first three status groups. The difficulties of 'those entirely dependent on wage-labor' have been described by Christopher Hill, 'Pottage for Freeborn Englishmen: Attitudes to Wage Labour' in *Change and Continuity in 17th Century England*, revised edition (New Haven: Yale University Press, 1991), 223-231.

[151]Raymond Brown, *English Baptists*, 10, suggests that 'the average normal size of Baptist congregations may not have exceeded fifty, though there were impressive exceptions'. He provides no documentation for this suggestion.

[152]Sex ratios for the general population in 1696 have been estimated at 77 men to every 100 women in London; 88 men to 100 women in other cities and towns, and 101 men to 100 women in villages and hamlets. See John Caffyn, *Sussex Believers: Baptist Marriage in the 17th and 18th Centuries* (Worthing, West Sussex: Churchman Publishing, 1988), 167. Caffyn depends on Roger Thompson's use of the late seventeenth-century statistics of Gregory King. Roger Thompson, *Women in Stuart England and America: A Comparative Study* (London: Routledge & Kegan Paul, 1974), 31. Roy Porter, *English Society in the Eighteenth Century*, rev. ed., (New York: Penguin Books, 1990), 48, 71, considers some related statistics of King to be too low.

CHAPTER 2

'Those thus called, he commandeth to walk together in particular societies, or churches': The Nature of the Church

While the Particular Baptists and their churches were closely allied with the congregational Independents and Separatists in the 1640s, it was the idiosyncrasies of their doctrine of the church which eventually pulled the groups apart[1] Close ties could not be maintained between parties with fundamentally different notions regarding the complexion of the Christian assembly. This is not to say that their views were mutually exclusive, it is simply to say that ecclesiology was the driving force behind the Baptist movement, and provided it with a self-conscious identity distinct from that of the Independents.

With this *proviso*, the early Particular Baptists brought to their new churches their experiences within the Independent and Separatist communities.[2] As noted in chapter 1, the relations between the groups were friendly, and the ecclesiology of the Particular Baptists was molded, in many ways, by the views of the paedobaptists with whom they were previously identified. They did not jettison the existing polity with which they had been familiar, rather they modified it to suit their own understanding of what the church ought to be. Throughout the seventeenth century, the Baptist Doctrine of the Church bore a close family resemblance to that of the Independents.[3]

Chapter 26 of the Second London Confession of Faith provides the theological framework upon which the practical ecclesiology of the Particular Baptists was built. Based primarily on a redaction of material from the Savoy *Declaration* and *Platform of Polity*, but incorporating subtle changes and

---

[1]B. R. White, 'The Doctrine of the Church in the Particular Baptist Confession of 1644', *Journal of Theological Studies*, n.s., 19, pt. 2 (Oct. 1968): 581.

[2]White, 'Doctrine', 572.

[3]On the Confessional level, the ecclesiological statements bear purposeful similarity. On the practical level there were significant similarities as well, at least between Particular Baptists and Congregationalists. One writer has identified four characteristics of the Congregational churches in their formative period: Separation from the world, Fellowship among believers, Freedom from external compulsion, and Fitness for membership through holiness. All of these may be found active in the Particular Baptist churches. See Nuttall, *Visible Saints*.

reflecting peculiarly Baptist views, it provides us with a concise and detailed explanation of their understanding of the nature of the church. A close investigation of its contents demonstrates that it may be divided into two general divisions, the Church Universal (paragraphs 1-4), and the Church Local (paragraphs 5-15). Samuel Waldron structures his exposition of this chapter according to this simple division.[4]

The Church Universal

The first four paragraphs of Chapter 26 state:

> 1. The Catholick or universal Church, which (with respect to the internal work of the Spirit, and truth of grace) may be called invisible, consists of the whole (a) number of the Elect, that have been, are, or shall be gathered into one, under Christ the head thereof; and is the spouse, the body, the fulness of him that filleth all in all.
>
> (a) Heb 12.23. Col 1.18. Eph 1.10,22.23. & ch. 5.23,27,32.
>
> 2. All persons throughout the world, professing the faith of the Gospel, and obedience unto God by Christ, according unto it; not destroying their own profession by any Errors everting the foundation, or unholyness of conversation, (b) are and may be called visible Saints; (c) and of such ought all particular Congregations to be constituted.
>
> (b) 1 Cor. 1.2. Act. 11.26.
> (c) Rom. 1.7. Eph. 1.20,21,22.
>
> 3. The purest Churches under heaven are subject (d) to mixture, and error; and som have so degenerated as to become (e) no Churches of Christ, but Synagogues of Satan; nevertheless Christ always hath had, and ever shall have a (f) Kingdome in this world, to the end thereof, of such as believe in him, and make profession of his Name.
>
> (d) 1 Cor. 15. Rev. 2.& ch. 3.
> (e) Rev. 18.2. 2 Thes. 2.11,12.
> (f) Mat. 16.18. Ps. 72.17. & 102.28. Rev. 12.17.
>
> 4. The Lord Jesus Christ is the Head of the Church, in whom by the appointment of the Father, (g) all power for the calling, institution, order, or Government of the Church, is invested in a supream & soveraigne manner, neither can the Pope of *Rome* in any sense be head thereof, but is (h) that Antichrist, that Man of sin, and Son of perdition, that exalteth himself in the Church against Christ, and all that is called God; whom the Lord shall destroy with the brightness of His coming.

---

[4]Waldron, *Modern Exposition*, 312-330.

(g) Col. 1.18. Mat. 28.18,19,20. Eph. 4.11,12.
(h) 2 Thes. 2.3-9.[5]

These paragraphs teach that there is a universal church in existence in the world. It is invisible in that its true members are those who have been the recipients of an 'internal work of the Spirit,'[6] and it consists of the sum total of the Elect of all the ages. In the world, there are those who profess faith in Christ, hold sound doctrine and live in holiness; these are called 'visible saints' and provide concrete form to the universal church as they are gathered into local churches. No church on earth is completely pure, but some have so degenerated from the standard that they must be rejected as true churches. In spite of this, there have always been expressions of the kingdom of God in the world. Christ himself is the head of the church and has received the right to all power and authority in it, and in established reformation style, the Pope is identified as the Man of Sin of 2 Thessalonians,[7] having no place by right in the visible church. The 'headship' of the Universal Church did not center on any human or earthly authority, but found its focus on Christ. For this reason, the Pope, or any other making similar claims must be considered a usurper and an enemy of the duly instituted right of Christ to be Lord and Prince over the church.

According to Benjamin Keach, 'in the universal Church are many particular congregations or communities of Christians.'[8] The substance of the universal church is evidenced in the visible local churches. Hanserd Knollys, in his exposition of Song of Solomon 1.5, likened the 'Church of God on Earth' to Jerusalem, and the churches to the 'daughters'. Jerusalem is the 'City of the great King', the 'Throne of God', a 'free city honored with many privileges'. The 'daughters' are double in nature: 'all the Churches of the Saints' who share a common name, nature and power; and also 'All the Saints in every Church of Christ'. The whole is 'the Mother', and the parts are 'the daughters'.[9] By using this figure, Knollys intended to demonstrate the intimate relationship existing between the visible and the invisible. The universal church consists of the sum total of the parts, and the parts give visibility to the whole. As will be seen below, it was this doctrine that prevented the Particular Baptists from unchurching the paedobaptists with whom they differed. While they may have come to very different conclusions on the nature of baptism and its relationship

---

[5]*A Confession of Faith*, 85-87.

[6]Waldron, *A Modern Exposition*, 313-14.

[7]For an examination of the relationship between Luther's eschatology and that of some of the Particular Baptists see Frank Engehausen, 'Luther und die Wunderzeichen: Eine englische Übersetzung der Adventspostille im Jahr 1661', *Archive für Reformationsgeschicte* 84 (1993): 276-288.

[8]Benjamin Keach, *Preaching from the Types and Metaphors of the Bible* (Grand Rapids: Kregel Publications, 1972), 687.

[9]Hanserd Knollys, *An Exposition of the first Chapter of the Song of Solomon* (London: W. Godeid, 1656), 20-21.

to church membership, they nevertheless considered the Independent and Presbyterian churches to be true churches, and part of the universal church. Such was not the case with the Church of England parishes, nor with Roman Catholic congregations, though they could recognize that true Christians remained in those communions, even Rome.[10]

The 'one' and 'many' motif accounts for the realistic assessment of history given in paragraph 3. No church is in this age perfected. There is a constant process of growth or decay, and sometimes decay wins the battle. In this case, at some point, a church ceases to be a church, and becomes an ally of Christ's great enemy, the Devil.

Particular Baptist polemics did not overlook this theme. Several writers sought to address the perceived defection, calling any true saints remaining in these communions to come out and join forces with the true (and often persecuted) church.[11] Rome was vilified as the Beast,[12] 'the great Whore',[13] full of 'false Prophets'.[14] Knollys contrasted the strategies of the two churches by pointing out that Christ gives liberty and freedom of conscience, while Antichrist uses 'coercive power to force' obedience to its 'Inventions, and Superstitious Traditions'.[15] DeLaune described 8 ways in which Rome differed from the true church: (1) In its head, the Pope versus Christ; (2) In its members, citizens of an empire versus visible saints gathered 'in distinct congregations'; (3) In the object of worship, God and various saints versus God alone; (4) In the place of worship, a consecrated building oriented to the east versus no consecrated place; (5) In the time of worship, feasts and saints' days versus the 'Christian Sabbath'; (6) In the priesthood versus the ministry of two offices, elder and deacon; (7) In the rites and ceremonies of worship, liturgy versus simplicity based on Scripture injunction; and (8) In the use of compulsion and persecution versus 'the exercise of all Love, Patience, and long suffering'.[16] These are fascinating examples of the key issues the Baptists perceived divided

---

[10]The premise of some of their polemic writings against Anglican and Roman churches was that there were true Christians present who needed to see the error of their ways and come out of the false churches to those which were authentic. Hanserd Knollys wrote 'to the People of God to come out of Mystical-*Babylon*, and to *Separate* from the Church of Rome', *Mystical Babylon Unvailed* (n.p., 1679), 27 (see 25-30), emphasis his; Hercules Collins, *Some Reasons for Separation from the Communion of the Church of England* (London: John How, 1682), 24.
[11]Notable examples are Collins, *Some Reasons for Separation*; Knollys, *Mystical Babylon Unvailed;* and T[homas] D[eLaune], *The Image of the Beast, Shewing, by a Parallel Scheme, what a Conformist the Church of Rome is to the Pagan, and what a Nonconformist to the Christian Church, in I'ts [sic] Rites, Service and Ceremonys, the better to Exemplify the True and False Church* (n.p., 1684).
[12]DeLaune, *Image*, 1; Knollys, *Mystical Babylon Unvailed*, 5.
[13]Knollys, *Mystical Babylon Unvailed*, 13.
[14]Knollys, *Mystical Babylon Unvailed*, 22.
[15]Knollys, *Song of Solomon*, 15-16.
[16]D[eLaune], *The Image of the Beast*, 1-6.

them from Rome. It will be noted that justification by faith is not present in Delaune's list. This is not because it was considered to be unimportant,[17] but because Rome was identified with paganism as exemplified by Babylon. The Roman system was rejected *in toto*. It was perceived to be an utter departure from the religion of Christ, more akin to ancient pagan worship than to the faith of the New Testament. These were the 'Inventions, and Superstitious Traditions' mentioned by Knollys. They were corruptions of the purity intended in Scripture and deserved an almost prophetical condemnation. For this reason, Rome was given such pejorative sobriquets, often taken directly from Scripture.

The Church of England did not fare much better. Hercules Collins' *Some Reasons for Separation from the Church of England* identified similar concerns, though he avoided some of the fiery rhetoric. He rejected the notion of a National church as opposed to congregational churches, criticized alterations in the observance of the ordinances and the imposition of unwarranted rites and ceremonies, and lamented the use of coercion in church attendance.[18] The Western Association had determined in 1656 that it was unlawful for any 'baptized believers to hear a person in the exercise of his gift preaching as a parochial or national minister'. To do so would give the appearance of evil in conforming to worship from which separation was commanded, could encourage immature members to follow suit, would give credence to their faulty principles, would provide support for their notion of a national church, would give offense to the other members who view such an action as contrary to Scripture, and would be 'a consenting to the evil doings of such as take the word of God into their mouthes and hate to be reformed, approving them in that which God reproveth them for'.[19] In the same year, the Abingdon Association asserted a corresponding position, calling the worship and ministry of the Church of England 'antichristian and Babilonish'.[20]

In all of these issues, the measure of practice was taken according to the precepts of Scripture. Primitivism was alive and active, governing perspectives and providing a standard by which both orthodoxy and orthopraxy could be evaluated. The universal church was not to be defined in terms of those who were in fellowship with the bishop of Rome and citizens of his empire, nor

---

[17]For an example of the importance of justification by faith in Particular Baptist theology see Henry Coleman, *Actual Justification Rightly Stated* (London: B. Harris, 1696). The lengthy preface to this book was apparently written by Benjamin Keach, Crosby, *CHEB*, 4:314. In it, Keach asserts the importance of the orthodox puritan doctrine of justification held by 'Dr. Owen, Dr. Goodwin and many other Reverend and Orthodox Divins, that say the same thing with us', Coleman, *Actual Justification*, 11. He also reminds his readers that the Baptists subscribed to an orthodox position on justification when the issue was discussed at the 1689 General Assembly. See 1689 *Narrative*, 14.

[18]Collins, *Some Reasons for Separation*, 3-24.

[19]White, *ARPB*, 61-62.

[20]White, *ARPB*, 169.

could it be visible in terms of the citizens of a nation. It was the sum total of the true gathered churches. They were the various parts of the universal church.

The fourth paragraph of Chapter 26 acts as something of a transition between the doctrine of the universal church expressed in the beginning of the chapter, and the doctrine of the local church fleshed out in its remainder. Christ the ascended mediator has received all power from his Father, and expresses that power in the calling, instituting, ordering and governing of the church. Its seat of authority is thus in heaven, and not on the earth. For this reason the Pope cannot in any sense be considered as the head of the universal church, but is a usurper subject to destruction upon the return of Christ.

The heavenly orientation of the church provides the driving impetus behind the Baptists' primitivism. The Scriptures attached to the assertion of the headship of Christ in the Confession speak of his absolute authority to rule the church, which he does through the gifts (Apostles, prophets, evangelists, pastors and teachers) he gives to the church. They are faithful when they do what 'he intrusts them with',[21] as opposed to what they might presume to be good and right. The government of the universal church consists of Christ as head, and the apostles and prophets as his instruments to give direction for 'institution, order and Government'. The local churches are subject to this government, which is the theme of the next paragraph.

The Church Local

The bridge between the universal church and the local church is the concept of Christ's power. Paragraphs 5 and 6 state:

> 5. In the execution of this power wherewith he is so intrusted, the Lord Jesus calleth out of the World unto himself, through the Ministry of his word, by his Spirit, (i) those that are given unto him by his Father; that they may walk before him in all the (k) ways of obedience, which he prescribeth to them in his Word. Those thus called he commandeth to walk together in particular societies, or (l) Churches, for their mutual edification; and the due performance of that publick worship, which he requireth of them in the World.
>
> (i) Joh 10.16. chap. 12,32.
> (k) Mat. 28.20.
> (l) Mat. 18.15-20.
>
> 6. The Members of these Churches are (m) Saints by calling, visibly manifesting and evidencing (in and by their profession and walking) their obedience unto that call of Christ; and do willingly consent to walk together according to the appointment of Christ, giving up themselves, to the Lord & one to another by the will of God, (n) in professed subjection to the Ordinances of the Gospel.

---

[21] *A Confession of Faith*, 89.

(m) Rom. 1.7. 1 Cor. 1.2.

(n) Act. 2.41,42. ch. 5.13,14. 2 Cor. 9.13.[22]

In these paragraphs, the nature of the local church is described. It comes into existence through the present execution of power by Christ who calls individuals to serve him and commands them to join together into churches. These whose lives demonstrate the validity of their profession freely unite into congregations 'in professed subjection to the Ordinances of the Gospel'. At this point, a detailed examination of the nature of the church is requisite.

The Identity of the Church

Curiously, the Confession does not provide a succinct definition of the local church. It indicates that these assemblies come into being by the work of Christ, and asserts a variety of stipulations which are to be followed closely, but it does not provide a summary statement on the nature of the church.

This deficiency is well supplied in various ecclesiological writings. Hercules Collins, perhaps not unexpectedly, relies on John Owen for a definition of the church:

> Quest. What is an instituted Church of the Gospel?
> Answ. A Society of Persons called out of the World, or their natural worldly state, by the Administration of the Word and Spirit, into the Obedience of Faith or the Knowledge of the Worship of God in Christ, joyned together in a holy bond, or by Special Agreement for the Exercise of the Communion of Saints and due Observation of all the Ordinances of the Gospel.[23]

This definition reflects many of the elements of paragraphs 5 and 6 of the Confession, including people being 'called out of the world', the activity of the Word and Spirit, the importance of obedience and worship, mutual commitment to be a church and the necessity of the ordinances. This is a positive definition of the church, collating a variety of theological strands into one. The differences between Baptists and paedobaptists could be comprehended in this statement. Certainly Collins would understand the 'due Observation of all the Ordinances of the Gospel' differently from Owen, but no one would miss that point. In spite of this distinct sense, they could share the same basic concept of what a church was to be.

Benjamin Keach similarly defined the church positively as:

---

[22]*A Confession of Faith*, 87-88.

[23]Collins, *Some Reasons for Separation*, 4. Cf. William H. Gould, ed., *The Works of John Owen* (Edinburgh: The Banner of Truth Trust, 1965), 15:479. The Banner of Truth edition reads 'Holy Band' instead of 'Holy Bond'. The latter seems to fit more precisely the context of the statement.

> A Church of Christ, according to the Gospel-Institution, is a Congregation
> of Godly Christians, who as a Stated-Assembly (being first baptized upon
> the Profession of Faith) do by mutual agreement and consent give
> themselves up to the Lord, and one to another, according to the Will of God;
> and do ordinarily meet together in one Place, for the Publick Service and
> Worship of God; among whom the Word of God and Sacraments are duly
> administred, according to Christ's Institution.[24]

The only additional factor added by Keach is the presence of Believer's
Baptism. This reflects his strict views on the relationship between the ordinance
and the Christian congregation. Keach was here writing for a Baptist audience,
seeking to bring together all of the possible strands contributing to the essence
of a church. He did not intend by this to imply that non-Baptist assemblies were
by definition not churches.[25] In every other facet of his statement, Keach
reflects the perspectives of Collins and Owen.

Hanserd Knollys, while using some of the same language, defined the
church more negatively by contrasting it with that which he perceived to be
false:

> A true visible Constituted Church of Christ under the Gospel is a
> Congregation of Saints, 1 *Cor.* 1.2. Called out of the World, *Rom.* 1.7.
> Separated from Idolaters and Idol Temples, 2 *Cor.* 6.16,17. from the
> unbelieving Jews and their Synagogues and all legal observations of holy
> dayes, Sabbath dayes, and Mosaical Rites, Ceremonies and shadows, *Act.*
> 19.9. *Col.* 2.26,27. and assembled together in one place, 1 *Cor.* 14.23. On
> the Lord's Day *the first day of the Week*, Acts 20.7. to worship God visibly
> by the spirit and in truth, *Joh.* 4.23,24. in the holy Ordinances of God, 1 *Cor.*
> 11.2. according to the faith and order of the Gospel, *Col.* 2.5.[26]

Knollys differentiates between true churches and false, based on a variety of
Scriptures. In order for the assembly to be one thing, it cannot be another. This
reflects the degeneration of the church described in paragraphs 3 and 4 of
Chapter 26. Knollys brings these two aspects together in his definition.

The Devonshire Square, London, church wrestled with the issue from a
different but very practical perspective. They were approached by three women
from Leonard Harrison's church seeking membership. The records state that
these three women

> have proposed to this church for communion who were members of ye late
> church under ye care of Bro: Leond Harrison: We have seriously considered
> their proposall, & Whereas there hath been an unhappy Breach & devission
> amongst them, to yt degree yt there is noe Pastor or Elder, noe Deacons, noe

---

[24]Benjamin Keach, *The Glory of a True Church, and its Discipline display'd* (London:
n.p., 1697), 5-6.
[25]See below.
[26]Hanserd Knollys, *The Parable of the Kingdom of Heaven Expounded* (London:
Benjamin Harris, 1674), 5-6.

> Church discipline noe administration of ye ordinance of ye Lds Supper in a
> word noe Answering ye great ends of our Lord Jesus in ye Institution of a
> Church here on earth we cant but conclude their church state to be dissolved
> ....[27]

From their standpoint, the absence of officers, church discipline, and administration of the Table effectively signified that their church relation had ended, and so these women could be received into membership without a breach of inter-church relations. What was once a church was no longer, the absence of these things serving as evidence of its demise.

In all of these cases, the church was defined in terms of its members, their commitments, its government, and its functions. Christian assemblies were religious organizations, brought into being by the active presence of Jesus Christ. They took visible form through mutual agreements, and engaged in certain activities delineated in the Scriptures.

The Particular Baptists did not consider their churches to be the only true churches. Paedobaptist assemblies, though defective, were nevertheless genuine. Benjamin Keach addressed the issue twice. In his *Exposition of the Parables Series 2*, he stated that a good minister

> ought to know how many essentials, or fundamental principles there are contained in the constitution of a true regular gospel church, and also know how, and where to place them in order; for if a church want but one essential principle, it is defective, and no complete congregation, according to the primitive constitution: if it hath six, as it appears it hath, and wants but one, it is imperfect; the six are these, viz., 'Repentance, faith, baptism, laying on of hands, the belief of the resurrection of the dead, and the eternal judgment', Heb. 6:1-2, Heb. 5:12. Acts 8:12,17; Acts 19:6. These are called fundamentals or foundation principles. But certainly 'baptism, and laying on of hand', are not fundamentals of salvation: for none can be saved but such that are baptized, &c? evident it is, the penitent thief was saved, but he was not baptized. These six principles therefore, as here laid down, are fundamentals of a gospel church: and as some are such, so they all belong to babes in Christ, or are the ABC of a Christian man, in order to his regular admittance into the church. True, a church may be materially a true church, and formally true, too, (i.e. they may give themselves up to the Lord, and to one another, as a congregation, to walk together in the fellowship of the gospel) who may not be baptized, nor own laying on of hands; but then they must be considered, not a complete gospel church, but in some things defective, in respect to its constitution and regular gospel form, or as wanting a pillar, &c. A house may be a real house, though it may want a principal post it stands on; it may be pretty firm, and may stand though one be missing, however, it is not so safe, to want one principle of the doctrine of Christ.[28]

---

[27]Devonshire Square *CMB*, 59.
[28]Benjamin Keach, *Exposition of the Parables Series Two* (Grand Rapids: Kregel, 1991), 32.

By this standard, complete churches rest on all six pillars of Hebrews 6.1-2, though the absence of one or two pillars does not eviscerate the congregation's status as an authentic assembly. Especially interesting is his insistence on laying on of hands.[29] This was a ceremony related to the reception of members in Keach's church, where the elder would actually place hands on the head of each and every new member, and pray over him or her individually at the time of reception. The inclusion of this practice in Keach's list signals a disagreement with many of the churches the Horselydown church recognized in formal association. It was not affirmed universally among the Particular Baptists in the seventeenth century, in fact, it was probably a minority report among them. Yet Keach incorporates it as one of the pillars of the church. He would not unchurch these with whom he shared a common Confessional commitment, nor would he unchurch his paedobaptist friends. He explicitly stated that a paedobaptist church was a true church, though deficient in a basic matter.

In *A Counter-Antidote to purge out the Malignant Effects of a Late Counterfeit prepared by Mr. Gyles Shute* (1694), Keach replied to a paedobaptist, Gyles Shute, who attacked the Baptists on a variety of issues. Among other things, Shute apparently tried to press his perception of the Baptists' doctrine to its logical conclusion: either the Independent churches were true churches, or the Baptist churches were true churches, but they could not both be genuine. Keach replied:

> In page 191 of this last book he says that they (meaning the Independent Congregations) are not true Churches, or else we are not: I know no reason for this, for I doubt not but they are true churches, as well as we, they being godly Christians, tho' I do believe they may be less compleat Churches: Then those who are Baptized upon the profession of Faith, or not so orderly in their constitution.[30]

He was not willing to concede the point, and accept Shute's reasoning. Baptism was not constituent to the *esse* of a church. The Independent congregations were legitimate visible expressions of the Universal church.

Hanserd Knollys counseled his readers to be cautious of perfectionistic tendencies in their evaluation of churches. Relying on and expanding the Confessional language 'The most pure Churches of Saints on Earth, are subject to mixture' he urged his readers to remain in their defective churches until they have 'faithfully and orderly born their testimony against' the disorders or false doctrines, 'humbly entreated' the church and ministers to reform, and were convinced that there was no evidence that change was in the process.[31] Every

---

[29]See Chapter 5, *infra*, for an brief examination of this practice.

[30]Benjamin Keach, *A Counter-Antidote to purge out the Malignant Effects of a Late Counterfeit prepared by Mr. Gyles Shute* (London: H. Bernard, 1694), 53-54

[31]Knollys, *The World that Now is*, 96-97.

church has defects, many of which do not hinder the fundamental validity of their claim to be churches.

The catholicity present among the Particular Baptists is evident in the presence of open-membership churches at the London General Assemblies.[32] The *Appendix* to the Second London Confession expressed the matter in these terms:

> We are not insensible that as to the order of God's house, and entire communion therein there are some things wherein we (as well as others) are not at a full accord among our selves, as for instance; the known principle, and state of the consciences of diverse of us, that have agreed in this Confession is such; that we cannot hold Church-communion, with any other than Baptized-believers, and Churches constituted of such; yet some others of us have a greater liberty and freedom in our spirits that way; and therefore we have purposely omitted the mention of things of that nature, that we might concurre, in giving this evidence of our agreement, both among ourselves, and with other good Christians, in those important articles of the Christian Religion, mainly insisted on by us.[33]

A careful reading of the Confession will demonstrate that baptism is never explicitly tied with church membership. This was purposely done in order to comprehend churches of both kinds. At the London Assemblies, the majority of churches would have been closed membership, but open membership churches were present as well.[34] The more strict churches were willing to unite with others whose views were slightly different from their own.

In these ways, the Particular Baptists sought to define carefully their understanding of the nature of the church. While on the one hand, their practice was, in their own understanding, the fullness of the expression of New Testament principles, they did not exclude others from recognition as authentic assemblies. Hercules Collins could use John Owen's definition, and the editors of the Confession could use the Savoyans' explicit language, because at the root of the matter, there was a mutual recognition and fellowship. The

---

[32]B. R. White, 'Open and Closed Membership among English and Welsh Baptists', *BQ* 24, no. 7 (July 1972): 330-334, 341.

[33]*A Confession of Faith*, 137-38.

[34]Broadmead, Bristol was indisputably open-membership. In addition, Plymouth and Stevington were most likely the same. The Plymouth church unanimously called a paedobaptist, Robert Brown, as minister in 1687. This could not happen in a closed membership church. In addition, the presence of Samuel Buttall, a former member of the open-membership London church previously under the ministry of Henry Jessey points to open-membership practices. See Plymouth (George St.) Church Manuscript Copy Extracts from Church Book 1648-1776, The Angus Library, Regent's Park College, Oxford, 13, 26. The Stevington church endured a division when they 'altered their judgments about the practice of baptisme', apparently in the early 1690s (though it may have been as early as 1688). They adopted a closed-membership stance. See Tibbutt, *Some Early Nonconformist Church Books*, 36, 37, 59.

Universal church was not a Baptist body, but a Christian body, incorporating assemblies of various types, and even individuals within the confines of apostate communions. Various congregations, whatever their constituting principles may have been, were true churches when visible saints were called out of the world, and united together in obedience to Christ.

Membership in the Local Church

The substance of each local assembly was people, men and women who had been recipients of the grace of God, who gave evidence of their conversion, and who were willing to be subject to the government of that congregation. Churches were not abstractions, but communities with defined memberships and set procedures for the administration of their government. We will notice the process by which churches were constituted, examine the procedures used for receiving members into established churches, describe the responsibilities of members, and consider the enacting of discipline in the assemblies.

THE CONSTITUTING OF A LOCAL CHURCH

Among the Particular Baptists, two different positions regarding the constituting of churches may be noticed. In some, there was an emphasis on the necessity of a church covenant.[35] This provided a concrete form by which the membership of the church could be disciplined. Some, however, scrupled at the use of covenants, arguing that they were not based on precept or example in Scripture, and were thus an imposition upon the church.

John Spilsbery and Benjamin Keach may serve as examples of the former group. In his 1643 work *A Treatise Concerning the Lawfull Subject of Baptisme*, Spilsbery argued that a covenant was the initiating document of a church. It preceded baptism, and en-churched those who committed themselves to it. Basing his argument on an analogy with the priority of the covenant of grace, which was the first 'forme' God used to bring his people into relationship with himself, Spilsbery sought to demonstrate that the same type of form was necessary when people join together as a church. He said, 'the covenant is the forme'.[36] More than fifty years later, Keach wrote that individuals 'when admitted Members, before the Church they must solemnly enter into a Covenant, to walk in the Fellowship of that particular Congregation, and to submit themselves to the Care and Discipline thereof'.[37]

---

[35]Samples of several seventeenth century Baptist church covenants may be found in Timothy and Denise George, ed., *Baptist Confessions, Covenants and Catechisms* (Nashville: Broadman & Holman, 1996), 173-183.

[36]J[ohn] S[pilsbery], *A Treatise Concerning the Lawful Subject of Baptisme* (London: n.p., 1643), 41.

[37]Keach, *The Glory of a True Church*, 7.

The White Street, London, church covenant is printed at the end of *The Glory of a True Church, and its Discipline dispay'd.*[38]

Hanserd Knollys' perspective was somewhat different. When challenged with the assertion that the new Baptist churches in London required subscription to a covenant, he responded by stating that some of the churches were gathered 'without urging or making a particular covenant with Members upon admittance'. For Knollys, this satisfied the requirements of Scripture. A formal covenant was unnecessary.[39]

The differences between Spilsbery and Knollys in the 1640s may be explained by the purpose of their writing. Spilsbery was attempting to exonerate himself and the other new Baptist assemblies from the allegation that their baptism was a novelty and a nullity. His opponents charged that the recovery of Believer's Baptism by immersion was invalid, as it implied that the unbaptized, of necessity, must have been the administrators at the time of recovery, an unthinkable condition according to their presuppositions. Spilsbery's retort was that the church had temporal priority over baptism, and being in existence, could appoint some of its own, though unbaptized, as proper administrators of the ordinance: 'The covenant and not baptism formes the church.'[40] Knollys, in contrast, was not seeking to address the matter of the recovery of baptism. He was simply explaining the method used in the gathering of some of the churches. Men preached, people believed and were baptized, and they were organized into churches.[41]

Knollys provides a detailed account of a procedure employed in constituting new churches. On a solemn day of prayer and fasting, an 'Able minister of the Gospel' along with 'the Elders and Chief Brethren of some particular Churches of Saints' (should they be able to come) assisting should meet with the new group. After preaching about 'their respective Duties in a Church Relation', these elders may 'constitute and make them a particular Visible Church of God' as the members agree to form a congregation, to assemble in

---

[38]Keach, *The Glory of a True Church*, 71-74. The White Street church was constituted with this covenant on 5 June 1696. It had been 'fostered' by Keach, and the first pastor was Richard Robbins. See W. T. Whitley, *The Baptists of London 1612-1928* (London: The Kingsgate Press, n.d.), 124. The Bromsgrove, Worcs. Church also used a covenant for members. Bromsgrove Baptist Church Record Book Volume One 1670-1715, Peter Wortley, transcriber, (Bromsgrove: Bromsgrove Baptist Church and the Baptist Historical Society, 1974), 5-10.

[39]Hanserd Knollys, *A Moderate Answer unto Dr. Bastwicks Book*, 20.

[40]This phrase was used on the title page as a summary of one of the 'particulars' addressed in the book. See Spilsbery, *A Treatise Concerning the Lawful Subjects*, 40-43.

[41]Knollys defended the new practice of baptism by arguing that the command of Christ in Scripture, especially Matt. 28.18-20, provided sufficient warrant for duly ordained church officers and/or recognized gifted brothers to serve as administrators of baptism. See Hanserd Knollys, *The Shining of a Flaming fire in Zion* (London: Jane Coe, 1646), 12-14. Knollys did not consider baptism to be of the essence of the church. See Hanserd Knollys, *The World that Now is*, 96-97.

one place each Lord's Day for public worship, to be subject to the 'Laws of God's house', to abide by apostolic doctrine and observe the ordinances together. When these commitments have been made,

> The same Minister ought to declare them to be a Church of Saints, and the Ministers and Brethren of other Churches being also present, ought to own and acknowledge them to be a Sister-Church, by giving them the Right hand of Fellowship; and so to commend them by Prayer unto God.[42]

The act of constituting the church depends on the engagements made by the founding members. So long as they are willing to commit themselves to one another and demonstrate the determination to be subject to the stipulations of Scripture, they could be formed into a church. The presence of visiting ministers was for assistance. They confirmed the validity of the action taken by extending recognition after the New Testament pattern. In this way, the new assembly could immediately lay claim to the due rights and privileges of a church with the approbation of others previously in a similar state.

Accounts of the formation of several churches are extant and reflect this methodology. Bampton, Devonshire, Maze Pond, London, and Bridlington, East Yorkshire were all constituted in the 1690s. In addition, the Porton, Wilts. church amicably divided into two distinct assemblies. Each of these serves as an example of the process used in forming new churches.

In 1690, a church was organized in Bampton, Devonshire. According to the Church Book, individuals from Bampton had traveled to the nearby[43] Tiverton church 'either of curiosity or for divertion', and had been convinced of the necessity of Believer's Baptism by immersion. The number of those traveling increased to the point 'as rendered us capable (as was thought by ourselves and others) to sett down in A distinct Society'. On 'the 5th day of the 9th Month, 1690', a church meeting was held at Bampton at which time it was determined that a sufficient number of people could unite to form a new assembly, 'distinct from that Congregation and Church of Christ usually meeting at Tiverton'. This was done 'in the presence, and with the advice, of Elders of other Churches', who are named as Tristram Truvin, Robert Stone and Thomas Dunsford from Tiverton, Andrew Gifford from the Pithay Church, Bristol, Thomas Whinnel from Taunton, Somerset, and William Phips from Exeter, Devon.[44] Eighteen men and twenty-one women formed this new assembly.

---

[42]Knollys, *The World that Now is*, 48-50.

[43]Approximately 7 miles.

[44]Bampton Church Book 1690-1825, The Angus Library, Regent's Park College, Oxford, 2. Of the men listed, all but Stone and Dunsford had been present at the 1689 General Assembly. One of the founding members of Bampton, John Ball, represented Tiverton at that meeting, 1689 *Narrative*, 19, 20, 24. Ball's name is the first among the male members listed in the church book, and he was nominated to serve as a ruling elder on the 23rd of the same month, Bampton *CB*, 3, 5.

At the beginning of the Church Book is a preface which seeks to place the Bampton church into the history of redemption. This congregation was viewed as a visible expression and fulfillment of the mission of Christ in coming to the world, and used the language of the Confession to describe the process by which a church is formed. Christ has received all power and through the gospel

> many being called and separated from the world giving themselves up first unto the Lord and to one another by the will of God by mutual contract forming themselves into distinct communities or societies for the maintenance of the worship of God according to the institutions given them by Christ their Lord yt taking on them the denomination of his churches ... which is the thing aimed at by a remnant of his people in assuming to themselves the name of a Church of Christ or their giving themselves one to another having first professedly in Baptism given themselves up to the Lord ....[45]

The church is formed 'by mutual contract' in which baptized individuals accede to be a society 'for the maintenance of the worship of God'. They agree together to do this, but in practice the act was confirmed by the presence of elders from several different churches, who apparently assented by their presence and participation that the new group was a true and duly constituted church. There was no covenant *per se*, though there was mutual 'contract'. The method of constituting is essentially the same as that advocated by Knollys.

In Bridlington, East Yorkshire, a church was formed on 16 September 1698 in the presence of four visiting elders. Their records state,

> The gratious God having to the Praise of his free grace chosen a people out of the world unto himself in and about Bridlington they were formed into a church state ... by declaring them selves willing to resign up themselves to his will Power & Authoritie of Christ promising his grace & Spirit assiting them to walk obedient to his blessed gospel by giving themselves one to another to walk together in the fellowship of the gospell.[46]

This act reflects the central issues in the Confession, and follows Knollys 'method of enchurchment. They did not adopt a covenant.

The Maze Pond, London, church was constituted on 9 February 1693/94 by a group of dissidents from Benjamin Keach's Horselydown church. While they may have been quite unhappy with Keach's introduction of singing in public worship, their actions reflected his views on formation of churches. On a special day of prayer and fasting, and assisted by several elders and observers from other churches, they adopted a covenant as the formal means of

---

[45]Bampton *CB*, 1. The preface is one exceptionally long sentence.
[46]Bridlington Church Book, Public Record Office Microfilm R64-3019, The Public Record Office, London, 1.

constituting themselves into a church.[47] Six men and thirteen women signed the original covenant. The Church Book is structured in such a way that there is a lengthy membership list at the front of the book. It appears that as members were added, they were required to sign their names to the covenant. In 1695/96, after a disruption among the founding members, the church renewed its commitment to the covenant on a solemn day of prayer and fasting.[48] It was a vital part of their state, serving as the means by which the members formalized their pledge to the church.

A circumstance of a slightly different kind took place when the Porton, Wilts. church divided into two distinct and independent bodies in 1690. The manuscript account of the action states,

> At a meeting at Sarum of the Brethren formerly bearing the Denomination of the Church of Christ at Porton, being then and there met together to consult what would be the most effectual method in order to promote the publick interest of Christ in converting Souls & building up each other in the Faith & Order of the Gospel, do jointly agree that in order to accomplish this their design, it will be most expedient for Time to come to sit down in two distinct Congregations (viz) Those in & about Sarum to sit down together having Br. Penn to their Pastor, who formerly belonged to the whole in that capacity: and the other Part to sit down in the country at what Place they think most for their conveniency, having Br. Read for their Pastor formerly in the same capacity with Br. Penn.[49]

The proposal was unanimously approved and signed by 15 men. In this case, an established church agreed to divide in order that their mission might be better accomplished. The two existing elders each became pastor of one of the succeeding churches.

All of these examples, whether making use of a covenant or not reflect the concerns of the Confession of Faith. The members of the churches are called out of the world by the present action of God, they entrust themselves to him and to one another, and they agree to function together as a church. The reality of the work of God was exemplified in the visibility of the church.

---

[47]The elders and observers were Edward Man, John Scott, Richard Baxter, George Barrett and Keach's chief nemesis, Isaac Marlow. All had been part of the General Assemblies. Maze Pond Church Book 1691-1708, The Angus Library, Regent's Park College, Oxford, 3, 91-92; 1689 *Narrative*, 22, 24; 1692 *Narrative*, 18. Baxter is not to be confused with the famous paedobaptist of the same name.

[48]Maze Pond *CMB*, 9.

[49]Broughton Baptist Church Collection Manuscript B 5/2, The Angus Library, Regent's Park College, Oxford. A brief mention of this manuscript and the act it describes may be found in Arthur Tucker, 'Porton Baptist Church, 1655-85', *TBHS* 1 (1908-1909): 60. 'Sarum' was the Roman name for Salisbury.

MEMBERSHIP

Churches are made of members, and the procedure for receiving new members was very carefully defined in the Particular Baptist congregations. In light of the Confessional statement that 'the members of these churches are saints by calling' who show evidence of their profession of faith in their lives, the churches adopted a careful means of managing the admittance of prospective members.

Generally, applicants who were not church members elsewhere would be 'propounded' or proposed to the church as a whole.[50] They would be asked to give testimony to their Christian experience, usually before the whole church[51] but in unusual circumstances to a representative selection of the church.[52] In some cases, messengers were sent to the homes, neighborhoods and/or employers of the applicants, inquiring into the validity of the profession of faith being made.[53] Current members could raise objections against the candidates.[54] If everything was in order, the individual would be received.[55] If any objections were placed or obstacles discovered, the person's membership could be deferred or refused.[56]

In the case of transfer of membership, the circumstances were slightly different. Members from distant churches could be received upon the presentation of a letter of commendation from their home churches.[57] When such a letter was not at hand, communication would be sent to the distant assembly in order to ascertain the status of the individual.[58] Instances are known of admittance to transient membership pending the arrival of a letter from the home church,[59] or if the individual was not permanently domiciled in the new location.[60] When a church was more local, messengers could be sent to

---

[50]Petty France *CMB*, 3, 4 and *passim*; Devonshire Square *CMB*, 69; Tibbutt, *Some Early Nonconformist Church Books,* 29.

[51]Devonshire Square *CMB*, 26; Broughton *CB1*, 21; White *ARPB*, 185; Benjamin Keach, *An Answer to Mr. Marlow's Appendix* (London: John Hancock, 1691), 33.

[52]Tibbutt, *Some Early Nonconformist Church Books*, 27, 29, 33-34; Keach, *The Glory of a True Church,* 6, 16-17.

[53]Petty France *CMB*, 6; Hayden, *The Records of a Church of Christ*, 216; Keach, *The Glory of a True Church*, 6, 17.

[54]Knollys, *A Moderate Answer*, 16; Hayden, *The Records of a Church of Christ*, 139; Warwick Baptist Church Book 1698-1760, Warwickshire County Record Office, Warwick, 4.

[55]Devonshire Square *CMB*, 51, 63; Hayden, *The Records of a Church of Christ*, 216.

[56]Hayden, *The Records of a Church of Christ*, 139; Tibbutt, *Some Early Nonconformist Church Books*, 39; Keach, *The Glory of a True Church*, 18.

[57]Petty France *CMB*, 7, and *passim*; Tibbutt, *Some Early Nonconformist Church Books*, 15, 26.

[58]Petty France *CMB*, 32 (mispaginated as 30).

[59]Petty France *CMB*, unnumbered page 42.

[60]Petty France *CMB*, 3, 4, 30 (mispaginated as 28); Devonshire Square *CMB*, 69.

probe into the character of each inquirer.[61] In one case, transfer was readily made because 'our Chch being in ye same Asociation wth them they readily dismissed her to our care'.[62]

Membership in a church of a different faith and order could be transferred into some of the subscribing churches. Petty France received a woman from the Pinners' Hall Independent church under the ministry of Anthony Palmer,[63] Broadmead, Bristol accepted a letter for their new pastor's wife from a Presbyterian congregation in London,[64] and Stevington, Bedfordshire received a woman from an Independent church in Newport Pagnell, Buckinghamshire.[65] Even General Baptist practice could be recognized as valid. Petty France received a woman 'upon profession of her faith ... she having been baptized into an Arminian church many yeares before'.[66]

Several letters of transfer have been preserved. The Stevington church book transcript includes letters of commendation one of which is addressed in typical style: 'To any church of Jesus Christ walking in the order and fellowship of the Gospell'. They are signed by various men including Samuel Buttall, Thomas Hardcastle and Hanserd Knollys.[67] The letters name the individual concerned, speak to her character, and commend her to membership in any church willing to receive her.

In every case, membership was a serious process, entered with caution. The necessity of regeneration and the attending visible fruits required scrutiny of potential members. When admitted, expectations were high.

RESPONSIBILITIES OF MEMBERS AND CHURCH DISCIPLINE

The responsibilities of church membership could be understood in two ways. On the one hand, there were positive duties which were incumbent upon all of

---

[61]Petty France *CMB*, 10, 27 (mispaginated as 24); Bagnio/Cripplegate *CMB*, unnumbered page facing page 13; Devonshire Square *CMB*, 26, 49, 59.

[62]Devonshire Square *CMB*, 29.

[63]Petty France *CMB*, 1. On Palmer and the Pinners' Hall church see Walter Wilson, *The History and Antiquities of Dissenting Churches and Meeting Houses, in London, Westminster and Southwark* (London: For the Author, 1808), 2:256-258.

[64]Hayden, *The Records of a Church of Christ*, 186. The London church's pastor was Thomas Vincent. The letter indicated that the 'Presbyterian' church admitted members '1. *Upon Enquiry* of ye parties' Knowledge of God, and ye Doctrine of Salvation. 2. *Upon Enquiry* of ye Work of Grace upon their *Hearts*. 3. *Upon Enquiry* of a Good and blameless *Conversation*'. The scribe says this was 'as wee doe', emphasis in original.

[65]Tibbutt, *Some Early Nonconformist Church Books*, 26.

[66]Petty France *CMB*, unmarked page 40; See also Keach, *The Glory of a True Church*, 18; Tibbutt, *Some Early Nonconformist Church Books*, 17; Maze Pond *CMB,* 152.

[67]Tibbutt, *Some Early Nonconformist Church Books*, 26. Buttall represented Plymouth at the 1689 Assembly and later became its pastor; and Hardcastle became Pastor of Broadmead, Bristol.

the members to perform. On the other hand, there were sanctions to be enacted against them if they failed to live according to these requirements.

Benjamin Keach summarized the positive obligations in terms of two broad categories: relations with the pastor and with one another. To the pastor each member owes 8 things: (1) prayer, (2) 'reverential esteem', (3) submission, (4) vindication from the reproaches of opponents, (5) information, i.e. going to them in times of trouble, (6) adequate financial support, (7) adherence in times of trials, and (8) attendance at meetings called by the pastor.[68] To one another, each member owes (1) submission to the church as a whole, (2) 'peace, unity and sweet concord', (3) willingness to follow the Scriptural process of settling offenses, and (4) impartiality in the exercise of discipline.[69]

The Confession tied the privileges and responsibilities of membership together with discipline. The demands placed on members were great, but it is presumed that the expectation that members would be true 'saints' in and of itself implied a high standard of behavior. Paragraphs 12 and 13 of the Confession describe the duties of members:

> 12. As all Believers are bound to joyn themselves to particular *Churches*, when and where they have opportunity so to do; So all that are admitted unto the priviledges of a *Church*, are also (b) under the Censures and Government thereof, according to the Rule of *Christ*.

> (b) 1 Thes. 5.14. 2 Thes. 3.6.14,15.

> 13. No Church-members upon any offence taken by them, having performed their Duty required of them towards the person they are offended at, ought to disturb any *Church* order, or absent themselves from the Assemblies of the *Church*, or Administration of any Ordinances, upon the account of such offence at any of their fellow members; but to wait upon *Christ*, (c) in the further proceedings of the *Church*.

> (c) Mat. 18.15,16,17. Eph 4.2,3.[70]

Hanserd Knollys brought the responsibilities of members and the exercise of discipline together. Using the explicit words of paragraphs 3 and 13 of Chapter 26, he argued that church members should not separate themselves from their churches in the cases of offenses or defections, until such time as the offenders are proceeded against 'and those offenses be reformed or removed by the Laws of God's House, or Christ removes 'the Candlestick' from the church. Even in the Scriptures, elements of 'unsound Doctrines, and corrupt Manners' may be noticed, and Christ 'did not presently forsake those Churches, nor did he

---

[68]Keach, *The Glory of a True Church*, 11-15.

[69]Keach, *Preaching from the Types and Metaphors of the Bible* (Grand Rapids: Kregel, 1972), 712-714.

[70]*A Confession of Faith*, 91-92, emphasis in original. The formal procedure of invoking church discipline is discussed in chapter 3 on Church Government.

command any of the Ministers, or Members thereof to separate themselves from them'.[71] Membership could not be lightly severed, but required a major departure in order to be justifiable.

Among the most common entries in the extant church books are cases of church discipline. The churches were regularly concerned with ensuring that their members were living as they ought, separate from the world and in holiness unto God. Purity in the congregation was an essential feature. If the assembly was God's temple, and if worship was carried on in his holy presence, sin could not be tolerated. When it was uncovered, it had to be confronted. There seem to have been three levels of church discipline: suspension, withdrawal and excommunication.[72] Suspension was, according to Keach, a interim measure used in cases of sin requiring further investigation. Other churches used it as a temporary removal of privileges pending demonstrable repentance.[73] Withdrawal was the punishment enacted on a 'disorderly' member, and involved two things. (1) A Public admonition or warning, followed by a period to allow for repentance,[74] and (2) in case the admonition was ignored, the church restricted its fellowship with the offender, though still considered him or her as a member.[75] Excommunication was the ultimate act. It cast the guilty party out of the church, to be handed over to Satan. The excommunicated person was not considered to be a believer, but was viewed as a 'heathen' or 'publican'.[76] The churches practiced these forms of discipline regularly, but seem to have done so often with a tender spirit and a genuine concern for the restoration of the offender. Examples of the matters for which individuals were placed under various levels of discipline are replete in the Church Books. Among the sins for which censures were necessary are laxity in attendance,[77] inter-personal strife,[78] neglect and/or abuse of family,[79] marriage to an unbeliever,[80] breaking a marriage engagement,[81] disobedience to parents,[82]

---

[71]Knollys, *The World That Now is*, 98-99. He argued primarily from the cases of the seven churches of Asia Minor in Revelation 2 and 3.

[72]Keach, *The Glory of a True Church*, 21-25.

[73]Tibbutt, *Some Early Nonconformist Church Books*, 15; Bampton *CMB*, 6.

[74]Hayden, *The Records of a Church of Christ*, 188, 191, 226; Tibbutt, *Some Early Nonconformist Church Books*, 29, 33; Warwick *CMB*, 1.

[75]Hayden, *The Records of a Church of Christ*, 217-18; Tibbutt, *Some Early Nonconformist Church Books*, 16, 28; Petty France *CMB*, 8.

[76]Hayden, *The Records of a Church of Christ*, 214, 217; Tibbutt, *Some Early Nonconformist Church Books*, 15; Devonshire Square *CMB*, 22; Petty France *CMB*, 9.

[77]Devonshire Square *CMB*, 21; Petty France *CMB*, 1; Broughton *CB1*, 52.

[78]Devonshire Square *CMB*, 22, 35; Bagnio/Cripplegate *CMB*, 4, 6, 11; Hayden, *The Records of a Church of Christ*, 190-91.

[79]Petty France *CMB*, 22, 28 (mispaginated as 26); Warwick *CMB*, 4-5; Maze Pond *CMB*, 116.

[80]Devonshire Square *CMB*, 29; Tibbutt, *Some Early Nonconformist Church Books*, 16, 28; Hayden, *The Records of a Church of Christ*, 226.

[81]Tibbutt, *Some Early Nonconformist Church Books*, 14.

failure to pay bills, financial irregularities and bankruptcy,[83] theft,[84] drunkenness,[85] various moral offenses,[86] attendance at Church of England[87] or Quaker[88] meetings, theological heresy,[89] witchcraft and visiting a 'conjuror',[90] Sabbath breaking,[91] and many others. In some cases, members were restored to full membership after their repentance.[92] Typically, some kind of inquiry would be made to ensure that the confession and repentance were genuine.[93] Lest it be thought that the churches were overwhelmed with trouble and full of sinning members, the words of H. Wheeler Robinson concerning the Bagnio/Cripplegate church must be considered:

> During the eleven years of Steed's pastorate, he kept a Discipline Book, which records about a score of cases for that period. This is a high testimony to the general morality of a Church of more than a hundred members when we consider the severity of their scrutiny of each other's conduct.[94]

This evaluation is undoubtedly true. In the larger churches, such as Petty France, London, there were more people, and more opportunities for difficulty. But the subjects of these cases are only a small minority of the total membership in the churches. Roger Hayden asserts that there was only one case of fornication noted in the Broadmead records over a period of forty seven years.[95] Apparently, the 'visible saints' for the most part lived up to expectations.

---

[82]Devonshire Square *CMB*, 29.

[83]Petty France *CMB*, 3, 8-9, 16-17, 20; Bagnio/Cripplegate *CMB*, 11.

[84]Devonshire Square *CMB*, 23; Petty France *CMB*, 9; Broughton *CB1*, 23; Bagnio/Cripplegate *CMB*, 2, 7; Tibbutt, *Some Early Nonconformist Church Books*, 35.

[85]Petty France *CMB*, 12; Hayden, *The Records of a Church of Christ*, 129, 187, 192, 194, 196-97, 201; Tibbutt, *Some Early Nonconformist Church Books*, 15.

[86]Devonshire Square *CMB*, 19; Petty France *CMB*, 1; Bagnio/Cripplegate *CMB*, 3.

[87]Petty France *CMB*, 2; Broughton *CB1*, 55, 62; Tibbutt, *Some Early Nonconformist Church Books*, 16; Maze Pond *CMB*, 112, where a woman was admonished for 'standing at the Sprinkling of a Child as a Godmother'.

[88]Devonshire Square *CMB*, 57; Petty France *CMB*, 2, 11; Tibbutt, *Some Early Nonconformist Church Books*, 25; Hayden, *The Records of a Church of Christ*, 112-13.

[89]Bagnio/Cripplegate *CMB*, 8, where a member was cast out for holding Arian views of the person of Christ.

[90]Petty France *CMB*, 1; Broughton *CB1*, 44; Tibbutt, *Some Early Nonconformist Church Books*, 36.

[91]Petty France *CMB*, 18; E. B. Underhill, *Records of the Churches of Christ, Gathered at Fenstanton, Warboys, and Hexham. 1644-1720* (London: The Hanserd Knollys Society, 1854), 297; Hayden, *Records of A Church of Christ*, 193.

[92]Petty France *CMB*, 4; Tibbutt, *Some Early Nonconformist Church Books*, 30; Bampton *CMB*, 6.

[93]Petty France *CMB*, 2, 4, 5, 12, unnumbered page 23.

[94]H. Wheeler Robinson, 'Baptist Church Discipline 1689-1699', *BQ* 1 (1922): 112.

[95]Hayden, *The Records of a Church of Christ*, 56.

In summary, the local church, considered to be the direct product of the sovereign work of Christ, was to be a house built from living stones. Believers were united together into a united body, set apart and dedicated to the service of God. Their orientation was heaven-ward, and they were expected to manifest evidence of conversion in order to be admitted, and to maintain this evidence throughout their period of membership. The close relationship existing between church members was not to be treated lightly, and required careful scrutiny. When sin was observed, it had to be excised, and the churches regularly carried out the established processes of discipline.

At the root of the identity of the church, and all of the practices associated with it was the primitivist urge to fulfill the dictates of Scripture. Innovation and novelty was unwanted and unwarranted. These churches ransacked the pages of the Bible in order to establish their deeds with a heavenly authority.

The Spread of the Churches

Our examination of the Particular Baptist understanding of the nature of the church up to this point has been an inward look—an examination of the mechanisms at work in the settled churches. But the Particular Baptists also had an outward look—believing in the necessity of planting churches throughout the nation.[96] They could not be content with enjoying their own privileges, but actively engaged in seeking to bring their views to others. This was primarily done by means of evangelists. This was not an office in the church, though the men involved were often elders, but rather appointed emissaries charged with the task of spreading the gospel and establishing churches. They carried with them authority from the sending churches. Two early examples of the convictions resident among these churches provide the basis for later actions.

In 1649, the Glaziers' Hall, London church held a day of prayer 'to seek the Lord that he would send labourers into the dark corners and parts of this land'.[97] On the next day, John Myles and Thomas Proud appeared in their midst, concerned for the needs of Wales. They were apparently baptized and sent, within a fortnight, back to Wales for the purpose of planting churches. On 1

---

[96]Cf. Christopher Hill, 'Puritans and "the Dark Corners of the Land"', in *Change and Continuity in 17th-Century England,* rev. ed. (New Haven: Yale University Press, 1991), 3-47. Hill demonstrates that a concern for the spread of the Gospel (and its attendant influences) was a significant concern among leading Puritans in the first half of the seventeenth century.

[97]Cited from the Ilston Church Book by B. R. White, 'John Miles and the Structures of the Calvinistic Baptist Mission to South Wales, 1649-1660', in Mansel John, ed., *Welsh Baptist Studies* (Llandysul: The South Wales Baptist College, 1976), 36; See also Henry Melville King, *Rev. John Myles and the Founding of the First Baptist Church in Massachusetts* (Providence, R.I.: Preston & Rounds, Co. 1905); Joshua Thomas, 'The Histories of Four Welsh Baptist Churches c. 1633-1770', in Carroll C. and Willard A. Ramsey, *The American Baptist Heritage in Wales* (Gallatin, Tenn.: Church History Research and Archives, 1976), 40-66.

October 1649, baptisms began to take place, and the Ilston church was organized, having forty-three members by October 1650.[98] Myles engaged in an aggressive plan to bring other churches into existence, so that within a year of the first baptism two more assemblies had been formed, and the first 'General Meeting'[99] in South Wales was held on 6 and 7 November 1650.[100] White, citing the Ilston church book, states that the commission given to Myles and Proud by the London church was 'to gather a "company or society of people holding forth and practising the doctrine, worship, order and discipline of the Gospel according to the primitive institution"'. He then comments,

> The terms in which they understood their mission are of considerable importance: they saw their task not only as concerned with the conversion of individuals to Christ but also with the foundation of congregations rightly ordered according to what they believed to be the one, unchanging, apostolic pattern.[101]

White is undoubtedly correct in this assessment. The well-ordered church was so central to the redemptive purposes of God that any kind of evangelistic thrust must seek, as its highest goal, to establish new assemblies. For these Welsh evangelists, one church was insufficient. The needs of the countryside were so great that only the founding of many churches would satisfy. This early perspective was active among the Particular Baptist churches.

The London church under the ministry of Hanserd Knollys sent Thomas Tillam[102] to another one of the 'dark corners of the land', the north in December 1651. He was appointed to a lectureship by the 'Committee for the Propagation of the Gospel' established by Parliament in February 1649/50,[103] and used this post as the base to plant a Baptist church in Hexham. In seven months, sixteen individuals were baptized and a church was formed. Tillam saw this as the great end of his mission:

> upon the 21st day of the 5th month, 1652 ... after serious consideration and some gospel preparation, a living temple began of these living stones.... These, solemnly giving themselves to the Lord and one to another, to walk in communion together, with submission to all the ordinances of the Gospel,

---

[98]White, 'John Miles', 37.

[99]I.e. association.

[100]White, 'John Miles', 40; White, *ARPB*, 3-4.

[101]White, 'John Miles', 36.

[102]Ernest A. Payne, 'Thomas Tillam', *BQ* 17:2, (April 1957): 61-66; David Douglas, *History of the Baptist Churches in the North of England, from 1648 to 1845* (London: Houlston and Stoneman, 1846), 8-69; Underhill, *Hexham Records*, 289-96. Tillam used the phrase 'dark corner' in the first entry to the Hexham records, and the church, in a letter sent to Knollys' assembly in London, used the full phrase five months later, 289, 304.

[103]Underhill, *Hexham Records*, 304; Payne, 'Thomas Tillam', 61. On the 'Committee' see Hill, 'Puritans and the Dark Corners', 32-44.

> I, Tho. Tillam, espoused to one husband; hoping that I shall present them a
> chaste virgin to Christ.[104]

The formula for church planting was at the front of this action. Evangelism was
not carried out simply to seek after conversions. Churches had to be planted.
This is an essential part of the latter Confessional doctrine of the church. Those
who received the gift of salvation were expected to become part of a well-
ordered church. The Baptists could not conceive of evangelism apart from
church planting. Converts were to be baptized, and formed into a church by a
(to use Keach's term) 'wise master builder'.

The difficulties of the Restoration Era hindered the spread of churches, but
in the relative freedom of the 1690s, several attempts were made to form new
congregations. Benjamin Keach argued that ministers should be active in
preaching in the towns and villages near where they were located, so that new
churches might be planted.[105] The Bromsgrove, Worcestershire, church
ordained David Crosley as an evangelist in 1692 stating 'we by virtue of
authority given unto us by our Lord Jesus Christ, have called our Brother forth
to preach the gospel and baptize wheresoever the Providence of God shall open
a door to his ministry'.[106] This 'roving commission'[107] was not simply to
preach. It included the necessary attendant for converts, baptism, implying the
next logical step, the formation of churches.

This evangelistic impulse was the driving force behind the 1689 General
Assembly's initiative to begin a fund intended (along with other purposes) 'to
send Ministers ... to preach, both in City and Country'.[108] In the 1690 *Narrative*,
they rejoice at the good work already done through the fund, 'especially in
Essex and *Suffolk*, where were no Baptized churches', because the mission was
so well received that 'two churches are like to be gathered'.[109] According to
Murdina MacDonald, Richard Tidmarsh had been sent into those counties, with
two new churches as the apparent result.[110]

These examples give some indication, at least from among the leaders of the
movement, for the spread of their message and the desire to see churches
multiplied. For them, the church was not simply a society of holy people
gathered for fellowship with one another, but was an instrument to bring light
and life to the darkest places. When they were able, they encouraged and

---

[104]Underhill, *Hexham Records*, 289.

[105][Benjamin Keach], *The Gospel Minister's Maintenance Vindicated* (London: John
Harris, 1689), 92-96; cf. Keach, *Parables: Series Two*, 362-63, where he likened
ministers to 'planters' whose fruit is to be 'planted in a visible church of Christ'.

[106]Bromsgrove *CB*, 51.

[107]W. T. Whitley, *Baptists of North-West England, 1649-1913* (London: The Kingsgate
Press, 1913). 76. See also Frederick Overend, *History of the Ebenezer Baptist Church
Bacup* (London: The Kingsgate Press, 1912), 71.

[108]1689 *Narrative*, 12.

[109]1690 *Narrative*, 4-5, emphasis in original.

[110]MacDonald, 'London Calvinistic Baptists 1689-1727', 42.

engaged in mission efforts within their capabilities. Undoubtedly, the relative poverty of many of the churches and their ministers hindered expansion.[111] But efforts were made, at times with positive results.

Conclusion

In Particular Baptist Ecclesiology, the church was fundamentally the result of the personal and sovereign activity of Christ in calling sinners out of the world to salvation. From its roots in the New Testament, it was intended to be a holy community, separate from the world and focused on heaven. It was invisible in that the renewed hearts of its constituent members were not apparent to the naked eye, but had a real visibility in the formation of local churches.

The universal church was understood as the sum total of the true churches in existence in the world. It had no human authority or power center, could not be national, or incorporate the political subjects of an empire, but gathered at the feet of its present 'head', Jesus Christ. None of the assemblies of Christians were perfect, but they nevertheless showed the characteristics of the work of God and so demonstrated to those who would notice the reality and validity of their claim to be churches. Realistically, churches had trouble, and some departed so far from the standards of orthodoxy and orthopraxy that they lost the right to bear the title 'church of Christ'.

There is a 'one' and 'many' motif present in their thinking. The one church is the true universal church with Christ as its head. The many are the local churches scattered throughout the world, consisting of truly regenerate women and men, dedicated to the service of God. They maintained catholicity in that they did not view themselves as the only true churches. Though paedobaptist churches were 'defective' in their doctrine of baptism, they were nonetheless true churches.

Whether formed by a covenant or simply a mutual agreement, the act of becoming a church was a serious matter. Membership was a high privilege with great responsibilities. Careful inquiry was made into the conversion experience of each applicant, and all were subject to scrutiny and corrective discipline if they fell into sin. Some transgressions required a verbal rebuke; an habitual pattern of sin would demanded a withdrawal of privileges and fellowship, while indulging and remaining in serious sins would result in excommunication, sending the guilty party out of the congregation and back to the world as an unconverted person.

So important was the existence of the local church that programs were established to promote the organization of more churches. Funds were raised, men were ordained and sent, in an attempt to replicate the pattern existing among themselves.

---

[111]In the 1689 *Narrative*, this point is explicit. They mourned the financial neglect of ministers who must be 'so incumbred with Worldly Affairs, that they are not able to perform the Duties of their Holy Calling, in preaching the Gospel ....' 1689 *Narrative*, 5.

In all of this, the Particular Baptist ecclesiology may be seen as a fundamental part of the self-identity of their churches. They were Calvinists like the Presbyterians and Independents around them, and their rejection of any notion of a national church resembled the broad patterns of Independent ecclesiology. But at root, their Baptist identity was fleshed out in their own understanding of the nature of the church.

CHAPTER 3

'To each of these churches ... he has given ... power and authority': Church Government

There is some disagreement over the nature of church government as it was practiced among the Particular Baptists. Michael A. G. Haykin argues that these churches were, from the start, congregational in their polity.[1] Hywel Jones, in a review of Dr. Haykin's book, questions whether they 'were truly "congregational", with authority vested in the gathered congregation, or were more akin to John Owen's view on "independency"'.[2] Poh Boon Sing has recently asserted that the Particular Baptist assemblies should not be considered as congregationalists, but were in fact Independents along the lines of John Owen.[3]

Dr. Poh argues that a distinction needs to be drawn between 'Congregationalism' and 'Independency'. According to him, the former, as a result of the writings of Robert Browne, 'began to mean that the congregation has power to rule the church, or, otherwise expressed, the power of self-rule'. The latter, while recognizing that each assembly is autonomous, does not imply popular democracy, but rather rule by elder.[4] The issue is confused by the fact that the terms were used interchangeably in much of the literature.[5]

What were the views of the Particular Baptists on church government? How should they be categorized in this discussion? The Particular Baptists expressed their ecclesiological views in their Confessions, in various theological writings, and in several manuscript documents, especially Church books. Each of these contributes to an understanding of their practical ecclesiology.

---

[1]Haykin, *Kiffin, Knollys and Keach*, 38.

[2]Hywel Jones, review of *Kiffin, Knollys and Keach—Rediscovering Our English Baptist Heritage* by Michael A.G. Haykin, in *The Banner of Truth* 401 (February 1997): 32.

[3]Poh Boon Sing, *The Keys of the Kingdom: A Study of the Biblical Form of Church Government* (Kuala Lumpur: Good News Enterprises, 1995), 16-29.

[4]Poh, *Keys*, 22-26.

[5]Poh, *Keys*, for other examples see: Collins, *Some Reasons for Separation*, 4; Benjamin Keach, *A Counter Antidote to Purge out the Malignant Effects of a Late Counterfeit, Prepared by Mr. Gyles Shute* (London: Printed for H. Bernard, at the Bible in the Poultry, 1694), 16, 18, 53; Nuttall, *Visible Saints*, 42, quoting Matthias Maurice.

Church Government in the Confession of Faith

The Second London Confession of 1677/89 provides the primary framework against which the convictions concerning Church Government among the Particular Baptists must be understood. Of course, it does not reflect a set of doctrines bursting on the scene *de novo,* and must itself be considered in terms of its theological precedents. Nevertheless, it is the most important source to define the Particular Baptist practices.

The relevant sections of Chapter 26 of the Confession are as follows:

> 5. In the execution of this power wherewith he is so intrusted, the Lord Jesus calleth out of the World unto himself, through the Ministry of his word, by His Spirit, (i) those that are given unto him by his Father; that they may walk before him in all the (k) ways of obedience, which he prescribeth to them in his Word. Those thus called, he commandeth to walk together in particular societies, or (l) Churches, for their mutual edification, and the due performance of that publick worship, which he requireth of them in the World.

> (i) Joh. 10.16. chap. 12,32.
> (k) Mat. 28.20.
> (l) Mat. 18.15-20.

> 6. The Members of these Churches are (m) Saints by calling, visibly manifesting and evidencing (in and by their profession and walking) their obedience unto that call of Christ; and do willingly consent to walk together according to the appointment of Christ, giving up themselves, to the Lord & one to another by the will of God, (n) in professed subjection to the Ordinances of the Gospel.

> (m) Rom. 1.7. 1 Cor. 1.2.
> (n) Act. 2.41,42. ch. 5.13.14. 2 Cor. 9.13.

> 7. To each of these Churches thus gathered, according to his mind declared in his word, he hath given all that (o) power and authority, which is in any way needful, for their carrying on that order in worship, and discipline, which he hath instituted for them to observe; with commands, and rules, for the due and right exerting, and executing of that power.

> (o) Mat. 18.17,18. 1 Cor. 5.4,5 with v.13. 2 Cor. 2.6,7,8.

> 8. A particular Church gathered, and compleatly Organized, according to the mind of Christ, consists of Officers, and Members; And the Officers appointed by *Christ* to be chosen and set apart by the Church (so called and gathered) for the peculiar Administration of Ordinances, and execution of Power, or Duty, which he intrusts them with, or calls them to, to be continued to the end of the World, are (p) Bishops or Elders and Deacons.

(r)[6] Act. 20:17,[7] with v.28. Phil. 1.1.[8]

This section of the Second London Confession has typically been understood to teach a form of rule by elder, what Poh Boon Sing calls 'independency'.[9] Samuel Waldron likewise asserts that this form of government is the one taught in the Confession.[10] Poh argues that the Confession advocates this position in opposition to Congregationalism, and makes the following distinctions which are important to notice:

> Congregationalism holds to the view that Christ has given power to the local church and it is the membership of the church that has the authority to rule. Decision-making is achieved by voting to procure a consensus of opinion from the church. Church officers are elected by the local congregations, so their office is limited to that local church alone. The office bearers have the authority to exercise rule only by delegation of the church....

> Independency holds to a position between Presbyterianism and Congregationalism. Like Congregationalism, it is believed that Christ gives the power of the keys to the church 'immediately'. [*sic*] Like Presbyterianism, this power is to be exercised by officers 'instrumentally' or 'actually'. [*sic*]

> Unlike Congregationalism, church officers do not have their authority delegated by the church. Instead, that authority is communicated *from* Christ immediately, and *through* the church.[11]

The question at hand is this: Where is the seat of authority for the government of the church? Is it in the church as a gathered body, and thus delegated to the elders as their representatives, or is it in the elders as a ruling body, delegated directly from Christ? The answer to these questions makes all the difference in understanding the church government of the seventeenth-century Particular Baptists.

According to Dr. Poh, the ecclesiological polity of the Particular Baptists is best understood in the light of the practices of the well-known Independents with whom they were known to have close fellowship.[12] He asserts that their practices were the same as the Independents: 'The early Particular Baptists consistently upheld the principle of "rule with congregational consent" just as

---

[6] The text erroneously reads 'r' instead of 'p.'

[7] In this case, the text places a colon between chapter and verse references instead of the more regular period.

[8] *A Confession of Faith*, 87-89.

[9] Poh, *Keys*, 89.

[10] Waldron, *Modern Exposition*, 319-326.

[11] Poh, *Keys*, 89, emphasis his.

[12] Poh, *Keys*, 26.

the paedobaptist Independents did.'[13] There is no question that the Second London Confession is a recension of the Savoy Declaration, and more specifically that Chapter 26 is heavily dependent on the Savoy Platform of Polity. The editors of the London Baptist Confession took the ecclesiological statements from the Platform of Polity and placed them directly into their Confession. They were not content to append a statement on polity, they desired to incorporate it into the body of the Confession itself. This dependence and direct borrowing has, for Poh, significant ramifications. In several places he relies upon a quote taken from Isaac Watts,

> In church government they (that is the Particular Baptists) are Independents.... the [*sic*] generality of Independents follow rather Dr. Owen's notion: their tenets are such as these: 1st. That the power of church government resides in the pastors and elders of every particular church, and 2nd. That it is the duty of the people to consent.[14]

Watts is used as a witness to the polity of the Baptists based on the fact that

> as a well-respected minister during the period immediately after the death of John Owen, and the re-affirmation of the 1677 Confession by the Particular Baptists in 1689, he must be considered to have been a competent judge of the church situation of his day.[15]

While there can be no doubt that Watts was 'well-respected', and that he lived in the generation after Owen and the reaffirmation of the Confession, it is not certain that he was a competent judge of the polity of the Particular Baptists. The material quoted by Poh is drawn from a letter written by Watts and addressed to his brother. Poh does not provide a date for the letter, nor does he provide specific support to the assertion that Watts was a 'competent judge' of the 'church situation' of his day. While he may have been intimately acquainted with the practices of the Baptists, he may also have been merely a casual observer. Was this letter written early on in Watts' life (1674-1748) or was it written towards the end? These factors must be weighed prior to depending on his statements.

Based on his understanding of these factors, Dr. Poh depends heavily on the writings of John Owen to illustrate the ecclesiological convictions and practices of the Baptists. While there can be no question that Owen was very influential in his time, and that the Particular Baptists regularly cite Owen in support of their views, it is simplistic to draw a straight line from one author to a whole group of churches. Some of the men involved with the Particular Baptists at the 1689 Assembly (specifically William Kiffin, Hanserd Knollys and Henry Forty) had been part of the movement from its beginnings in the 1640s. Kiffin

---

[13]Poh, *Keys*, 256.
[14]Poh, *Keys*, 25, 151, 257.
[15]Poh, *Keys*, 25.

and Knollys had both been part of the circle of churches related to the Jacob/Lathrop/Jessey church, and had observed the development, both in theory and practice, of Independency from its beginnings. The radical separatism present in the movement at the start cannot and should not be discounted. The ecclesiology of the Particular Baptists was shaped by a variety of forces.[16] Owen did have significant impact on them, but so also did many others. There were modifications to Owen's theoretical system.

Poh argues that two components contribute to the practice of Independency:

> The church has chosen elders to rule over them. The church voluntarily agrees to act 'with them and under them in all duties of rule'. Using Owen's words further, '1. All authority in the church is committed by Christ unto the officers or rulers of it, as unto all acts and duties whereunto office-power is required; and 2. Every individual person hath the liberty of his own judgment as unto his own consent or dissent in what he is himself concerned'.[17]

From this, Dr. Poh argues that in the Independent system, and thus by extension among the Particular Baptists, the elders rule in the church, by the authority of Christ. They deliberate on matters to be brought to the church business meetings, and the members of the church give consent to these decisions made by the elders. The agenda for the meeting is set by the eldership, and 'under normal circumstances, the congregation has a duty to give its consent'[18] to the matters proposed by the eldership. The elders are thus responsible for the teaching ministry of the church and 'the exercise of judicial power: the making of decisions, the drawing up of rules, for the church with respect to its discipline, worship, and government'.[19] This is in contrast to Congregationalism, which 'operates in practice ... that the church members raise issues in the church business meeting, and the decisions are made by obtaining a consensus of opinion from all the members through voting'.[20]

Poh seems to argue for extensive rule by the elders. They are responsible for 'the making of decisions, the drawing up of rules, for the church with respect to its discipline, worship, and government'. He bases this on a quote from Owen who says 'by "jurisdiction", [sic] *the rule, government, or discipline of the church is designed*'.[21] Poh then states,

> Rule is exercised when the eldership brings a decision pertaining to the welfare of the church to the membership for its consideration. The members, after weighing up the decision of the eldership, give their consent or otherwise. Note that it is a *decision* that is brought to the congregation, and

---

[16]See Chapter 1, *infra.*
[17]Poh, *Keys,* 239; *The Works of John Owen,* 16:40.
[18]Poh, *Keys,* 253-54.
[19]Poh, *Keys,* 239.
[20]Poh, *Keys,* 264.
[21]Poh, *Keys,* 240, emphasis his.

it is the *consent* of the congregation that is sought by the eldership. The congregation does not make the decision for the elders to consent, but *vice versa.*[22]

Based on this description, Independency places the onus of rule in all matters upon the elders. They deliberate together, and then bring their conclusions to the church for consent. When such consent has been obtained, the matter is complete.

It is not certain that Poh has properly understood the ecclesiology of John Owen and the Independents, nor the application of these principles in the seventeenth-century Particular Baptist churches. He argues that Owen taught, and the Baptist churches practiced, an extensive form of rule by elder. But the evidence seems to point in a different direction. The Second London Confession, and the Savoy Platform of Polity on which it is dependent, do not necessarily imply this position. Their words need to be noted carefully:

> the Officers appointed by *Christ* to be chosen and set apart by the Church (so called and gathered) for the peculiar Administration of Ordinances, and execution of Power, or Duty, which he intrusts them with, or calls them to, to be continued to the end of the World, are Bishops or Elders and Deacons.[23]

But what is the 'execution of Power, or duty which he intrusts them with or calls them to'? Poh assumes that it extends to all aspects of the life of the church.

At this point, we must turn to an examination of the primary sources as they relate to the Baptists. Conclusions about their practices may be drawn from their own writings.

Church Government in Ecclesiological Writings

The ecclesiological writings of the Particular Baptists provide much information by which to determine the nature of their theological positions concerning church government. Several examples may be provided which address the topic under consideration.

Hanserd Knollys: Modified Independency

Hanserd Knollys was part of the Particular Baptist movement from its very beginnings, having come through a process which took him by stages out of the ministry of the Church of England and into a fully developed Baptist position.

---

[22]Poh, *Keys*, emphasis his.

[23]*A Confession of Faith*, 89. This paragraph is identical to article IX of the Savoy Platform of Polity except for the officers named at the very end.

In his ecclesiological writings, he discusses issues of church government in several places.

In his 1645 work *A Moderate Answer unto Dr. Bastwicks Book; Called, Independency not God's Ordinance*, Knollys argues for what he denominates a 'Presbyterian-Independent' form of church government.[24] Bastwick, according to Knollys, argued for the classic Presbyterian position, in which a particular church was subject to the ascending jurisdiction of church courts, while Knollys sought to defend the developing system of Independency being adopted in many churches through the influence of men like John Cotton.[25] Knollys considers Bastwick's exegesis to be faulty, and that the Scriptures teach the Independent position, which he defines as 'a Presbyterian-Government, which hath not Dependencie upon any in matters meerly Ecclesiastical (but upon the Lord Jesus Christ, who is the Head of the Church)'.[26] He denies Bastwick's insistence that there was one church in Jerusalem which consisted of many sub-congregations and were ruled jointly by the elders of the one church.[27] At a glance, Knollys seems to argue for rule by elder as understood in Poh Boon Sing's definition: the elders rule and the congregation consents. He says, 'It is not denied by the Brethren, that the Presbyters in all the Churches were the men in the Government of the Churches in which they are Elders.'[28] Throughout the book, however, he insists on participation from the members in the affairs of the church. He argues that the whole congregation has power to judge and admonish in matters of discipline, that 'the whole church, the multitude' were present and approved of the decisions at Jerusalem recorded in Acts 15, and that 'the Brethren' of the church have a right to participate in the admission of new members.[29] These statements recognize some participatory rights among the church members.

---

[24]Knollys, *Moderate Answer*, 1.

[25]Cotton's *The Keys of the Kingdom of Heaven* had been published in London in 1644, with a recommendatory preface written by Thomas Goodwin and Philip Nye. Cf. Larzer Ziff, ed., *John Cotton on the Churches of New England* (Cambridge, Mass.: The Belknap Press, 1968), 27. Cotton's work was so persuasive that it convinced John Owen to adopt Independent polity. Owen says, 'I professed myself of the presbyterian judgment, in opposition to democratical confusion; and, indeed, so I do still, and so do all the congregational men in England that I am acquainted withal.... I set myself seriously to inquire into the controversies then warmly agitated in these nations.... I fixed on one ... Mr. Cotton's book of the Keys.... I was prevailed on to receive that and those principles which I had thought to have set myself in an opposition unto.' Owen, *A Review of the True Nature of Schism, with a Vindication of the Congregational Churches in England from the Imputation Thereof*, in *Works*, 13:223.

[26]Knollys, *Moderate Answer*, (unnumbered) 2.

[27]Knollys, *Moderate Answer*, 11.

[28]Knollys, *Moderate Answer*, 11.

[29]Knollys, *Moderate Answer*, 7, 13, 16. Bastwick had argued that 'The Presbyters alone without the consent of Brethren may admit members and cast out members, and that the

In 1681, Knollys published *The World that Now Is, and The World That is to Come*[30] which provides a detailed description of his views on church government, and seems to reflect some modifications of what he had printed 35 years earlier. In several places, he asserts that there should only be one church in each city or locality, though there may be several congregations or churches which make up this one church. He says

> The Church at Jerusalem was the first of all those Gospel-Churches ... Which Church was at its first Constitution a particular Congregation of sanctified Believers baptized with Water ... And although the number of the Disciples were multiplied from one hundred and twenty ... to three thousand ... yea to five thousand ... So that the Apostles had their own distinct Companies, Societies, or Congregations in Jerusalem [Act. 4.13, 19, 23 ....] Yet they all being of one heart, and of one soul, were but one church ... And so were all the particular Congregations in every City denominated and called .... Gospel-Oneness which maketh very much for the Well-Being of a particular Church is threefold: First, That there be but ONE Church in one City; and that all the Congregations of Saints in that City (called Churches) bear but one Name, to wit, the Church of God in that City, as in the Apostles daies, Act. 15.4.22. 1 Cor. 1.2. That so there may be no Schism, Divisions, nor sinful Separations from the Church of God; but that the whole church may be perfectly joyned together in ONE, As a City that is compact together, Psal. 122.3. as an House or Building fitly framed together, Ephes. 2.21,22. and as a Body fitly joyned and compacted by every joynt of supply, Eph. 4.16.[31]

While this seems to be a concession to Bastwick's Presbyterianism, it is not, for Knollys says plainly, 'The Churches of God under the Gospel, are not *National*, but *Political*, and *Congregational*.'[32]

The 'Well-Being of a particular church' consists of three things, Oneness, Order, and Government. Oneness involves being of one heart and soul, seeking to love one another, and that all of the saints must walk by the same rule, submitting to the bishops, pastors, teachers, presbyters, or elders set over them. Order requires a careful attention to all of the commands Christ gave for the life of the Church (such as in the proper administration of the ordinances), and Government finds its source in Christ who delegated authority to 'Apostles, Prophets, Evangelists, Pastors and teachers, called Bishops, Presbyters, or Elders' and who express their government in

---

Brethren or the congregation hath nothing to doe to hinder any such thing' as quoted by Knollys, 17.

[30]Hanserd Knollys, *The World that Now is; And The World that is to Come* (London: Tho. Snowden, 1681).

[31]Knollys, *The World that Now is*, 44-45, 50-51. See the discussion below.

[32]Knollys, *The World that Now is*, 45.

Church-Censures of Admonition, 2 *Thes.* 3.15. and *Titus* 3.10. Suspension (or withdrawing from a Brother or Member, that hath, and doth walk disorderly,) 2 *Thes.* 3.6. and Excommunication of those Members that live in gross and scandalous sins, 1 *Cor.* 5.1,4,5,13.[33]

At another place, Knollys says,

The Office of a *Pastor, Bishop*, and *Presbyter*, or *Elder* in the Church of God, is to take the Charge, Oversight, and Care of those Souls which the Lord Jesus Christ hath committed to them, to feed the Flock of God; to watch for their Souls, ... to Rule, Guide and Govern them (*by virtue of their Commission, and Authority received from Christ, Mat.* 28.28,19,20. & *Titus* 2.15.) according to the Laws, Constitutions and Ordinances of the Gospel.[34]

These two quotations help to define Knollys' latter understanding of church government, and they need to be read carefully in the light of each other. He did believe in the Independent principle of rule mediated by Christ, but, there is a subtle factor of great significance that must be noted. Rule in the church does not mean general oversight of all the affairs of the church. It is carefully circumscribed to certain specific actions, primarily centered on discipline (admonition, suspension and excommunication). These things, together with the ministry of the Word, make up 'the Laws, Constitutions and Ordinances of the Gospel'. The rule of elders is specifically defined and carried out in certain spheres. It is not an absolute rule, but a limited rule, circumscribed by Christ's commands. Knollys' position is not identical to the Independency described by Poh, but reflects a more limited rule by the elders in church polity.

Nehemiah Coxe: Congregational Consent/Rule by Elder

As one of the Pastors of the Petty France Church, the congregation from which the Second London Confession is thought to have originated, Nehemiah Coxe's views take on some importance. In 1681, he preached a sermon at the

---

[33]Knollys, *The World that Now is*, 50-54.
[34]Knollys, *The World that Now is*, 56-7. Further on in the book, he gives lengthy attention to his conviction that the church in each city should choose one of the elders of the churches to have 'Priority, Presidence, and Pre-eminence' over the other elders! He says, 'I mean and intend any one of the Bishops, Pastors, Teachers, Presbyters, or Elders, who are, or shall by the Consent, Approbation and Choice of the rest be appointed, ordained, and set over them as Chief Bishop or Presbyter of the Church in any City and Villages adjacent, who for Order sake in Gospel-Government, hath Priority, Pre-eminence, and Authority above the rest of the Presbyters or Bishops of the same Church, not alone, nor without them, but when Convened with them, to Act, Rule, Guide, Order and Govern with their Consent, Suffrage and Assistance, according to the Laws of the Lord Jesus Christ, the Constitutions and Commandments, the Practice and Example of his Holy Apostles, Act. 15.2, 6, 19, 22', 68-69 (see 55-69). I can find no indication that such a view was ever put into practice.

ordination of officers in one of the London churches, in which he explains some of his own understanding concerning these matters.

In the midst of a discussion of the duties of an elder, Coxe says

> It is his Duty to take care of the due exercise of *Discipline* in the Church, and the right ordering of all things pertaining to the Government therof; He is the *Overseer* of God's House, and is to *rule* therein, not in a despotical or lordly Way, but by the Testament of Christ, as becomes a *Minister*, and as one set over the *Lord's Heritage* who are a voluntary People, and to be governed not with force and rigor, but with their own consent. All the Brethren have an Interest in the management of Church-Affairs, in the admission, and ejection of Members; yet this denies not a peculiar Concernment of the Elder in these things, and a neglect of their due Administration will especially be charged upon him, if guilty thereof. And in these things, great Prudence, Tenderness, Diligence, and Impartiality is required of him. It is a Matter of great importance, that the Gates of the Lord's House, the goings out and comings in thereof be well look'd to. If Members be not received with due caution, our Number may be increased, but not our Joy, and if any be precipitantly, and without just cause ejected, the scandal and inconvenience will be as great.[35]

In this paragraph, Coxe defines the duties of elders as overseers in the church. He admits that all of the 'brethren' of the church have a proper 'interest in the management of Church-Affairs, in the admission, and ejection of Members' but that elders have a special concern in these things. While 'brethren' probably means male members, it nevertheless points towards the active involvement of (at least) the men in the church in business matters. The rule of elders is ministerial, not lordly, and must reflect the authority of Christ among a voluntary people.

This joint participation does not remove the obligation of church members to submit to their elders. Coxe says,

> You owe Submission and Obedience to them in the discharge of their Office, and in the exercise of that Rule and Oversight which Christ hath committed to them for your Edification; Obey them that have the Rule over you, and submit your selves, Heb. 13.17. It is not a blind Obedience that the Apostle requires, nor such as shall suppose a Legislative Power in Church-Officers, but an orderly subjection to them acting in their Office according to the Law and testament of Jesus Christ; even a ready obedience to the Word of God dispensed by them, and humble submission to their just Reproofs and Ministerial Correction, when rendered necessary by any miscarriage.[36]

---

[35]Nehemiah Coxe, *A Sermon Preached at the Ordination of an Elder and Deacons in a Baptized Congregation in London* (London: Tho. Fabian, 1681), 27.
[36]Cox, *Sermon*, 33-4.

Here Coxe further defines the nature of rule by elder. It is not 'legislative power', a freedom to make decisions for the church; it is rather ministerial, applying the Word of God in the church. Ministerial rule has boundaries, defined by 'the Law and testament of Jesus Christ'. Elders exercise their rule within the sphere set by Scripture. When they can rely upon a passage by asserting 'thus says the Lord', the people are to submit. But they do not have legislative power to go beyond the Scriptures in setting church policy. In addition, they have a special responsibility to bring 'reproofs and correction' to church members who sin. They have no authority to go beyond these boundaries. The people of God demonstrate their submission to the Word as they submit to their elders in these things. Coxe's doctrine maintains the notion that Elders receive their authority by delegation from Christ through the Apostles while restricting that authority to specific spiritual issues. In this way Coxe's position resembles Knollys'.

Benjamin Keach: Congregationalism/Rule by a Single Elder

Benjamin Keach also deals with the subject of rule by elder, and confirms the position put forward by Coxe. Relying heavily on Thomas Goodwin, he responds to the question 'Why is a steward, or pastor of a church, called a ruler?' with the answer

> Not that the whole government of the church is committed to him; he is not to rule without the brotherhood. 'If he will not hear the church,' Matt. xviii,17; it is not said, if he will not hear the pastor.

> 1.... He is invested with authority and power, as the chief ruler in the church, though there be helps of government, and for any to plead for an absolute or sole power of rule and government, to be in a pastor, and so a worse government in its nature, than many civil constitutions among men. In a particular church rightly constituted, is the fixed seat and subject of all ordinances of public worship, and hath the seat of all officers, or organical members, that serve for the use of the whole; and that these with their officers, have the seat of that government that is judicially to bind or loose the soul. The government of Christ's household is ordained or appointed by himself, and not left to men to order and govern it as they think good.

> 2. A ruler is to govern by law, and the constitution of the land, city, or corporation, where he is placed, and so an elder must govern according to the gospel constitution or laws and rules left by Jesus Christ.

> 3. Some rulers, or chief magistrates, can pass no act, law, or sentence, without the people, either to acquit, or condemn, (according to the constitution of the government) it must be with, and by their assent and

consent. So the steward or pastor of Christ's household, can pass no act, to receive in, or cast out, &c., without the assent and consent of the church.[37]

The pastor cannot rule 'without the brotherhood'. To do so is potentially tyrannical and despotic. The seat of government is in the church, and the elder's rule is carefully and explicitly circumscribed by the 'constitution or laws and rules left by Jesus Christ'. The third point noted, focusing on the 'sentence ... to acquit ... or condemn' underscores the point. The elder is a 'steward' and can only do that which is consonant with his stewardship. He is not a legislator, but a servant to Christ and the Church, charged with conveying the rules of the Lord, and not his own. This closely circumscribes the authority of the elder.

Keach also seems to approach a form of polity in which one pastor serves a congregational church. He frequently speaks of the officer in the singular. It is curious that when the prosperous London jewel merchant Isaac Marlow cried out against ministerial domination, Benjamin Keach is assumed to be the target of his denunciation.[38]

Thomas Crosby records an interesting event in the life of Keach's church which directly contributes to this discussion. A certain Benjamin Grosvenor was baptized and joined the Horselydown church in 1689. After seven or eight years of membership, he was thought to be a promising candidate for the pastoral office, and was sent off for 'instructions to be better fitted for the work of the ministry'. Upon his return from the unnamed place of study, Grosvenor announced 'that *infants* ought to be *baptized*; that the *government* of the church ought to be in the *eldership*, and not in the *members*; and that *unordained* persons ought not to preach'.[39] These three positions are part and parcel of classic Presbyterianism, and caused a great stir in the church. Crosby says,

> These things moved the church to deal plainly with him   ... and [they] appointed proper persons to discourse these points with him. After much time spent between the church and him in *controversy* upon these points, without any effect, he desired a dismission ... [they] did dismiss him from his membership with them.[40]

The inclusion of the second point is notable. One would expect that the adoption of paedobaptism would cause a controversy, and the rejection of the legitimacy of Gifted Brethren was contrary to accepted practice among the

---

[37]Keach, *Parables: Series Two*, 196. The material from Goodwin that stands behind Keach may be found in *The Works of Thomas Goodwin*, vol. 11, *The Government and Discipline of the Churches of Christ* (Eureka, Calif.: Tanski Publications, 1996 reprint), 495.

[38]Brown, *English Baptists*, 46-7. Marlow was a bitterly vocal opponent of Keach in the Hymn singing controversy, and probably wrote more on the subject than anyone besides Keach.

[39]Crosby, *CHEB*, 4:203, emphasis his.

[40]Crosby, *CHEB*, 4:203-04.

Particular Baptists.[41] But from Crosby's expressions, it is evident that the change of view with regard to the seat of government in the church was just as troubling to Keach's assembly. For them, church government was not in the hands of the elders, but in the membership of the church.

The execution of church power was the responsibility of appointed men. Benjamin Keach provides a detailed description of the method to be followed by the church and its officers in cases of discipline. He urges the churches to set aside one day a month for discipline, though smaller churches might only need to hold such a day once in two or three months. This meeting is based on the fact that

> The Power of the Keys, or to receive in and shut out of the Congregation, is committed unto the Church: The Political Power of Christ ... is in the Church, whereby it is exercised in the Name of Christ, having all lawful Rule and Government within it self....
>
> This power of Christ is exerted as committed to them by the Hands of the Elder appointed by Christ ... And that the Power of the Keys is in the Church, appears to me from Mat. 18. *If he will not hear the Church*; it is not said, if he will not hear the Elder, or Elders. As also that of the Apostle, in directing the Church to cast out the Incestuous Person, he doth not give this Counsel to the Elder or Elders of the Church, but to the Church; so he commands the Church to withdraw from every brother that walks disorderly.[42]

The judicial power of the keys is in the church, and the execution of power is in the elder(s). He admits into membership, or speaks the sentence of discipline, on behalf of the church. He does not act in this alone, nor as a representative of the eldership, but as the one duly charged with the responsibility of being the mouthpiece of the church. Keach provides further detail with regard to discipline. If the process of reconciliation commanded in Matthew 18 does not produce the desired response, then the church must act. The elder presents the case to the church, and they deliberate and determine that the offender is 'incorrigible' and so must be cast out of the assembly. When the decision has been reached,

> the Pastor after calling upon God, and opening the nature of the Offence, and the Justness of their Proceedings, in the Name and by the Authority of Christ, pronounces the Sentence of Excommunication to this effect.
>
> *That A.B. being guilty of great Iniquity, and not manifesting unfeigned Repentance, but refusing to hear the Church, I do in the Name, and by the Authority of Christ committed unto me as Pastor of this Church, pronounce and declare that he is to be, and is hereby excommunicated, excluded or*

---

[41]See Chapter 4, Church Officers, *infra.*

[42]Benjamin Keach, *The Glory of a True Church, And its Discipline display'd* (London: n.p., 1697), 19-21.

> *cast out of the Congregation, and no longer to be owned a Brother, or a Member of this Church; and this for the destruction of the Flesh, that his Spirit may be saved in the day of the Lord Jesus.*[43]

This is the execution of power or duty mentioned in the Confessional statement. The church does not simply express its power of discipline in the act of voting and concluding on the matter. There must be judicial sentence passed, and it was the duty of the elder to execute that power. He expresses the sentence 'by the Authority of Christ committed unto me as Pastor of this Church'. Christ appointed pastors in churches to exercise power. This is how it was enacted.

A potential problem with this method might arise in the case of an elder who sins. Keach anticipates this difficulty, indicating that the members of the church should in meekness follow the process contained in Matthew 18, and if the pastor is obstinate in his sin, the church must proceed to formal discipline. He says, 'but before he be dealt with they must appoint one from among themselves, qualifyd for the *work* of a Pastor, to execute the Church's Censure against him'.[44] Only an elder could pronounce the judicial sentence of the church.

Keach's language must be attentively noted. He said, 'this power of Christ is exerted as committed to them by the Hands of the Elder appointed by Christ'.[45] Power is in the church, but exerted by the elders who have been appointed by Christ. The church judges, the elder pronounces the sentence. This is a deliberately balanced and defined wielding of power. The elders cannot and do not act alone, and the church does not fulfill its responsibility by a simple vote. Both the action of the church and the sentence pronounced by the elder are necessary in order to bring the judicial verdict to fruition.

In the Confessional statement this balance is carefully developed. The term 'power' is used in a succession of paragraphs. In Paragraph 4, Christ is said to have received power for the origin, order and government of the church in a supreme and sovereign fashion. He expresses his power, according to paragraph 5, by calling people to salvation and commanding them to walk together as churches. Paragraph 6 does not use the word 'power', but expresses the conviction that these converted church members are to submit to Christ in the 'ordinances of the Gospel'. Paragraph 7 indicates that each church has been 'given all that power and authority, which is in any way needful for their carrying on that order in worship and discipline', and Christ has provided 'rules for the due and right exerting, and executing of that power'. And in paragraph 8, officers, namely 'bishops or elders and deacons', are said to be 'chosen and set apart' for the 'execution of power, or duty, which he entrusts them with, or calls them to'.[46] There is a logical and theological progression in the definition

---

[43]Keach, *Glory*, 27-28, emphasis his. The solemnity of the act is evident in the words spoken.

[44]Keach, *Glory*, 38, emphasis his. Keach is quoting an unnamed author.

[45]Keach, *Glory*, 21.

[46]*A Confession of Faith*, 86-89.

of power described here. Christ has supreme power. The church, as his institution, derives power from him for worship and discipline. Within the church there are some who hold office, and to them is granted a specific execution of power. There is a diminishing sphere of the exercise of power in these statements. Christ's power is all-encompassing. The church's power, received from him, extends to its proper functions of worship and discipline. It does not extend to other spheres. The elders' power is 'peculiar' or specific in its expression as well.

In putting this teaching into practice, the Particular Baptists did not interpret these words in a broad sense. The 'execution of power or duty' was limited and specific. When the Word of God spoke, or when necessity required the church to act in matters of discipline, the elders were authorized to speak or act. But they did not possess an authority that extended to every issue in church life.

These examples move away from the type of Independency explained by Poh Boon Sing. Knollys and Coxe seem to view elder authority as derived from Christ, while Keach says that the seat of authority is in the gathered congregation. This may indicate that there were theoretical differences on the details of ecclesiology among the Particular Baptists. In any case, the expression of rule by elder is limited to the specific actions described in the Confession, and not expanded beyond them.

John Owen himself seems to circumscribe the sphere in which elders rule. He says,

> The means whereby the Lord Christ communicates this power unto men is by his law and constitution, whereby he hath granted, ordained, and appointed, that such and such powers shall be exercised in his church, and that by such and such persons, to be derived unto them in such a way and manner; so that the word of the gospel, or the laws and constitutions of the Lord Christ therein, are the first recipient seat and subject morally of all church-power whatever, Matt. 16:19, 18:17-20.
>
> This authority is comprised in the law and constitution of Christ, which themselves exert only *ministerially*; and therefore, when ever they act any thing *authoritatively*, which they are not enabled for or warranted in by the word of the gospel, or do any thing without or contrary unto rule, all such actings, as to any spiritual effect of the gospel, or obligation on the consciences of men, are 'ipso facto' null, and are no way ratified in heaven, where all their orderly actings are made valid,—that is, by Christ himself in his word.[47]
>
> As this *whole church-power* is committed unto the whole church by Christ, so all that are called unto the peculiar exercise of any part of it, by virtue of office-authority, do receive that authority from him by the only way of the communication of it,—namely, by his word and Spirit, through the ministry of the church;

---

[47]Owen, *Works*, 15:500-501, emphasis his.

[Christ] hath determined and limited the powers and duties of the officers.

They who are called unto rule and authority in the church by virtue of their office are not thereon admitted unto an unlimited power, to be exercised at their pleasure in a lordly or despotical manner, but their power is stated, bounded, limited, and confined, as to the objects of it, its acts, its manner of administration, its ends, and as unto all things wherein it is concerned.

This authority in the rulers of the church is neither *autocratical* or sovereign, nor *nomothetical* or legislative, nor *despotical* or absolute, but *organical* and ministerial only.

Church-rule is a due care and provision that the institutions, laws, commands, and appointments of Jesus Christ be duly observed, and nothing else.[48]

Owen argues that the rule of elders 'may be reduced to three heads'. They are (1) The Admission and Exclusion of Members; (2) The Direction of the Church, that is, encouragement to mutual love, holiness, and service to others; (3) The conduct of worship, business meetings and other special meetings.[49] The expression of rule by the elders in Independent churches is to be limited by the Word of God. Owen does not argue for extensive rule by elder, but limited rule by elder. This is exactly what is found in the ecclesiological writings of the Particular Baptists.

If this is the case, how then did the congregations function? The minute books of the seventeenth-century churches provide further details on how this theoretical framework was put into practice.

Church Government in Church Minute Books

The best portrait of the implementation of church government principles among the Baptists may be found in the existing manuscript church books. Nehemiah Coxe's Petty France church book is still extant. The surviving book from Knollys' church begins in 1691, apparently written by his assistant and successor, Robert Steed. There are no extant church books from Keach's church until 1717. There are, nevertheless, many books from churches around the country. Together, they establish a pattern which explicates the practices of the Particular Baptist churches.

When these manuscripts are examined, the expressions of Independency, and the limitations on elder rule as suggested above are confirmed. In some places, the details are made very explicit, while in others they are evident in the regular activities of the church as a whole.

---

[48]Owen, *Works*, 16:36, 37, 39, 131, 138, emphasis his.
[49]Owen, *Works*, 16:136-37.

In Bromsgrove, Worcestershire, a church was planted under John Eckells, a man who had been trained for the ministry by the great anti-paedobaptist John Tombes.[50] On page 17 of the church book, the following is entered:

> On the 21st.day of ye 7th.month
> In ye year 1673   The Church being then assembled at one place, did appoint and determine of as a standing decree that on every second day of that week preceeding the monthly day, at 6 of ye clock in ye evening, precisely, ye brethren of ye congregation should meet to regulate ye affairs of ye Church.[51]

In this case, the men of the church were decreed to meet monthly for the purpose of settling the business of the church. No indication is given that these meetings were held for the purpose of giving consent to the prior decisions of the elder(s). The men met 'to regulate ye affairs of ye church'. This is unquestionably a form of democratic congregationalism. There are scanty records entered into the book for the 1670s and '80s, so that it is impossible to determine how faithfully this decree was put into practice. The meetings that are recorded generally have to do with discipline cases. But there is evidence that this congregationalism characterized the life of this church. On 21 April 1690, they state 'It is agreed that the next general meeting be on the 27th of September for the regulating of Church affairs.'[52] Throughout this period of time, John Eckells was pastor of the church, and a comparison of the names in membership in 1670 with those listed as full members in 1690 reveals that twenty-eight men remained in membership throughout this period. There is every reason to assume that their practice remained consistent during the intervening years.

The records of the Broadmead, Bristol church indicate that they established a 'Monthly meeting of ye Brethren only, to Consider of Persons or things amisse in ye Congregation'.[53] Throughout the following decades, the church acted on such matters as discipline, receiving members, choosing officers, the purchase of a burial place, and finances.[54] In 1670, they state

> And ye Church, though they had no Pastor, yett they did notwithstanding deale with Members that walked Irregular in their conversations; and they cast out some from amongst them, and Received in others to be members

---

[50]Eckells career is summarized in Ivimey, *HEB*, II:594-96. For Tombes, see *BDBR*, s.v. 'Tombes, John', by T. L. Underwood.
[51]Bromsgrove *CB*, 17. The Typescript pages are unnumbered, and frequently include more than one page from the original book. 'Page 17' refers to the original.
[52]Bromsgrove *CB*. According to the typescript, at this point in the original pagination begins again with the number 1 (it is actually page 74).
[53]Hayden, *The Records of a Church of Christ*, 121.
[54]Hayden, *The Records of a Church of Christ*, 128, 126, 130, 173, 134-36.

with them. Thus, having Ruling Elders, by them they carried on and managed ye *Church-Power*, and kept up all their meetings duly.[55]

Although the congregation did not have a pastor, the presence of recognized elders allowed them to continue to function as a church. The meetings of the 'brethren' would settle the business, and the elders enacted the decisions. They held the 'power of the keys', and were able to admit members and declare the judgment in cases of church discipline. In the cases of discipline, the elders would pronounce the verdict, exerting 'church power'. No one but an elder could express the sentence of discipline determined by the church. An incident from 1670 illustrates: a certain Philip Sciphard was several times rebuked for excessive drinking. Two men of the church saw him 'overcome in drinke', brought the matter before the church and

> therefore at a Church-meeting, he being present, his Evils were laid before him, and by ye Eldest Ruleing Elder Brother Ellis, at his house, ye said Philip Sciphard was cast out of ye Congregation.[56]

The balance between congregation and elders was carefully maintained. When the church had a pastor, he generally presided at the discipline meetings and expressed the judgment of the church.[57]

Perhaps the most explicit statement of congregationalism is found in the Bagnio/Cripplegate church book. Robert Steed, co-pastor and successor to Hanserd Knollys, noted in the manuscript,

> The church being assembled did unanimously agree that for the better carrying on of the work of God in it. That division might be prevented and peace preserved and purity and love maintained. That ten or twelve Brethren be desired to meet together to prepare matters for this church soe as that no materiall affaire be presented or transacted in the church till they have considered and agreed about it.
> This was consented to with these limitations:
> 1. That none of the Brethren be excluded who shall be willing to be with them when they meet & to help in theire consultations.
> 2. That they shall determine nothing but only present theire consultations and agreement to the church for theire consideration, whose consent shall be the determination of it.

---

[55]Hayden, *The Records of a Church of Christ*, 128, emphasis his.
[56]Hayden, *The Records of a Church of Christ*, 128-29. In 1679, just prior to the arrival of their new pastor, ruling elders officiated at several discipline cases, and welcomed in a new member, cf. 213-218.
[57]Hayden, *The Records of a Church of Christ*, 188, 192, 196, 201, 226. At a meeting held in February 1677/78, the pastor pronounced one sentence of withdrawal, while in a different case at the same meeting, a ruling elder pronounced the sentence, 196-97.

3. That when theire time or season of meeting is come any 5 or 7 of them shall be a sufficient number to consider of such things as might be presented to them if the rest be absent.[58]

It may be that the meetings of the church were becoming unwieldy. In any case, ten or twelve of the men of the church were appointed to meet together as a screening committee for business brought to the church as a whole. These men were not elders alone,[59] for 'none of the Brethren' who might want to attend could be excluded.

Ten years later, this decision was reaffirmed and expanded.

Agreed to by ye church before Bro: Steed died
1st That 12 Brethren (not excluding others) be appointed by ye church to prepare all matters for ye church. (Every last Monday of the month, at one a clock at ____ house.)
2 That nothing be finally concluded by them.
3 That 7 of them be capable to act
4 That no extraordinary collection be made (wthout advis of ye Br)
    That no stranger be admitted to preach
    That no matter of discipline whatsoever be brought into ye church untill first considered by these brethren
5 That no stranger be present when any declare ye dealing of God with their Soules: or any other matter in ye church but members only (unless allowed by ye pastor)
6 That all those members yt frequently are absent from their comunion wth the church, be carefully and constantly observed, and our Elders acquainted therewith; that they may be visited, & admonished according to rule.
7 That when any difference or offence is between members, and it is in debate in ye church; both parties be desired to withdraw while in debate: And to forbear their communion at ye Lords Table untill they are reconciled or ye case determined according to rule.
8 That none be admitted privatly to declare ye dealing of God wth their soules: except in extraordinary cases
9 That in all debates in ye church, there be observed a sober orderly behaviour as becometh saints: and but one speaking at a time
10 That ye list of the members be completed & read in ye Church once in 6 months.
11 That every member that doth not contribute towards the maintenance of ye Ministrie &c. according to their ability be visited & admonished according to rule.
12 That all matters & things that are finally concluded in & by the Church, be recorded in the Church Booke.

---

[58]Bagnio/Cripplegate *CMB*, unnumbered page facing page 2. The minutes for 1689-99 have been reprinted in H. Wheeler Robinson, ed. 'Baptist Church Discipline 1689-1699', *BQ* 1 (1922): 112-28; 179-85. The manuscript Church Book is mistitled because the entries are chronologically mixed, with the first dated entry being 1695.
[59]There is no indication in the Church Minute Book that the church recognized ruling elders.

13 That ye power of determining & concluding all matters & things be in &
by the Church: The actuall exercise of all power (ministerially) &c. be by ye
Elders or those the Church shall appoint, According to ye rule of our Lord
and Law-giver Christ Jesus in ye Holy Scriptures.[60]

This is a remarkable statement. It affirms the decision made ten years earlier,
and provides a more detailed explanation of how this worked, as well as a brief
assertion of the theological basis upon which it rested.

For this church, final authority was vested in the gathered congregation. All
'matters & things' were to be determined and concluded upon by the church.
These conclusions would then be enacted by the elders of the church. This is
the same procedure as found in the Broadmead records above, though it is
made more explicit. The power of the elder is ministerial. He alone has the
right to make the pronouncement of the church, but he does so on the basis of
the decision of the church.

When business needed to be transacted, it was presented first to this meeting
of the brethren. At the same church meeting where this statement was
approved, the deacons were charged to acquaint 'ye Brethren at their sd
meeting wth the state of ye poor & how provide for their releef in point of
stock'.[61] The deacons were subject to the decisions of this meeting, which was
itself subject to the meeting of the church.[62]

The priority of the church is evidenced in the decisions made immediately
after the constituting of the Maze Pond church in London in 1693/94. The
nucleus of this group was made of a handful of dissidents from Benjamin
Keach's Horselydown church. When he introduced hymn singing into the
public worship, they broke away and eventually formed the Maze Pond church.
On 9 February 1693/94, they were constituted as a church with the help of
several London pastors. They called James Warburton as pastor, and on the
twenty-first of the month decreed 'that Brother James Warburton in an especall
manner shall move to the church such things as may be thought necessary, and
take the churches answers and declare them, and the like'.[63] Though he was
pastor, he was subject to the church and acted at their order. Just over a year
later, when he wanted to go away for three weeks, he had to request permission
from the church to leave.[64]

---

[60]Bagnio/Cripplegate *CMB*, 12.
[61]Bagnio/Cripplegate *CMB.*, Unnumbered page facing page 13. In cases of emergency,
the deacons were free to act, 'yet yt it is expedient the Deacons should acquaint and
advise wth ye Brethren at their next meeting on church affairs'.
[62]The Broadmead, Bristol Church in 1680 appointed two deacons to receive collections
'not only for ye Poor, but for any other Use for ye Good of ye Congregation' stipulating
that 'they must not lay it out without ye Consent of ye Church, at least ye Elders'.
Hayden, *The Records of A Church of Christ*, 225.
[63]Maze Pond *CMB*, 91. The church book actually begins with the events leading to the
separation from Keach in 1691.
[64]Maze Pond *CMB*, 115.

David Crossley was ordained to the ministry of the Bagnio/Cripplegate church in February, 1702/30. Several visiting elders assisted the church, but not until one of them spoke to the people in these words,

> Now you Brethren & Sisters of the Church that this blessed work may more solemnly & effectually be done, if you do desire these reverend Elders to constitute & Ordaine this our Dear Bro: to this office, manifest the same by holding up your hands which was againe unanimously by all ye members present.[65]

They would not act without the explicit consent of the church. They could not act 'effectually' on their own, even as 'reverend elders'. An act of the church was required prior to their participation in the ordination. In 1704, the church ordained six deacons. Crossley led the ordination, but was careful to point out that he was acting for the church: 'while I say we ordain we mean is of ye church & not our selves'.[66] In a similar fashion, when Mark Key was to be ordained as co-pastor with Richard Adams at Devonshire Square, London, Adams was instructed to say 'I now declare by ye authority of Christ and this church yt my Bro: Mark Key is by this church appointed or ordained a joynt elder Pastor or overseer wth my self over her.'[67] In this case, the church determined the form and the content of the ordination. Their ecclesiological perspectives always gave priority to the local church.

While in most cases elders took the lead in exercising the power of the keys, in the absence of elders gifted brothers could be charged with these responsibilities. When the Bampton, Devon, church was without a settled pastor in 1702, they requested their supply preacher James Murch 'to be our mouth in pronouncing the sentence of ejection ... which he accepted and it was solemnly done'.[68] He could do this because of his qualifications as a gifted brother (he would later become their pastor) and because the church empowered him to do so. Both of these needed to be in place in order for the act to be authoritative.

At the 7 June 1699 meeting of the Northern Association, the question was asked, 'Whether it be lawful & expedient for an Elder or Ministering Brother to take ye whole time every Lords day when there are other Gifts little or nothing inferior belonging to the Church?' The answer was 'That it is neither lawful nor expedient for an Elder to take up the whole time contrary to ye Churches mind. I Cor. 3.27. I Cor. 2.3. I Pet. 5.5.'[69] In this case, even the preaching ministry of the elders was subject to the local church. They did not rule in this matter, but submitted to the wishes of the congregation.

---

[65]Bagnio/Cripplegate *CMB*, 22.
[66]Bagnio/Cripplegate *CMB*, 25.
[67]Devonshire Square *CMB*, 159.
[68]Bampton *CMB*, 36.
[69]Stephen L. Copson, *Association Life of the Particular Baptists of Northern England 1699-1732* (London: The Baptist Historical Society, 1991), 84. I Cor. 3 only has 23 verses.

In addition to the explicit statements of polity recorded in Church Books, an analysis of the records themselves demonstrates a high level of congregational participation in the decision making process. Many of the churches had a regularly scheduled 'monthly day'[70] on which business was transacted. The church minute books demonstrate patterns of business meetings. Petty France, London, met on an irregular but approximate two week schedule, sometimes increased in frequency to weekly.[71] The Maze Pond, London church met a staggering 37 times in the first eight months of its existence.[72] The Bampton, Devon, Church Minute Book is incomplete, but the extant entries indicate a similar pattern. Within the first month of their constituting, the church met for business five times. From 1702 through 1704, they transacted business almost weekly.[73]

These church meetings were distinct from worship. The entries in the Bampton Minutes frequently begin with the phrase 'after the publique worship was over'[74] indicating the distinction drawn between worship and business. The topics considered range over every issue relevant to the life of the church. New Members were 'propounded', 'approved', and welcomed into membership;[75] discipline was discussed, determined and enacted;[76] financial matters were

---

[70]Broadmead, Bristol, Bromsgrove, Worcs., Bagnio/Cripplegate, London have all been noted above. Keach advocated 'that a monthly day be appointed for Discipline   ... tho in small Congregations perhaps a day in two or three Months may be sufficient'. Keach, *The Glory of a True Church*, 19-20. Devonshire Square, London generally followed a four-week pattern in 1701-05. Devonshire Square *CMB*, 25-131. They called this a 'monthly meeting' even though some months had two meetings (one very early and the other very late in the calendar) while others (because of two in the previous month) had none, 55.

[71]Petty France *CMB, passim*. As an example, the Church Book records that in 1679 (January to January, modern reckoning), a typical year, the church met on: 26 January; 9 February; 2 and 23 March; 13, 20 and 27 April; 4, 11 and 25 May; 15 and 22 June; 6 and 27 July; 3, 10 and 31 Aug; 7, 21, and 28 September; 12 and 19 October; 9 and 30 November; and 28 December. This is twenty-five meetings in less than fifty-two weeks.

[72]Maze Pond *CMB*, 91-105. The period covered is 9 February to 31 October 1694. On four occasions, they met for business three times within a week (21, 25 and 18 March; 2, 6 and 9 May; 20, 23 and 27 May; 22, 25 and 29 July); and once they did this in the space of 5 days (Oct. 9, 10 and 14). Many of these meetings concerned new members.

[73]Bampton *CMB*, 2-5, 19-58.

[74]Bampton *CMB*.

[75]Petty France, *CMB*, 1 and *passim*; Maze Pond *CMB*, 92-120. From 18 February 1694 until 18 August 1695, this church admitted 78 women and 28 men by profession of faith and baptism; Broughton (Porton) Church Book 1 1657-1684, The Angus Library, Regent's Park College, Oxford, 21.

[76]Petty France, *CMB*, 1 and *passim*; Bagnio/Cripplegate *CMB, passim*, see also the transcription of the early portion of this manuscript in Robinson, 'Baptist Church Discipline', 116-28, 179-185.

approved;[77] benevolence was determined;[78] officers were chosen;[79] inter-church difficulties were debated,[80] and associational matters were settled.[81] In addition, a whole host of practical questions related to each particular church was discussed. Stevington, Bedfordshire prayed for rain during a time of drought,[82] Maze Pond approved the use of their facility for a visiting preacher's special service[83] and for use as a school house.[84] They also decided to defray the cost of baptism for the poor and voted to give their pastor permission to take three weeks off for a trip to the country.[85] In 1692, the Wantage, Oxfordshire church approved a 2,000 year lease on a barn and property as a meeting place.[86] The Bampton, Devon, church allowed their pastor to preach in Plymouth 'for one Lord's Day and Bro: More appointed to goe with him to prevent any design there might be in the Church of Plym to indeavour the having our Bro: Murch away to themselves'. A special collection was taken to defray More's expenses.[87]

---

[77]Maze Pond *CMB*, 96, 143; Bourton on the Water, 'Accounts of Building First Church with List of Subscribers, 1701', The Angus Library, Regent's Park College, Oxford; 'Records and Letters Relative to the Baptist Church at Hexham from Oct 1651 to July 1680. Followed by Records of the Church at Hamsterley in the County of Durham. Rebound in One Volume at the request and Expense of Richard Pengilly, Newcastle 1832', The Angus Library, Regent's Park College, Oxford, 7 (of Hamsterley section); Ernest Kevan, *London's Oldest Baptist Church* (London: The Kingsgate Press, 1933), 46-49.

[78]Warwick Baptist Church Book 1698-1760, Warwickshire County Record Office, Warwick, 2; Maze Pond *CMB*, 114; Broughton *CB1*, 23;

[79]Petty France *CMB*, 1, 4, 23 (no page number in the manuscript); Devonshire Square *CMB*, 21, 131; Henley in Arden Church Book Minutes 1803-1885, Warwickshire County Record Office, Warwick, Microfilm MI 197 (this is the account of the call of John Beddome in 1697); Tottlebank Church Book 1669-1854, The Angus Library, Regent's Park College, Oxford, 5.

[80]Tibbutt, *Some Early Nonconformist Church Books*, 33; Petty France *CMB*, 41 (no pagination in original); Maze Pond *CMB*, 92, 102-104.

[81]Petty France *CMB*, 12, 13, 17, 21, 27 (mispaginated as 24), 28 (mispaginated as 26); Devonshire Square *CMB*, 39, 73; Maze Pond *CMB*, 98; Bagnio/Cripplegate *CMB*, 26-28.

[82]Tibbutt, *Some Early Nonconformist Church Books*, 32, 34.

[83]Maze Pond *CMB*, 95. The visiting preacher was the High Calvinist Independent Richard Davis.

[84]Maze Pond *CMB*, 112.

[85]Maze Pond *CMB*, 114-15.

[86]Wantage Baptist Church Book 1760-1824, Wantage Baptist Church, Wantage, Oxfordshire, unnumbered page at the back of the book entitled 'An Abstract of ye Writings of ye Barn now ye Meeting house near Grove Street Wantage'. The lease commenced 'from ye 16th year of Charles 2d king &c which happened in ye year of our Lord one thousand six hundred & seventy seven'. The purchase price was £40.

[87]Bampton *CMB*, 18-19.

In every case, even in the churches associated with the ministries of Hanserd Knollys and Nehemiah Coxe, it is the church that decides and acts. No evidence can be found to support the notion that the elders of the church brought decisions to the churches for their consent. To the contrary, the elders occasionally came to the church for permission to do certain things. It is at this point that the modification of Owen's theoretical system may be noticed. In these practices, the Particular Baptists carried a greater resemblance to the Congregationalism of the Brownists than the Independency of Owen. Poh's description of Congregationalism, '[it] operates in practice ... that the church members raise issues in the church business meeting, and the decisions are made by obtaining a consensus of opinion from all the members through voting'[88] fits precisely as a description of the Particular Baptist church meetings.

Conclusion

The assertions made by Poh Boon Sing do not fit the weight of the evidence presented here. Church Government in the Independent ecclesiological system was a carefully balanced interaction between elder rule and congregational democracy. An attentive reading of the Confessional statement will bear this out. It says,

> 7. To each of these Churches thus gathered, according to his mind declared in his word, he hath given all that power and authority, which is in any way needful, for their carrying on that order in worship, and discipline, which he hath instituted for them to observe; with commands, and rules, for the due and right exerting, and executing of that power.

> 8. A particular Church gathered, and compleatly Organized, according to the mind of Christ, consists of Officers, and Members; And the Officers appointed by *Christ* to be chosen and set apart by the Church (so called and gathered) for the peculiar Administration of Ordinances, and execution of Power, or Duty, which he intrusts them with, or calls them to, to be continued to the end of the World, are Bishops or Elders and Deacons.[89]

In paragraph 7, Christ is said to have given *to the churches*, power and authority for worship and discipline, and instructions by which this power might be executed. Paragraph 8 then follows, explaining how this power is executed. A church 'completely organized' has officers as well as members, and these officers have been appointed for specific tasks, namely the administration of the ordinances, and the execution of power or duty. As we have seen, this power or duty was not universal, but was strictly circumscribed by the Scriptures. In practice, this meant that the elders 'officiated' at those times when the expression of power or duty was necessary, but it did not mean

[88]Poh, *Keys*, 264.
[89]*A Confession of Faith*, 88-89.

that they exercised universal rule in the church. They were not, in Nehemiah Coxe's words, 'legislators' in the church, rather they were stewards of specific tasks under divine appointment. The completely organized church had everything necessary, within itself, to fulfill its tasks in the world.

Independency, at least as practiced by the Particular Baptist churches, was not a system emphasizing the rights of the elders so much as it was an attempt to maintain the rights of the people while carrying out the appointed tasks of the eldership. The people (or in most cases, the men) of the church were active participants in the regular decisions of the church. The elders administered the ordinances, and acted on behalf of the church when power or duty was executed.

CHAPTER 4

'The officers appointed by Christ ... are bishops or elders, and deacons': Church Officers

The Second London Confession identifies two offices in the local church, 'Bishops or Elders and Deacons'.[1] The first of these offices, described by the two terms bishop and elder, refers to the teaching and ruling office in the church, and the second, deacon, to the serving office. These were the only formal 'offices' recognized among the Particular Baptists.[2]

The Confessional statement says,

> 8. A particular church gathered, and compleatly Organized, according to the mind of Christ, consists of Officers, and Members; And the Officers appointed by *Christ* to be chosen and set apart by the Church (so called and gathered) for the peculiar Administration of Ordinances, and Execution of Power or Duty, which he intrusts them with, or calls them to, to be continued to the end of the World are (p) Bishops or Elders and Deacons.

> (d) Act. 20.17 with v. 28. Phil. 1.1.

> 9. The way appointed by *Christ* for the Calling of any person, fitted, and gifted by the Holy *Spirit*, unto the Office of Bishop, or Elder, in a Church, is, that he be chosen thereunto by the common (q) suffrage of the Church itself; and Solemnly set apart by Fasting and Prayer, with imposition of hands of the (r) Eldership of the Church, if there be any before Constituted therein; And of a Deacon (s) that he be chosen by the like suffrage, and set apart by Prayer, and the like Imposition of hands.

---

[1] *A Confession of Faith*, 89.

[2] Among the General Baptists, a third office, messenger, was recognized. This was something of an overseer or bishop of a number of churches in a geographic area. The *Orthodox Creed* of 1679 explicitly stated that there were three offices in the church, namely, 'Bishops, or Messengers; and Elders, or Pastors; and Deacons, or Overseers of the poor'. These bishops or messengers 'have the government of those churches, that had suffrage in their election'. Lumpkin, *BCF*, 319-320. Cf. J. F. V. Nicholson, 'The Office of "Messenger" amongst British Baptists in the Seventeenth and Eighteenth Centuries', *BQ* 17 (1957-58): 211-213. The Particular Baptists also had messengers, but they were simply representatives of the churches to the Association meetings and General Assemblies. Nicholson, 'Office of Messenger', 213.

(q) Act. 14.23: See the original.
(r) 1 Tim. 4.14.
(s) Act 6.3.5.6.

10. The work of Pastors being constantly to attend the Service of *Christ*, in his Churches, in the Ministry of the Word, and Prayer, (t) with watching for their Souls, as they that must give an account to him; it is incumbent on the Churches to whom they Minister, not only to give them all due respect, (u) but also to communicate to them of all their good things according to their ability, so as they may have a comfortable supply, without being themselves (x) [*sic*] entangled in Secular Affairs; and may also be capable of exercising (y) Hospitality toward others; and this is required by the (z) Law of Nature, and by the Express order of our Lord Jesus, who hath ordained that they that preach the Gospel, should live of the Gospel.

(t) Act. 6.4. Heb. 13.17.
(u) 1 Tim. 5.17,18. Gal 6.6,7.
(x) 2 Tim. 2.4.
(y) 1 Tim. 3.2.
(z) 1 Cor. 9.6-14.[3]

The officers are appointed by Christ, who has established qualifications and guidelines for those men to occupy their office. When installed, they have specific functions, and the pastors are to receive financial compensation for their work so that they are enabled to lay aside their secular employment and devote themselves to fulfilling their ministry.

The concept of 'office' was rooted in a belief that Christ is an active and present Lord over the Church who chooses and gifts certain individuals with the requisites for service. Hanserd Knollys understood office as something 'Divine and Sacred, but not *Lordly*'.[4] It was an appointed position, with the firm belief that Christ himself was active in the selection of those to be set aside, though it did not provide the appointed with any kind of aristocratic position.

Nehemiah Coxe considered office so important that he asserted that every 'particular Congregation hath not only *right*, but is in *duty* bound to dispose her self in that Order, and under that Rule and Government, which Christ hath appointed in his testament'.[5] To use the words of the Confession, a church was not complete until it was furnished with officers duly installed.

Office in the church was both ordinary and extraordinary. The extraordinary offices, Apostle, Evangelist, and Prophet, were considered to have ended with the completion of the canon of Scripture. But the ordinary officers, elders and deacons, continued on throughout the post-apostolic era.[6] Apostles were

---

[3] *A Confession of Faith*, 89-91.
[4] Hanserd Knollys, *The World that Now is*, 56, emphasis his.
[5] Coxe, *Ordination Sermon*, 8.
[6] Coxe, *Ordination Sermon*, 6-7. See below under 'Elders and the Local Church' for a further discussion of this issue.

'antecedent' to the church, and received their call and appointment directly from Christ. 'Ordinary ministers', are not 'of men' in that their authority derives from humanity, nor are they 'by men', that is, subject to the whims of human authority and appointment, but they are 'by men' in that they are 'brought to their Office by the Call of the Church'.[7] Benjamin Keach argued based on this distinction that ordinary officers could not exist apart from the prior existence of a church. It is the constituted church that chooses, ordains and installs its officers. A church without a 'pastor or pastors ordained' is 'very disorderly',[8] and a pastor without a church is impossible. The church had priority over the officers, but was incomplete without them. Ministers could not function without the call and approbation of a specific church.

The Confessional statement indicates that there were two classes of officers: bishops or elders, and deacons. The former occupied the office of serving by ruling in the church, while the latter were given over to be servants 'for the Relief of the Poor' in and around the church.[9] Each office deserves specific attention.

The Teaching/Ruling Office

The Teaching/Ruling office centered on elders, though there were other recognized teachers, specifically the Gifted Brethren.

Elders

The most significant of the ordinary offices of the church was pastor or elder. The relationship between this office and the local church was well-defined in Particular Baptist polity.

ELDERS AND THE LOCAL CHURCH

The notion that officers were essential to the *bene esse* of the church provides an important contextual pointer for an understanding of the relationship between the two. Although the church was prior, and circumscribed the office, it was insufficient apart from these officers. The role of office, especially of elder, was foundational to the successful mission of the church. Congregations without duly ordained ministers could not function in every way as they ought.

Current thinking on the nature of the relationship between elder and church was basic to their practice. The Baptists reflect the views of contemporary Independent writers on ecclesiology in this matter. To what extent were elders allowed to function in their offices? Was their ministerial authority universal, extending to all of the churches of the same faith and practice, or were they restricted in any way? Several writers addressed these issues. The views of two

---

[7]Coxe, *Ordination Sermon*, 6.
[8]Keach, *The Glory of a True Church*, 7-8.
[9]Coxe, *Ordination Sermon*, 10.

key Independent writers, John Owen and Thomas Goodwin, and several Particular Baptists shed light on the question.

Perhaps the most important writer of congregational polity in the second half of the seventeenth century is John Owen. His books defined the practices of the paedobaptists who participated in the adoption of or subscribed the Savoy Platform of Polity. He was esteemed as a careful exegete and discerning theologian, and his works had enormous influence among the non-conformists of the era, both paedobaptist and Baptist. In several places, Owen addresses topics related to this subject.

In his 1667 work entitled *A Brief Instruction in the Worship of God and Discipline of the Churches of the New Testament*,[10] Owen twice broaches the theme. Questions 21-31 address issues relating to the officers of the church. According to Owen, there are two types of officers, *extraordinary* and *ordinary*. The extraordinary officers of the church are apostles, evangelists and prophets, and the ordinary officers are 'those whom the Scripture calls pastors and teachers, bishops, elders, and guides'. Question 24 asks, 'What are the principal differences between these two sorts of officers or rulers in the church, extraordinary and ordinary?' Owen's answer is noteworthy:

> The former were called to their office immediately by Jesus Christ in his own person, or revelation made by the Holy Ghost in his name to that purpose; the latter by the suffrage, choice, and appointment of the church itself. The former, both in their office and work, were independent on, and antecedent unto, all or any churches, whose calling and gathering depended on their office as its consequent and effect; the latter, in both, consequent unto the calling, gathering, and constituting of the churches themselves, as an effect thereof, in their tendency unto completeness and perfection. *The authority of the former being communicated unto them immediately by Jesus Christ, without any intervenient actings of any church, extended itself equally unto all churches whatever; that of the latter being derived unto them from Christ by the election and designation of the church, is in the exercise of it confined unto that church wherein and whereby it is so derived unto them.* They differ also in gifts, which were suited unto their several distinct works and employments.[11]

Owen here draws a careful distinction between the spheres of authority granted to the two kinds of officers. The extraordinary officers, because their call derives directly from Jesus Christ, enjoy the privilege of universal responsibility and authority. They speak to each and every church. This is the doctrine of the government of the universal church. Jesus Christ is the head, and he has given some to serve as his instruments in laying the foundation for the church. The ordinary officers, however, have a different kind of authority. It is *confined* to the church in which they were called. The nature of the call defines the sphere of authority.

---

[10] Owen, *Works*, 15:445-530.
[11] Owen, *Works*, 15:492, emphasis mine.

A few pages further on, Owen expands on the issue in Question 26:

> May a person be called to, or be employed in, a part only of the office or
> work of the ministry; or may he hold the relation and exercise the duty of an
> elder or minister unto more churches than one at the same time?

The answer is tersely stated:

> Neither of these has either warrant or precedent in the Scripture; nor is the
> first of them consistent with the authority of the ministry, nor the latter with
> the duty thereof, nor either of them with the nature of that relation which is
> between the elders and the church.[12]

The Scriptures given in support are Acts 14.23, 1 Pet. 5.2, and Acts 20.28. It is
the second part of this question which is of importance for this study.

Owen says that his intent is 'concerning the relation of the same person to
more churches than one at the same time, and his undertaking to discharge the
duty of his relation unto them as an elder or minister'.[13] This is explicitly
related to the question under consideration. While Owen probably was
responding to certain practices characteristic of some in the Church of
England,[14] the principles he addresses are quite relevant. He envisions two
circumstances in which one might hold the relation of elder to two or more
churches: (1) 'Formally and directly, by an equal formal interest in them,
undertaking the pastoral charge equally and alike of them, being called alike to
them, and accepting of such a relation'. This is probably specifically a
description of pluralism. (2) 'Virtually, when, by virtue of his relation unto one
church, he puts forth his power or authority in ministerial acts in or towards
another.' Owen calls both of these 'irregular and unwarrantable'. The first,
pluralism, 'is unlawful, and destructive both of the office and duty of a pastor'
because the Scriptures speak to elders' obligations in specific local churches
where the Holy Spirit has set them, and they will give account for their
relations with that specific church. The Scripture verses cited above are
especially significant in this regard. Owen refers to them because they point to
a unique relationship between elder and church. Elders are appointed 'in every
church', they are to shepherd the flock which is 'among them', and the Holy
Spirit has made them overseers 'among' the people of a certain flock. The
second, performing authoritative ministerial acts in a congregation other than
his own, is 'unwarrantable', as there is neither precept nor example in Scripture
to countenance such a case.[15]

---

[12]Owen, *Works,* 15:496-97.

[13]Owen, *Works*, 15:197-98.

[14]Pluralism, i.e. the holding of two or more livings at the same time, was practiced in up
to a third of the parishes in some counties. John Spurr, *The Restoration Church of
England, 1646-1689* (New Haven: Yale University Press, 1991), 175.

[15]Owen, *Works*, 15:498.

For Owen, the relationship with a church is particular. The call and ordination to the ministry circumscribes the field in which ministerial acts are to be performed. An elder cannot and ought not to extend his ministerial authority beyond the sphere of that church's call.[16]

In his treatise *The True Nature of a Gospel Church and Its Government* (published in 1689), he reaffirms this same position:

> It is manifest ... how inconsistent it is with this office, and the due discharge of it, for any one man to undertake the relation of a pastor unto more churches than one, especially if far distant from one another.[17]

The weight of the account that must be given for the souls of men ought to be enough to condemn the practice of multiple church relations.

Another writer of importance is Thomas Goodwin. In his lengthy treatise *Of the Constitution, Right Order, and Government of the Churches of Christ*, apparently written while the Westminster Assembly was in session,[18] Goodwin speaks to the issue of inter-church communion. The ecclesiological debates of the Assembly are well-known, as Goodwin and the other 'Dissenting Brethren' (Burroughs, Nye, Simpson and Bridge) sought to argue against the prevailing Presbyterianism of the rest of the Assembly. Goodwin's treatise on church government is a carefully nuanced presentation of the principles of Independency as they were being fleshed out in the fledgling congregational churches. In chapters 9 and 10 of book 5, he addresses the subject of elders and their relations with a church or churches. Do elders as elders have a right to exercise their office beyond the sphere of their own local churches? For the Presbyterian party, the answer was clearly 'yes'. Such a notion is inherent to the Presbyterian system. But for Goodwin, the issue is more complex. He argues that elders must be viewed in terms of two basic kinds of power: the first is power of order, which derives from the elders' relation in dedication to God and Christ, is expressed in terms of activities such as preaching, and is carried with him wherever he goes; the second is power of jurisdiction, which is exercised along with other elders 'and with other elders not materially considered, but as formed up into the relation of a presbytery, to a church which is to be the seat of it'. The first power may receive the blessing of God wherever it is expressed, but the second 'is not to be extended beyond the seat, the church, to which he hath relation'. By this distinction, Goodwin is concerned to circumscribe the proper expression of the power of an elder. On the one hand, they must be 'reverenced' by those in other churches because they are elders, but on the other hand, 'it will be hard to shew wherein ministers have power of jurisdiction over persons that belong not to their own churches'. In his own words, 'a particular church may receive the elders of other churches,

---

[16]Cf. Keach, *Parables: Series Two*, 193: 'A true regular call to the ministry lies in a true church of Christ'.

[17]Owen, *Works*, 16:90.

[18]Goodwin, *Works*, 11:3-484. He mentions 'the assembly that now sitteth' on page 274.

and receive them as elders in respect of some acts, as preaching and the like, but not in respect of acts of jurisdiction'.[19]

It must be stated that Goodwin did make allowance for elders to exercise acts of jurisdiction in churches other than their own, but this is to be only occasionally, and at the specific request of the second church. He said:

> But if the elders of other churches were capable to exercise the acts of jurisdiction occasionally in some cases over churches which they have not a constant relation of eldership unto, by virtue of the catholic communion of churches, yet the seat in which, and the bounds of extent over which this jurisdiction is to be exercised, must still be a particular congregation. And the call by which this jurisdiction is to be exercised, should be occasionally from that congregation, in case of want or need; which therefore should in such cases, stand instead of a fixed and constant relation that elders do bear to that church, the call being occasional and from themselves, in case of need, as the jurisdiction they exercise is but merely occasional, and for that time. And so by this means, still as the right bounds, that Christ hath instituted for the seat of jurisdiction, is kept unto and not exceeded, so the power of the congregation itself is hereby also preserved.[20]

Goodwin then described the types of acts which he had in mind: 'a particular congregation may make use of the elders of another congregation to ordain, to assist them in excommunication, &c', though he was immediately careful to deny that these acts mediate power to the visiting elders in the visited church.[21]

The position espoused here by Thomas Goodwin has similarities to that of John Owen. For each of these men, the local church as a body has primacy in terms of pastoral relations and authority. According to Owen, the formal relationship established between one church and its elder(s) precludes such a formal relationship with other churches. In Goodwin, the emphasis is on the distinction between ministerial acts and power of jurisdiction. If a special circumstance were to arise, in which one church needed to call upon the elders of another church for assistance, it was free to do so, but only for a specific and clearly delimited reason. The notion that elders could function in formal pastoral relationships with two or more churches is unfounded. Their ministerial activities were largely restricted to the churches in which they held office.

It is very likely that this was the prevailing opinion among the Independents and the Particular Baptists. W. T. Whitley records the minutes of an association meeting held 21-23 September 1695, at Barnoldswick, in the north of England. The churches present were Independent in polity, and on the brink of adopting a full-blown Particular Baptist ecclesiology which was clearly in place by 1696, though it is not certain that they had taken this step definitively in 1695. At that meeting, the following question was proposed, and answered as follows,

---

[19]Goodwin, *Works*, 11:270-71.
[20]Goodwin, *Works*, 11:272.
[21]Goodwin, *Works*.

> Whether a pastor & Elder of one Congregation can Regularly perform
> pastorall acts in another Congregation where he hath neither Relation, office
> or membership yea or no

> Answere in the negative but yet we judge yt it may be done comfortably &
> profittably in some cases of absolute nesesity provided it be no longer
> continued then whilst those cases remain such; we further add yt no pson
> can prform such acts by vertue of membership, or relation, only unless
> called to office.[22]

These churches reflect the concerns of Owen and Goodwin. The pastoral office
is circumscribed by membership in a specific local church, though in unusual
cases elders may assist other assemblies.

Not only did the Independent divines address the issue, but so also did the
Baptists. They reflect the same concerns and convictions as found in Owen and
Goodwin. The theoretical framework erected by the Independent divines
provided the structure necessary for the Baptists' practices.

In the 1640s and especially the 1650s, several formal associations of
churches sprang up in London and in the counties. At the meeting of the
Midlands Association of Particular Baptists, on 4-6 June 1656, the following
question was asked and answered:

> Whether an aproved gospell minister, who hath gathered many churches,
> which churches have no administrator of the ordinances but himselfe, hee
> may be chosen into office by any of the said churches without the full
> consente of the others.

> Answer: such a gospell minister cannot be orderly chosen as an officer by
> any church unless he be orderly a member of the same, Acts 6.3; 14.23. And
> that church of which he is an orderly member ought in this cause to do that
> and only that which shall be most for the churches' good and for the glory of
> God, 1 Cor. 10.31.[23]

This answer is of importance. For the Baptists, membership in a local church
was a prerequisite for ministerial service in that church. A man cannot be called
to office in a church unless he is first a member in that church. Anything less is
disorderly. This answer, though expressed prior to John Owen's published
writing on the subject, shares the same perspective. These Baptists considered
church membership in priority over office, and could not envision an officer
holding formal relations with more churches than one, since he could not be in
orderly membership with more churches than one at the same time.

Twenty-six years later, Hercules Collins, wrote a work entitled *Some
Reasons for Separation from the Church of England.* This tract is something of

---

[22]W. T. Whitley, *Baptists of North-West England, 1649-1913* (London: The Kingsgate
Press, 1913), 79.
[23]White, *ARPB*, 26.

an imaginary dialogue between a member of the Church of England (Conformist) and a Baptist (Non-conformist). At one point in the discussion, the Baptist asks the Conformist

> Whether the Scriptures will Authorize any Minister, Pastor, Elder or Bishop to take the care and charge of any more than one Church or Congregation at a time, and whether all the seven Churches in Asia, had not a particular Angel and Pastor, and whether we read not in Acts the 20. That there was Elders in the Church of Ephesus. So James 5. Send for the Elders of the Church, and whether these Scriptures Canons not be against your 41 [canon] which doth allow of more places then one for a Minister, provided [he be] a publick and sufficient Preacher, and taken the degree of Master of [Arts]. pray see D. Owen's brief instruction in the Worship of God.[24]

Clearly, Collins was writing against pluralism as it was practiced in the Church of England, but his words carry weight for this subject. Of especial importance is his dependence on John Owen at this point. He wanted to send his conformist friend off to the writings of the great Independent divine, in order to demonstrate the validity of the position he himself held. In this case at least, it may be fairly asserted that Owen's view reflects the convictions of this London Baptist pastor.

Another leader of the Particular Baptist cause in London, Benjamin Keach, addressed the issue in his 1697 work *The Glory of a True Church and it's Discipline Display'd*. This book is essentially a church manual, written to provide the members of his assembly and of the other 'baptized churches' with a brief understanding of the polity which should characterize a well ordered church. On page 16, Keach asked and answered this question:

> May an Elder of one Church if called, warrantably administer all Ordinances to another?

> Answ. No surely; for we find no warrant for any such Practice, he being only ordained Pastor or Elder of that particular Church that chose him, &c. and hath no right of Authority to administer as an Elder in any other where he is not so much as a Member.[25]

Keach's concern is very similar to both Owen and Goodwin. His words need to be noted carefully. At first glance, they may appear to be an absolute prohibition of any kind of ministerial activity outside of the elder's own church, but such is probably not the case. The question is framed in terms of ministering 'all ordinances' to another church. This should presumably be taken to mean officiating at all of the formal functions of the church as if he were elder of that church. At the 1689 General Assembly, a meeting at which Keach

---

[24]Collins, *Some Reasons for Separation from the Communion of the Church of England*, 14.
[25]Keach, *The Glory of a True Church*, 16.

was present and of which he was an integral part, the following resolution was passed:

> Q. *Whether an Elder of one Church may administer the Ordinance in other Churches of the same Faith?*
>
> A. That an Elder of one Church, may administer the Ordinance of the Lord's Supper to another of the same Faith, being called so to do by the said Church; tho not as Pastor, but as a Minister, necessity being only considered in the Case.[26]

While this question appears to be very similar to that of Keach, they should probably be regarded as addressing different issues. The General Assembly resolved on the specific matter of the administration of the Lord's Supper in the case of necessity, and decided in favor of the participation of an outside elder, functioning not as an elder in the church, but as a minister. This is similar to Goodwin's position.

Keach addressed a much more broad set of issues, as he used the term 'ordinances' in the plural, and modified it with the word 'all'. He may have been responding to the idea that elders of one church could function as elders in another church, fulfilling in two places all the necessary functions of the ministry. Keach recoiled at the prospect. This is probably also very similar to Goodwin's idea. While the Assembly resolved that in the specific case of necessity at the Lord's Supper, an elder may minister, though not as an elder, they went no further. Keach may have been addressing the more broad issue of elders taking formal ministerial roles in churches other than their own. Two further examples may help to make the point, each involving Keach. The Narrative of the 1690 General Assembly records these resolutions:

> That this Assembly do desire the Elders and Brethren in *London*, to send down one Elder or two to assist our Brother *Henry Austin*, in the Ordination of Brother *Henry Brett* of *Pulham*; That we do desire our Brother *Benj. Keach*, and one Brother more, to visit our Friends at *Colchester, Suffolk,* and *Norfolk, &c.* to preach the Gospel, and to assist them in all those things they need, for the settlement in the Faith and Order of the Gospel, as the Lord shall open a Door of opportunity to them.[27]

In 1692, the London Association sent a letter to 'the Association at Southampton' signed by Richard Adams, Benjamin Keach and William Collins 'in the name and by the order of the whole assembly'. Among other things, it said,

> Beloved Brethren Some time since we received a letter from you signifying the great need you have of two or more Elders to be sent down to you to

---

[26]1689 *Narrative*, 18.
[27]1690 *Narrative*, 7.

ordain Elders amongst you and to set in order what things are wanting. Now these lines are to Enforme you that we have taken into consideration your circumstances and are willing to answer your desire (viz) to send two or three of our brethren down and that the charge of their journey shall be discharged out of the fund, it being as we conceive an Extraordinary case, yet nevertheless we have thought it necessary to signifie to you that you ought to look out from amongst you such persons that you judge compedently qualified for the sacred office and to elect such persons in a soleme manner in a day or days of prayer and fasting that so all things may be done that are previous in order to that great worke before such Elders come down that so the worke may the sooner be dispatched when they come.[28]

Considering the rest of the transcript, it is probable that Keach himself was sent to these churches. In each of these cases, elders from one church were sent to another to do precisely the type of thing that Goodwin described. Keach's words in *The Glory of a True Church* should be read in the light of these types of practices. Of course, it may be that Keach changed his views between 1692 and 1697, but such an assertion is not necessary if the differences in terms are noted. The distinctions provided by Goodwin help to sort out a possible harmony between these statements.

In any case, neither Keach nor the General Assembly could countenance the view that elders may have pastoral authority outside of their own congregations. Owen's insistence on the priority of membership, and Goodwin's distinction between the kinds of power attached to office both function to govern the perspectives of the Particular Baptists. Elders acted primarily within their own churches, though there were special occasions in which their assistance could be given to others. In every case, the priority of the specific church was paramount. The elders contributed to the 'completion' of the work of each assembly. Without them, a serious deficiency was present. Their regular 'seat' was found in the congregation in which they were members.

TEACHING ELDERS AND RULING ELDERS

The Confessional statement indicates that there are two offices in the church, bishops or elders, and deacons. It does not address possible distinctions made within the office of bishop or elder itself. Samuel Waldron argues, based on his

---

[28]This quote is taken from a transcript of letters and documents known as 'A Collection of Manuscript Letters Relating to the Calvinistic Baptist Church at Whitchurch' deposited in the Angus Library of Regent's Park College, Oxford. See page 14, Number A3, entitled 'Letters from the London Association sent to the Association at Southampton A Copy of which was sent to Whitchurch by John Sibley of Southampton Feb. 18th 1691'. In modern reckoning, 18 February 1691 would actually be 18 February 1692, as the New Year was not considered to start until 25 March.

reading of the Confession, that no distinction can be drawn between pastor and elder. All are equal in a relationship of parity within the eldership.[29] Poh Boon Sing disagrees with Waldron, arguing that there are distinctions to be noted between ruling and teaching elders.[30] How did the Particular Baptists practice this aspect of their ecclesiology?

The majority of the writers and churches did not recognize a distinct office of ruling elder. In 1656, the Abingdon Association messengers determined that 'the office of pastors, elders and overseers or bishops is but one and the same and that it is the duty of everie elder as well to teach as to rule in the church whereof he is an elder'.[31] Similarly, Nehemiah Coxe stated with regard to '*Elders, ... Bishops* or *Overseers, ... Pastors* and *Teachers*' that 'it is evident the Holy Ghost intends no distinction, or preeminence of Office among those that bear these Characters, by any of these different Terms'.[32] The Church records from his Petty France, London Assembly, perhaps written in his own hand, state 'On ye 21th of ye 7th M: bro Collins & Bro: Coxe were solemnly ordained pastors or elders in this church.'[33] Throughout the book until Coxe's death, they function as equals in the church. There is no indication that they recognized ruling elders in their congregation. In 1690, when Richard Adams was inducted into the eldership of the Devonshire Square, London church alongside William Kiffin, the minutes state simply that he was ordained into 'sayd worke & office of an elder amongst them, in conjunction wth Bro. Wm Kiffin'.[34] No distinction is drawn between Adams and Kiffin. Likewise, in 1706 when Mark Key was ordained into office with him, Adams was instructed to say '... my Bro: Mark Key is by this church appointed or ordained a joynt elder Pastor or overseer wth my self over her'.[35] At Devonshire Square, there was parity within the eldership. At Kensworth, Bedfordshire, in 1688, three men were chosen 'jointly and equally to offitiate in the room of [the deceased pastor] Brother Hayward in breaking bread, and other administration of ordinances, and the church did at the same time agree to provide and mainetane all at there one charge'.[36]

Benjamin Keach addressed this subject by means of a question and answer in his *The Glory of a True Church and its Discipline display'd*. He said,

---

[29]Waldron, *Modern Exposition*, 321.

[30]Poh Boon Sing, *The Keys of the Kingdom*, 129-30, 145, 159.

[31]White, *ARPB*, 135, 138, 145. The Western Association had arrived at the same conclusion one year earlier. See *ARPB*, 60-61.

[32]Coxe, *Ordination Sermon*, 18.

[33]Petty France *CMB*, 1. See Chapter 1, *infra* for a discussion of Coxe's possible authorship of the Church Book.

[34]Devonshire Square *CMB*, 21.

[35]Devonshire Square *CB*, 159.

[36]Tibbutt, *Some Early Nonconformist Church Books*, 16.

Query, *Are there no ruling Elders besides the Pastor?*

Answ. There might be such in the Primitive Apostolical Church, but we see no ground to believe it an abiding Office to continue in the Church, but was only temporary.

1. Because we have none of the Qualifications of such Elders mention'd, or how to be chosen.

2. Because we read not particularly what their Work and Business is, or how distinct from preaching Elders; tho we see not but the Church may (if she sees meet) choose some able and discreet Brethren to be *Helps in Government*: We have Qualifications of Bishops and Deacons directly laid down, and how to be chosen, and their Work declared, but of no other Office or Officers in the Church, but these only.[37]

So far as Keach was concerned, the Scriptures did not give sufficient guidance to support the notion that the office of ruling elder continued beyond the Apostolic era. This is a forceful theoretical rejection of the validity of the office.

An interesting anecdote from the Bampton, Devon church points to the presence of differences among the Particular Baptist churches on this issue. In 1703, James Murch was ordained as pastor with the assistance of two men who had participated in the London General Assemblies, Andrew Gifford and Richard Sampson. After the service of installation for Murch and two deacons it is noted that

Diverse members of the neighbouring Ch[urs] [*sic*] being present the ordination of Bro: Frost a ruling Elder being proposed but both Bro: Gifford and Sampson declined it as having noe satisfaction in the thing so that it was concluded to be left as it was.[38]

Even though the host church recognized the office of ruling elder, neither of these pastors would participate as they did not accept it as valid.

This incident does demonstrate that at least a small number of the churches made a distinction between teaching and ruling elders. The South Wales Association considered the office to remain in force in 1654,[39] and the Broadmead, Bristol church also recognized ruling elders. The pastor was the 'chiefe of ye Elders of ye Church', while the ruling elders shared with him its oversight.[40] The South Wales churches, Bampton and Bristol are unusual in this

---

[37]Keach, *The Glory of a True Church*, 15-16, emphasis his.
[38]Bampton *CMB*, 46.
[39]White, *ARPB*, 11.
[40]Hayden, *The Records of a Church of Christ*, 193, 195.

practice. One wonders if the relative geographic proximity indicates that the idea was more accepted in the west than in the rest of the country.[41]

Hanserd Knollys contributed a different perspective when he argued that elders 'were not all of equal Dignity and Authority'. He believed that 'even from the Beginning of the Gospel' there was 'a Priority and Pre-eminence among the Ministers of Christ', one who was chosen from among them and called 'bishop'.[42] This priority was not, however, expressed within the eldership of a local church. It was, based on his unusual view that all of the congregation in one city should be considered as part of the one 'church' in that city,[43] the choice of one elder from the different congregations to have precedence in the one church there. He says,

> I mean and intend any one of the Bishops, Pastors, Teachers, Presbyters, or Elders, who are, or shall by the Consent, Approbation and Choice of the rest be appointed, ordained, and set over them as *Chief* Bishop or Presbyter of the Church in any City and Villages adjacent, who for Order sake in Gospel-Government, hath Priority, Pre-eminence, and Authority above the rest of the Presbyters or Bishops of the same Church, not alone, *nor without them*, but when *Convened* with them, to Act, Rule, Guide, Order and Govern with their Consent, Suffrage and Assistance ....[44]

This position is very unusual for Baptists, and I can find no evidence to demonstrate that it was ever put into practice among them. Knollys' view resembles the episcopalian structure of the National Church far more than the Independency with which the Baptists are commonly associated.

The majority of the Particular Baptists were committed to a plurality and parity of elders in their churches. This is not to say that all of the churches had such a plurality, in fact many did not. The 1689 *Narrative* rebuked churches that failed to ordain Pastors (and Deacons), and called upon them to reform.[45] But the theoretical basis for this exhortation rested on the belief that elders are necessary for a completed church. It is probably best to conclude that the Confessional statement was considered to be ambiguous at this point, and did not require adherence to any one specific order of polity. This ambiguity allowed churches of different practices to maintain communion with each other.

---

[41]Nevertheless, Andrew Gifford was pastor of the other Particular Baptist church in Bristol, meeting at the Pithay, and Sampson was pastor in Exeter, Devon, both also in the West.

[42]Knollys, *The World that Now is*, 57, 58, 63.

[43]See chapter 3, *infra*.

[44]Knollys, *The World that Now is*, 69.

[45]1689 *Narrative*, 5.

ORDINATION INTO OFFICE

Ordination, or the formal setting aside of called and chosen men to their office, was of great importance to the Particular Baptists. Hercules Collins considered it to be the *sine qua non* of the ministry. It was the pattern of installation to office throughout both Testaments, and could not have been an imposition by the Apostles, for then it would have been will-worship. It must have had the divine approbation, and thus continued in its importance for the churches.[46]

Collins described the 'import' of the ceremony:

> 1. A Dedication, and devoting the Person to the Office of a Pastor and sacred Imployment. 2. To let them know that the Hand of God is with them in all that they do in his Name, and by his Authority, to guide, strengthen and protect them. 3. And imploring the Gifts, Blessing, Protection, and Custody of the Holy Spirit upon them in a most plentiful manner, as being to take charge of the Souls of others.[47]

For Collins, the act of the imposition of hands consecrates the ordinand to office, symbolizes the presence of the hand of God, and provokes special prayer for a fruitful ministry.

The Particular Baptist writings are replete with discussions of the qualifications necessary for the eldership, based on Paul's instructions in 1 Timothy 3 and Titus 1.[48] So far as they were concerned, these character traits were a requisite for holding office in the church. When a duly qualified candidate was chosen by the church for office, a trial period would usually be established. Sometimes the interval was brief, but at others it was lengthy. Richard Adams was 'on trial' for three months at Devonshire Square, London,[49] while Daniel Negus of Stevington, Bedfordshire, waited two full years between his call and his ordination.[50] After the trial period, an election would be held. While unanimity was desired, it was not required. The Northern Association resolved this question in 1700:

> Qu. 3. If all the Church should be satisfied before a Person be called to Office?

---

[46]Hercules Collins, *The Temple Repair'd. or, An Essay to revive the long neglected Ordinances, of exercising the spiritual Gift of Prophecy for the Edification of the Churches; and of ordaining Ministers duly qualified* (London: William and Joseph Marshall, 1702), 58-61.

[47]Collins, *Temple*, 61.

[48]Collins, *Temple*, 53-56; Coxe, *Ordination Sermon*, 19-21; [Benjamin Keach] *The Gospel Minister's Maintenance Vindicated* (London: John Harris, 1689), 7-8; *idem*, *The Display of Glorious Grace: or, The Covenant of Peace, Opened* (London: S. Bridge, 1698), 147-48.

[49]Devonshire Square *CMB*, 21.

[50]Tibbutt, *Some Early Nonconformist Church Books*, 35.

It is most comfortable when it is so and should be laboured after notwithstanding if some be otherwise minded they are to shew their Reasons from the Scriptures which the rest of the Church cannot Answer otherwise their opposition is Judged invalid.[51]

Election to office was to be determined by Scripture and nothing else. Objections not based on an understanding of the text of the Bible were not legitimate, and could be ignored by the rest of those voting.

When it was finally determined that an ordination should take place, the matter was treated with the greatest sobriety. Several detailed accounts of ordinations are extant,[52] and they all point to the procedure described in the Confession: a day of 'fasting and prayer, with the imposition of hands'. In each case, visiting ministers assisted the churches. At Bagnio/Cripplegate and Bampton, there were no current elders, while at Devonshire Square, Richard Adams was in office as an elder. The presiding elder typically preached, and there were several relevant prayers offered. The churches were questioned concerning their willingness to proceed with the installation of the individual(s) concerned, and at the appropriate time, the ordinand would be called to the front, and questioned relative to his willingness to take the responsibilities of office. If all was positive, the participating elders would place their hands on his head and shoulders, (at Bampton and Bagnio/Cripplegate, the candidate kneeled while being inducted), prayer would be offered, and a pronouncement made on behalf of the church indicating that the recipient was now officially installed and duly empowered to fulfill his responsibilities and function with all the rights and privileges of office. From that time forward, he was an officer of the church.

THE FUNCTIONS OF ELDERS

The functions of church officers were carefully delineated in the Confessional statement. They were set aside 'for the peculiar Administration of Ordinances, and Execution of Power, or Duty' entrusted to them by Christ.[53] As demonstrated in chapter 3, these responsibilities should be interpreted quite literally. The Baptists entrusted their elders with the exact responsibilities enumerated in the Confession, no more, no less.

Nehemiah Coxe described the public duties of elders as prayer (leading worship), preaching, and the exercise of discipline; and the private duties as visiting the flock, encouraging, exhorting and rebuking them.[54] Basing his assertions on Titus 1.5, where the Apostle indicates that elders are to settle churches in Gospel order, Hanserd Knollys listed the duties of elders in greater

[51]Copson, *Northern Association*, 85.
[52]Bagnio/Cripplegate *CMB*, 22; Bampton *CMB*, 46; Devonshire Square *CMB*, 139, 157, 159.
[53]*A Confession of Faith*, 89.
[54]Coxe, *Ordination Sermon*, 22-29.

detail: 'Administration of God's Sacred Ordinances, ... the Admission of Members, ... the Ordination of Church-Officers and in withdrawing from every Brother that walketh *Disorderly*'.[55] He summarizes these duties by stating that

> The Office of a *Pastor, Bishop,* and *Presbyter,* or *Elder* in the Church of God, is to take the Charge, Oversight, and Care of those Souls which the Lord Jesus Christ hath committed to them, to feed the Flock of God; to watch for their Souls, to Rule, Guide and Govern them ... according to the Laws, Constitutions and Ordinances of the Gospel.[56]

Benjamin Keach asserted that these duties must be understood in the context of stewardship and servanthood: stewards responsible to their Master, and servants to their people.[57]

The Particular Baptist concept of the ministry was two-fold: it looked up to God and stood as his representative, and it looked around at the people of God in order to serve them. Elders who served well fulfilled both of these responsibilities.

MINISTERIAL SUPPORT

One of the most pressing matters handled at the 1689 General Assembly had to do with ministerial support. At several points in the *Narrative*, the issue is mentioned, and the development and erection of a Fund to assist in the matter was arranged. The messengers to the Assembly perceived that there was a general neglect on the part of churches to support adequately their pastors, and addressed the matter straightforwardly. So serious was the problem that they approved the contents of a recently published book, *The Gospel Minister's Maintenance Vindicated,*[58] and urged that 'some of the brethren of each church' ensure that copies were distributed in their assemblies.[59]

The original London Confession advocated pastoral remuneration,[60] and a similar statement was incorporated into Chapter 26 of the Second London Confession:

---

[55]Knollys, *The World that Now is*, 52.

[56]Knollys, *The World that Now is*, 58-59.

[57]Keach, *Parables: Series Two*, 195. He also discussed the matter at length in a section of *The Gospel Minister's Maintenance Vindicated* entitled 'The Great and Weighty Work of a True Gospel Minister Opened'. [Keach], *The Gospel Minister's Maintenance*, 113-132.

[58]The book was originally published anonymously, with a recommendatory preface signed by 11 London pastors. Thomas Crosby asserts that it was written by Keach. See Crosby, *CHEB*, 4:292-98, 311; Vaughn, 'Benjamin Keach's *The Gospel Minister's Maintenance Vindicated*', 53-60.

[59]1689 *Narrative*, 18.

[60]Lumpkin, *BCF*, 166. Paragraph XXXVIII states, 'That the due maintenance of the Officers aforesaid, should be the free and voluntary communication of the Church, that according to Christs Ordinance, they that preach the Gospel, should live on the Gospel

10. The work of Pastors being constantly to attend the Service of *Christ*, in his Churches, in the Ministry of the Word, and Prayer, (t) with watching for their Souls, as they that must give an account to him; it is incumbent on the Churches to whom they Minister, not only to give them all due respect, (u) but also to communicate to them of all their good things according to their ability, so as they may have a comfortable supply, without being themselves (x) [*sic*] entangled in Secular Affairs; and may also be capable of exercising (y) Hospitality toward others; and this is required by the (z) Law of Nature, and by the Express order of our Lord Jesus, who hath ordained that they that preach the Gospel, should live of the Gospel.

(t) Act. 6.4. Heb. 13.17.
(u) 1 Tim. 5.17,18. Gal 6.6,7.
(x) 2 Tim. 2.4.
(y) 1 Tim. 3.2.
(z) 1 Cor. 9.6-14.[61]

So important was the need to urge the support of ministers that these Baptists insisted on elevating the practice to be a matter of faith. Perhaps they hoped that in this way churches would more readily take up this concern.

Benjamin Keach indicates that the need was great:

I fear one thing that greatly hinders the flourishing of our churches, and obstructs some men who are gifted, from exercising their gifts, is that great neglect of the present pastors. Should we be called, say some, to that office, we and our families may be exposed to want, or to many straits, as we see others now are: Oh what provision did God make for his ministers under the law, and to be sure he would have his gospel ministers as well provided for. Such churches who are rich and do it not, are under great evil.[62]

This is a strong indictment, and perhaps provides some of the background for the concern at the General Assembly. Keach indicates that some pastors suffered great financial hardship in their ministries, and this scared off some likely ministerial prospects.

What was ministerial support like? There are not many specific indications. The Broadmead church provided its ministers with £80 per year around 1670, but this seems generous.[63] Robert Keate of Wantage received £40 per year in 1680.[64] When a certain Mr. Warner was offered £40 per year to come as pastor

---

and not by constraint to be compelled from the people by a forced Law'. The 'constraint ... by a forced Law' evidently refers to the state Tithe system.
[61]*A Confession of Faith*, 90-91.
[62]Keach, *Parables: Series Two*, 194.
[63]Foreman, 'Baptist Provision for Ministerial Education', 359. He draws this information from Hayden, *Records of A Church of Christ*, 134-6, 204-5.
[64]*A Historical Survey of the Baptist Church in Wantage* (Newbury: G. W. Simpson & Son, Ltd., 1949), 13.

to Plymouth in 1689, he refused because the amount was inadequate.[65] Roy Porter provides us with some meaningful comparisons:

> In the Georgian age, rock-bottom wages for males were about a shilling a day, but a man fully employed all the weeks of the year—and most were not—would not have been able to support a family on such a sum. For that, earnings in the region of £30—£40 a year would be required. A careful artisan family could hope to keep itself from hunger and out of debt on a pound a week, and members of the petty bourgeoisie would commonly have incomes of between £50 and £100 a year.[66]

At these rates, one can see the difficulty inherent in the lives of these ministers. Keach, Knollys, Kiffin and Coxe all supplemented their income with secular employment, as did other men in other places.[67]

The anonymous publication of *The Gospel Minister's Maintenance Vindicated*, and its approval by the General Assembly, was a calculated attempt to remedy this pressing need. Keach argues that the New Testament demands that churches support their pastors at a level suitable to their needs and which allows them the privilege of showing hospitality and benevolence to others. But he is careful to ensure that he does not encourage anyone to be guilty of the charge of entering the ministry for the sake of personal financial gain. In fact, he insists that it is wrong for a candidate for a pastoral position to negotiate a stipend or wage prior to the acceptance of a call to a church. It is the church's duty to be generous, but it is not for the minister to demand, or even inquire, into the financial prospect upon settlement. To do this is to give the impression (if not the reality) of being a hireling and not a servant.[68]

There is a delicate balancing act here. On the one hand, the church is responsible to ensure that the minister receives a comfortable supply, while on the other he must not be guilty of seeking after sinful financial gain. Probably, this is a further indication of the importance and priority of the church. The onus is on it to demonstrate obedience to Scripture by caring for its pastor(s). The final decision rests with the gathered congregation. This was the perspective stated in the First London Confession, consistently carried on forty five years later.

CONCLUSION

The importance of the office of elder in Particular Baptist ecclesiology is evident. The church's well-being depended on a fully functioning ministry. It was subject to the church, circumscribed by membership and focused on service to God and his people. Entry into office was made with great care, and attempts were made to recover the dignity attached to the office by advocating

[65]Plymouth Manuscript, 17.
[66]Porter, *English Society in the Eighteenth Century*, xv.
[67]See Chapter 1, *Infra*, for details.
[68][Keach], *The Gospel Minister's Maintenance*, 105-106.

full ministerial support. In order for a church to live well, it must have had resident elders.

Gifted Brethren

While the role of teaching and preaching centered on the office of elder/pastor/bishop, it was not confined to that office. The Particular Baptists made a place for others to serve the church in public ministry. The Second London Confession addressed this subject in paragraph 11 of chapter 26:

> 11. Although it be incumbent on the Bishops or Pastors of the Churches to be instant in Preaching the Word, by way of Office; yet the work of Preaching the Word, is not so peculiarly confined to them; but that others also (a) gifted, and fitted by the Holy *Spirit* for it, and approved, and called by the *Church*, may and ought to perform it.
>
> (a)   Act. 11.19,20,21. 1 Pet. 4.10.11.[69]

These words, dependent on (though slightly different from) the *Savoy Platform of Polity*,[70] reflect the Baptists' adoption of the position of the Congregational leaders in the long debate they carried on with strict Presbyterians over the propriety of the public ministry of 'Gifted Brethren' or lay preachers.[71] The Congregationalists advocated the right of some laymen, formally called and approved by churches after a trial period, to exercise a ministry of public preaching and teaching. These men were not ordained into the pastoral office, but were a special class of laymen who had been recognized and set apart for this ministry. Their opponents argued that the only men authorized to exercise any kind of public ministry were those who had been duly ordained after sufficient theological training at the universities.

The differences between the two positions may be illustrated from the records of the Broadmead, Bristol, church, which was among those criticized for its use of men who were unacceptable to the high Presbyterians. In his remarks for 1657, Edward Terrill says,

> Our friends called Presbyterians, Those of them that were bitter-spirited, or Rigid, they would vilifie our Ministry, because not Called and Ordained in their way by a Classical or Synodicall Assembly, and not brought up at ye university for such Literature.[72]

---

[69]*A Confession of Faith*, 91.

[70]Walker, *The Creeds and Platforms of Congregationalism*, 405.

[71]Geoffrey Nuttall, *The Holy Spirit in Puritan Faith and Experience* (Chicago: University of Chicago Press, 1992 reprint), 75-85; Nuttall, *Visible Saints*, 87; Richard L. Greaves, 'The Ordination Controversy and the Spirit of Reform in Puritan England', *Journal of Ecclesiastical History* 21, no. 3 (July 1970): 225-241.

[72]Hayden, *The Records of a Church of Christ*, 114.

In 1674, three of the four dissenting churches in Bristol were without ministers because their pastors had been imprisoned. The churches sought to maintain worship without them, but the Presbyterians nearly stopped meeting because their 'principle was not to hear a man not bred up at ye university, and not Ordained'.[73] This kind of clericalism was not atypical of much high Presbyterian argumentation.

In response to this position, the Independents countered that

> Every man ... to whomsoever the Spirit hath afforded a gift, either wisely to speak, and apply Gospel truths to the souls of others ... or understandingly to give an exposition of the Scriptures, every man that hath such gifts, it belongeth to his place and calling, to use those gifts ... else he crosseth the end of the Spirit.[74]

These authors argued that the gifts for public ministry were not confined to the ordained clergy, nor ought they be restricted to the graduates of universities. Spiritual gifts were given by the ascended Christ, and needed to be used by the recipients.

The Presbyterian critique held a double sting for the Baptists. On the one hand, it would eliminate the activity of the Gifted Brethren by circumscribing the public ministry to the ordained clergy, while on the other it would undermine the validity of the office of most of the Baptist elders, few of whom had received any university training.[75] Of course, by the end of the century the Presbyterians themselves had a shortage of university trained men, as Oxford and Cambridge were closed to dissenters after the restoration.

The inclusion of paragraph 11 in chapter 26 demonstrates that the Baptists accepted the Independent position. This is not to be unexpected, as the earlier 1644 London Confession had similarly provided for the ministry of lay preachers.[76] Hercules Collins is typical of the Particular Baptist position on this subject. Writing near the end of his ministry in London, in 1702, he relied on the material in *The Preacher Sent* to defend the propriety of recognizing and using Gifted Brethren. He identified five arguments from that book: (1) prior to

---

[73]Hayden, *The Records of a Church of Christ*, 149. I am indebted for this citation to Nuttall, *Holy Spirit*, 78 (though he quotes from the 1865 Bunyan Library edition of the Broadmead Records).

[74]Samuel Petto, John Martin and Frederick Woodal, *The Preacher Sent: or, A Vindication of the liberty of Publick Preaching, by some men not Ordained* (1658), quoted in Nuttall, *Holy Spirit*, 79.

[75]Of the first generation of Particular Baptist pastors, several did have university training. Among them were Benjamin Coxe, Daniel Dyke of Devonshire Square, London, George Fownes of Broadmead, Bristol (1679-83), and Hanserd Knollys. As the century progressed fewer pastors could fit the requirements demanded by the strict Presbyterians. For Coxe see *BDBR*, and W. T. Whitley, 'Benjamin Cox', 50-59; for Dyke and Fownes, see A. G. Matthews, *Calamy Revised*, (Oxford: The Clarendon Press, 1934), 176, 210.

[76]Lumpkin, *BCF*, 168.

choosing a man for office, the church must have some opportunity to evaluate his gifts; (2) the 'Gospel Commands' to exhort and speak require that 'this is to be done by every one who hath received the Gift'; (3) the 'Gospel Promise' of increase granted to everyone who uses his gifts mandates the 'improvement' of gifts for verbal ministry in each one to whom they have been given; (4) there are several 'Gospel-Precedents' such as Apollos and the scattered members of the Jerusalem church who provide warrant for the practice; (5) 'Gospel-Rules about Prophesying', such as Paul's exhortation to desire the gift of prophesy 'is to desire a Gift from God to expound and interpret the Scripture to the Churches Edification'.[77] For Collins, there was an important role to be filled by these Gifted Brethren.

Benjamin Keach was also concerned with encouraging the ministry of 'teachers'.[78] Using very similar argumentation, he makes a careful distinction between elders or pastors, and teachers. The former are responsible for the leadership of churches, but the latter have a more restricted role and function in the house of God. They supplement the ministry of the elders and pastors through the use of their public gifts.

Keach helps to define the nature of this position. He says that churches must extend a 'regular call' to these men, prior to the public 'exercise' of their gifts.

> When gifted, or thought to be gifted, the church may, nay, ought to admit them to exercise their gifts, and try them, nay, try them again and again....
> They should be employed privately at first only in the church.[79]

This trial was a very specific activity, and as Keach stated, a private matter carried out only before the church. In 1679, the Petty France, London, Church appointed 'Br. Austen ... to spend some time upon 1 Pet. 5.5 on ye Lord's day fortnight after ye publick exercise is over, for ye tryall of his gift before ye congregation'.[80] Since this activity was a trial, it was thought to be inappropriate to allow non-members to hear. Presumably, if the individual was not gifted for public ministry, there would be some embarrassment attached to poor preaching or teaching, but this could be avoided by a private trial.[81]

Nehemiah Coxe, one of the pastors of the Petty France Church in London from 1675 until his death in 1688, entered into the ministry through the process of being recognized as a Gifted Brother in John Bunyan's Bedford Independent church. He was received into membership on 14 May 1669, and by 1671 is

---

[77]Collins, *The Temple Repair'd*, 9-12. His church regularly placed men on trial to be recognized as Gifted Brethren. See Kevan, *London's Oldest Baptist Church*, 39-40.

[78]Keach, *Parables: Series Two*, 191-95. These teachers are clearly equivalent to the Gifted Brethren.

[79]Keach, *Parables: Series Two*, 193.

[80]Petty France *CMB*, 10.

[81]Keach states that the trial should be private in answer to the objection: 'Those that are called may be weak at first, and so it may not be honourable to employ them.' *Parables: Series Two*, 193.

found among those signing the official letters of the church, and was also deputed to bring the report of the church to a member under discipline. On 21 December 1671, at the same meeting where Bunyan was chosen as an elder, Coxe was among seven men of whom

> the church did solemnly approve the gifts of and called to the work of the ministry ... for the furtherance of the works of God, and carrying on hereof, in the meetings usually maintained by this congregation, as occasion and opportunity shall by providence be ministred to them.[82]

This was not a full and free call to exercise gifts, as the minutes immediately state that the church

> did further determine, that if any new place offer it self, or another people that we have not full knowledge of, or communion with, shall desire that any of these brethren should come to them, to be helpful to them, by the word, and doctrine, that then such brother so desired, shall first present the thing to ye congregation, who after due consideration will determine thereof: and according as they shall determine, so shall such brother act and doe.[83]

The distinctions in these words need to be noted. These men were called to be 'ministers' but not elders. They acted in subordination to the will of, and at the disposal of, the church as a whole. The strict rules circumscribing their activity demonstrate the sobriety with which the church treated the action. Public ministry of any kind was a high and holy calling, and could not be treated lightly.

Several records in the Devonshire Square Church Book provide further detail into this practice. On 31 December 1702 it was noted 'It is agreed allsoe yt Brõ: Bowler, & Brõ: Sandford doe exercise their gifts in ye church this day fortnight & this day 3 weeks.'[84] At the church meetings held on 4 February, 4 March, 3 June and 2 September, the same two men are asked again to 'exercise' their gifts at appointed times.[85] On 4 May 1704, the manuscript notes

> The Church having called Bro: Tho: Sandford to exercise his gift privately in ye church & upon frequent tryall have approved of him as having a gift profitable for instruction & edification doe call him forth to exercise his gift as ye necessity of ye people of God require, & as ye Lord shall enable him.[86]

---

[82]*The Church Book of Bunyan Meeting*, 27, 44, 46, 49, 50, 51.

[83]*The Church Book of Bunyan Meeting*, 51. These men are explicitly called 'gifted brethren' in the notation for 25 June 1672, see p. 52.

[84]Devonshire Square *CMB*, 41.

[85]Devonshire Square *CB*, 43, 45, 51, 57.

[86]Devonshire Square *CB*, 75.

The church was satisfied with Sandford's gift after this trial period, and issued the call to him. But Bowler did not receive approval until eighteen months later, on 6 December 1705:

> It is ... agreed that the church haveing often heard & had tryall of ye gifts & graces of our Bro: Cha: Bowler in ye exercising privately amongst us to our comfort & satisfaction, doe now call him forth, & accordingly doe now call him forth [sic] to exercise his gift in preaching ye gospel of our Lord Jesus as ye necessity of the People may require & as ye Lord shall enable and encline.[87]

Evidently, the church needed more time in their judgment of his capabilities, but their patience ultimately brought a positive response.

On 30 March 1704, in the midst of the trial period for these two men, the church meeting 'orderd that Bro Lamb do exercise his gift in the church this day fortnight'.[88] On 10 August, he was asked once more to 'exercise his gift before the congregation' and on 17 August, the following note is entered:

> The Church haveing had several Tryalls of ye gift of Bro: Robt Lamb, for ye work of ye ministry, have upon a serious hearing, & Judging thereof, come to the conclusion, that at ye present they believe he hath not a gift for ye ministry, to ye honoring of our God & our holy profession, & therefore have concluded our Bro: Lamb ought not to goe forth to preach ye Gospel of Christ untill endued wth a greater annointing to yt work.[89]

The recognition of Gifted Brethren was not automatic, and was taken very seriously. It is not unlikely that this example is typical of the practice of many churches. Lamb was not satisfied with the decision of the church and went out to preach on his own. In the record for 5 October the minutes state (after repeating the earlier decision) that

> Information being given that sence that time contrary to ye sd order he hath publickly preacht therefore it is now agreed that Bro: King & Bro Clark be appointed to goe to him and acquaint him with his disorderly practice in preaching ....[90]

On 9 November, King and Clark reported to the Church that Lamb refused to submit to their decision, and so the congregation 'therefore agreed that he shall have no further communion with this church till he return by giving

---

[87]Devonshire Square *CB*, 129.

[88]Devonshire Square *CB*, 73.

[89]Devonshire Square *CB*, 87, 89.

[90]Devonshire Square *CB*, 93.

satisfaction'.[91] His impropriety brought about expulsion. On 7 May 1705, Lamb returned to the church, confessed his sin in the matter, and they were satisfied.[92]

The 1693 meeting of the Western Association at Bristol had directly addressed this issue:

> Whereas we have heard of some persons, who being vainly puffed up by their fleshly minds, do presume to preach publicly without being solemnly called and appointed by the church thereto, and some administer all ordinances,
>
> We advise and desire, that every particular church would do what in them lies to discountenance this practice, and to prevent all such from exercising their pretended gift, it being contrary to Rom. x. 15. And also that they would not send forth any person among themselves, to preach publicly, of whose qualifications they have not had sufficient trial, and whom they have not called thereto; that the name of God may not be dishonoured, the peace of the churches disturbed, nor the reputation of the ministry blemished.[93]

Public ministry was a very important matter, and could not be treated lightly. Those who thought that they could act on their own needed to be brought under the regulating power of the Church. This was done in 1694 by the Bagnio/Cripplegate church in London. One of their men, Brother Kennington, established several 'publik meetings' even though he had not been approved by the church. They determined that he did not appear 'to be furnisht with competent gifts fitt for such solemne work'. He was 'admonished and warned by the Church solemnly in the name of the Lord', but gave no evidence of repentance and was 'withdrawn from'.[94] Unrecognized preachers were not tolerated.

At the 1689 General Assembly, a question relating to the status of the Gifted Brethren was debated:

> Q. Whether the continuing of Gifted Brethren many Years upon trial for Eldership, or any Person for the Office of a Deacon, without ordaining them, altho qualified for the same, be not omission of an Ordinance of God?
>
> A. Concluded in the Affirmative.[95]

In all probability, this question as it concerns the Gifted Brethren relates to the problem of ministerial support discussed previously. Churches called and approved men as Gifted Brethren, and functioned for long periods of time with these men as their preachers and (sometimes) administrators of the ordinances,

---

[91]Devonshire Square *CB*, 95.
[92]Devonshire Square *CB*, 111.
[93]Ivimey, *HEB*, 1:527-28.
[94]Bagnio/Cripplegate *CMB*, 9; Robinson, 'Baptist Church Discipline', 125-26.
[95]*1689 Narrative*, 13.

but they did not set them apart to the office of elder. The first section of *The Gospel Minister's Maintenance Vindicated* is entitled 'A Regular Ministry in the Church Asserted'.[96] Keach labors long to prove that churches must not be satisfied to exist without ordained elders functioning among them:

> How greatly then must those Churches be to blame, that unconcernedly live in neglect of so great a Duty, upon which the Edification of the Church, and her Well-being so much depends, as well as Gospel Order: For although the Essence and Being of a Church depends upon its Institution in respect both of Matter and Form: (A competent number of Believers may by mutual agreement lay the Foundation of the Being of a Gospel Church,) but they cannot be a Church Organical without Officers, which the Lord hath placed there for the orderly Exercises of his Authority committed to her; To neglect this, is to despise the Wisdom of Christ, who best knows what is for the good of His Church, and for Her Edification in this state. 2, To slight His goodness in so useful and beneficial an Institution. 3, Its a contempt put upon his Authority, as King of Saints, who has in his Sovereign Right, in and over the Church, ordained it so to be, for the Churches Good and Well-being.[97]

This was, based on Keach's language, a serious problem in some of the churches. He states, 'For Churches therefore to be so unconcern'd, whether they have Officers or not, according to Gospel Rule, ... are greatly blameable.'[98]

The lack of recognition of officers points to two things. On the one hand, it demonstrates the importance of the function of Gifted Brethren. The position was esteemed among the churches. But on the other hand, it demonstrates that the Gifted Brethren were not regarded as equivalent to elders. They were another class of men in the church. They had been called and approved upon completion of a trial, but that calling did not set them apart for the pastoral office. In many cases, it was the Gifted Brethren who were ultimately elected to office in the church,[99] but it seems that some of the churches were content to function under the ministry of these men, apart from duly recognized and ordained elders.

In summary, the ecclesiological doctrine contained in paragraph 11 of chapter 26 of the Second London Confession was regularly put into practice among the Particular Baptist churches. They encouraged the recognition of laymen who were gifted and able to preach, but only under specific and well-defined guidelines. Anyone who went out to preach on his own was disorderly,

---

[96][Keach], *Maintenance*, 1-13.
[97][Keach], *Maintenance*, 9-10.
[98][Keach], *Maintenance*, 12-13.
[99]In Plymouth, the gifted brother Samuel Buttall was chosen pastor in 1690; and in 1693, another gifted brother from the same assembly, James Murch, was called to be pastor at Dalwood. See the Plymouth Church Book, 26, 28; also see above on Nehemiah Coxe.

while those who were approved and called ministered with the blessings of the churches.

The Serving Office

In addition to the office of Elder, the Particular Baptists recognized that Scripture advocated a second office, that of Deacon. This was distinct from elder or pastor, and was carefully designated among them.

Deacons

In the Confession, Deacons are only mentioned twice, at the end of 26:8, when officers are listed, and again in 26:9 where it is stated that they should be ordained into office in a manner similar to that of elders. This serving office did not receive the prominence given to the teaching/ruling office. It was noble to serve as a deacon, but the office was never confused with eldership.

According to Nehemiah Coxe, deacons had one primary responsibility, the relief of the poor.[100] Benjamin Keach expanded on this by stating that 'The Work of Deacons is to serve Tables, *viz.* To see to provide for the Lord's Table, the Minister's Table, and the Poor's Table.' They furnish the elements for the observance of the Lord's Supper, canvas the membership to ensure that all members contribute to the financial support of the ministry and 'that each Member do give weekly to the Poor, as God has blessed him', and visit the Poor, 'especially the aged Widows' so that no one is neglected.[101] At Broadmead, Bristol, they were charged with keeping the funds of the church, distributing them to the poor and using them 'for any other Use for ye Good of ye Congregation' so long as they first sought the approbation of the church.[102] Bagnio/Cripplegate also required the Deacons to consult with the church before expending funds.[103]

Benevolence was an important part of the ministry of these churches. Devonshire Square, London, kept a detailed ledger of money collected and distributed for the poor. This concern was very practical. Funds were collected on a weekly basis, generally at the level of £1:10:00, with expenditures of £1:09:00.[104] With charges for bread and wine added, they were often slightly under balance. The ledger records that they regularly received and disbursed money to provide coal for heat in the homes of the poor. On 23 August 1695, £8:02:06 was passed out to the needy for coal. The names of the recipients are listed, all of them with the designator 'brother' or 'sister'. This would seem to indicate that this disbursement was intended for church members rather than the poor in general. The Broughton church regularly supported several widows

---

[100]Coxe, *Ordination Sermon*, 10; Petty France *CMB*, 4.

[101]Keach, *The Glory of a True Church*, 10-11.

[102]Hayden, *The Records of a Church of Christ*, 224-25.

[103]Bagnio/Cripplegate *CMB*, unnumbered page facing page 13.

[104]I.e. Pounds: Shillings: Pence.

designated by the term 'sister', but also note that they gave a shilling to 'a man at the door'.[105] In 1689, just after the death of Nehemiah Coxe, the Petty France church held a meeting 'where it was agreed that somethings [*sic*] should be raised by subscription for ye maintaining Br. Cox's son and yt the congregation should bee moved in it'.[106] This would have been a diaconal responsibility.

The number of deacons in a church was not fixed. Nehemiah Coxe argued that the seven original deacons in Acts 6 were 'suited to the present Necessity and convenience of that numerous Congregation', and thus could not be 'intended as a rule' for other assemblies.[107] His own church elected and installed four men in November, 1688.[108]

Deacons, like elders, were scrutinized to ensure that they met the qualifications of Scripture. Nehemiah Coxe argued that any requirement of a trial period for the office of Deacon was a misunderstanding of 1 Timothy 3.10, which only required that the candidates be examined for their moral qualifications, not with regard to their ability to serve.[109] In several cases, men were installed into office almost immediately after election.[110] Nominations for the office came from the elders,[111] and from the church.[112] Probably, each church had its own procedural method. At times, deacons advanced to the office of elder, but this is probably more an instance of the recognition of gifts for public ministry than an indication that the serving office was a stepping stone for the teaching/ruling office.[113]

The ordination service for deacons was as solemn as that for elders. In Bampton, Devon, the ordination of the pastor was open to all, but at the same service the 'public assembly' was dismissed prior to the ordination of deacons.[114] This may have been an attempt to keep the benevolence work of the church secret and unobservable to the general public. Since the Scriptures require charitable deeds to be done in secret (Matthew 6.1-4), one would expect that the primitivist impulse active in these churches would be evidenced in this way. In Bampton and at Bagnio/Cripplegate, hands were laid on the deacons-elect, while at Broadmead, Bristol, 'ye Pastor somewhat scrupled at it' and so it was omitted from the service.[115]

---

[105]Broughton *CMB1*, 92-106; Broughton *CMB2*, unnumbered page 7.

[106]Petty France *CMB*, 26 (page is mispaginated as '24').

[107]Coxe, *Ordination Sermon*, 10.

[108]Petty France *CMB*, unnumbered page 23.

[109]Coxe, *Ordination Sermon*, 11.

[110]Petty France *CMB*, unnumbered page 23; Devonshire Square *CMB*, 31, 33-34; Hayden, *The Records of a Church of Christ*, 224.

[111]Hayden, *The Records of a Church of Christ*, 224.

[112]Devonshire Square *CMB*, 31, 33.

[113]Tibbutt, *Some Early Nonconformist Church Books*, 29, 30, 35.

[114]Bampton *CMB*, 46.

[115]Bampton *CB*; Bagnio/Cripplegate *CB*, unnumbered page facing page 25; Hayden, *The Records of a Church of Christ*, 224.

In summary, the office of deacon was considered to be an important part of the life of the church. Primarily established for benevolence, similar responsibilities related to the keeping of funds were occasionally attached to it. Deacons were chosen by the church, and ordained into office by elders.

Deaconesses

In one case, deaconesses were recognized in a church. In 1679, the Broadmead church records stated

> *And* this said day ye Church chose 4 sisters of ye Church that were widdows, Each above 60 yeares of age, to be Deaconesses for ye Congregation, to looke after ye Sick Sisters; namely S. Smith, ye elder; S. Spurgeon; S. Webb, ye elder; S Walton; Deaconesses.[116]

Three of the women were present, and they were asked if they would be willing to serve. They accepted, and the church proceeded to install them. They were asked if they would take a pledge not to marry, and they all acquiesced. Then the ruling elder presiding declared them to be deaconesses, outlining their responsibilities as, (1) visiting the sick 'sisters', (2) visiting the sick brothers also, (3) to report to the elders deacons and congregation of the needs of the sick so that the church might supply them, (4) to speak a word of 'support or consolation' to the souls of those they visit, and (5) to attend the sick. Then 'those 3 sisters were set aparte as Deaconesses of this Congregation, by fasting and prayer, said day'.[117]

This act in the Broadmead church was clearly an attempt to implement the teaching of Paul in 1 Timothy 5.9-10. Paul's stipulations were scrupulously followed, even to the point of requiring the women chosen to promise not to marry again. It was specifically delimited and restricted by the church. These women were not considered to be in an office equivalent to the deacons, nor were they given status as officers in the church. They were special servants to the sick.

---

[116]Hayden, *The Records of a Church of Christ*, 208. Cf. also 117, 142. In the minutes of the South Wales Association for 1654, mention is also made, albeit briefly, of 'widows' who serve as assistants to deacons 'most probably in looking to the poor and sick'. The grammatical structure seems to imply that the recognition of this position was theoretical and not practical. See White, *ARPB*, 11. Leon McBeth says that 'among both groups of Baptists, women routinely served as deaconesses'. Leon McBeth, *A Sourcebook for Baptist Heritage* (Nashville: Broadman Press, 1990), 54. He provides no corroborating evidence, and my own research has uncovered none further for the Particular Baptists.

[117]Hayden, *The Records of the Church of Christ*, 208-209.

Conclusion

In their implementation of the teaching of their Confession, the Particular Baptists were determined to follow the rule of Scripture. This principle is regularly demonstrated in their practice concerning church officers.

The church, though it existed and could function, was incomplete without them. They were of the *bene esse* of the congregation. Both members and officers had to be in place, and when they were, the church was 'compleatly organized'. The church had priority over the ministry, and circumscribed the sphere of duties for each officer. Elders were generally restricted to serving in their own congregations, though special circumstances could permit their involvement at other places. In order to have jurisdictional power though, membership was a priority. In the majority of places, only two offices were recognized, elder and deacon. There were, however, a few churches that made a distinction between ruling and teaching elders. In addition, at least one church recognized deaconesses as a position (if not office) in the church.

The greatest challenge to the ministry as perceived by the ministers at the General Assemblies was the inadequate financial support given to so many of the pastors of churches. Specific steps were taken to attempt to rectify and ameliorate the deficiency.

The churches were also concerned with the work of benevolence, and ordered the office of deacon to take primary responsibility for the need. Many of the churches received regular collections designated for the poor, and distributed the funds received accordingly. In addition, they received offerings to meet special needs, administering the funds by the hands of the deacons.

In the case of both offices, the church had priority over the office. As in the Confession, the church calls men to serve, and they fulfill their roles in response to the call of the assembly. The officers fulfilled their responsibilities for the benefit of the congregation.

CHAPTER 5

'The due performance of that publick worship, which he requireth of them in the world': The Church at Worship

At the very heart of ecclesiology is the expression of worship in and by the church. The meeting of the Christian Assembly is not primarily for the transaction of church related business, but is first and foremost a meeting to worship God. Among the Particular Baptist churches, a fervent desire to worship is evident.[1]

The Proper Form of Worship: The Regulative Principle of Scripture

The Baptists considered their views and practices to belong to the flow of ideas which issued from the Reformation, and thought of themselves as the logical conclusion of the teachings of the Reformation.[2] Central to the teaching of the

---

[1] There are several treatments of Puritan Worship in general, but no comprehensive investigations into the specific practices of the Particular Baptists. In most ways, their worship seems to reflect that of the broader Puritan movement. See for example, Horton Davies, *The Worship of the English Puritans* (Westminster: Dacre Press, 1948); J. I. Packer, *A Quest for Godliness* (Wheaton, Ill.: Crossway Books, 1990), 245-257; Leland Ryken, *Worldly Saints: The Puritans as They Really Were* (Grand Rapids: Acadamie Books, 1986), 91-134; Leslie A. Rawlinson, 'Worship in Liturgy and Form' in *Anglican and Puritan Thinking* (London: The Westminster Conference, 1977), 71-88. A comprehensive treatment of worship among the seventeenth-century English churches may be found in Davies, *Worship and Theology in England: II. From Andrewes to Baxter and Fox, 1603-1690* (Grand Rapids: Eerdmans, 1996, reprint of 1975 edition). Davies himself provides only a brief treatment of the worship of the Particular Baptists, but defends his method by stating 'In fact, Baptism apart, it would be difficult to distinguish their worship from that of the Independents, for the latter were Calvinists in doctrine, demanded Scriptural warrants for all their ordinances, believed in extemporaneous prayer, and insisted upon the local autonomy of each gathered church.' *Worship and Theology II*, 507. A brief treatment of early Baptist worship may be found in Thomas R. McKibbens, 'Our Baptist Heritage in Worship' *Review and Expositor* 80 (1983): 53-69.

[2] Especially interesting in this regard is the twelve step description of the origin of his own church given by Edward Terrill in the Broadmead Records. Beginning with the

(Genevan) Reformers was the so-called 'Regulative Principle'. William Cunningham has described the intent of this principle in these words,

> There are sufficiently plain indications in Scripture itself, that it was Christ's mind and will that nothing should be introduced into the government and worship of the Church, unless a positive warrant for it could be found in Scripture.[3]

The Calvinist Reformers and their heirs believed that Scripture was clear and plain, and prescribed only certain forms which were permitted to be used in worship. Anything not specifically enjoined in Scripture was considered an innovation, and was therefore not to be brought into the worship of God.

The various Puritan Confessions of the seventeenth century give testimony to this conviction. It was clearly articulated in the Westminster Confession, and was likewise repeated in the Independent revision of this document, the Savoy Declaration. The Particular Baptists, incorporated it into their own Confession in these words:

> Chapter 1, Paragraph 6A
> The whole Councel of God concerning all things (i) necessary for his own Glory, Mans Salvation, Faith and Life, is either expressly set down or necessarily contained in the *Holy Scripture*; unto which nothing at any time is to be added, whether by new Revelation of the *spirit*, or traditions of men.
>
> (i) 2 Tim. 3.15,16,17. Gal. 1.8,9.
>
> Chapter 22, Paragraph 1B
> The acceptable way of Worshipping the true God, is (b) instituted by himself; and so limited by his own revealed will, that he may not be Worshipped according to the imaginations, and devices of Men, or the suggestions of Satan, under any visible representations, or (c) any other way, not prescribed in the Holy Scriptures.
>
> (b) Deut. 12.32.
> (c) Exo. 20.4,5,6.[4]

---

advent of the Reformation in the sixteenth century, he moves through twelve stages by which the people cast off 'Antichristian Worship' and adopted a fully Scriptural practice. Terrill moves from the global reformation in England to the specific implementation of it in the Broadmead church. He clearly considered his own assembly to be the logical fruit of the movement begun a century before. He says, 'Thus I have briefly recited Twelve steps that doth complete a demonstration that they, this Church, in their beginning, were truly reformed in a greate measure, in turning from ye Worship of Antichrist.' See Hayden, *The Records of a Church of Christ*, 93-96.

[3]William Cunningham, 'The Reformers and the Regulative Principle' in *The Reformation of the Church*, ed. Iain Murray (London: Banner of Truth, 1965), 38.

[4]*A Confession of Faith*, 6, 73-74. The Westminster statement may be found in *The Westminster Confession of Faith* (Edinburgh: Publications Committee of the Free

These two statements demonstrate that the Baptists shared in this concern for the purity of the worship of God. They were committed, through their Confession of faith, to this central tenet of Puritanism. God was to be worshipped only as He ordained, and not according to the inventions of man, regardless of how good they might seem to be.

Benjamin Keach articulated the principle well when he said,

> Whatsoever we do in the worship of God, we must see we have a command from God to warrant our practice, and also exactly to do it according to the pattern he hath left us, or directions he hath given us; we must not add to, nor diminish from, nor alter anything ... if we do, God will not hold us guiltless.[5]

Similarly, William Kiffin and three other pastors stated,

> It is a great Truth, that as we are not to omit any thing in the Solemn Worship of God that is of his Appointment; so we are not to admit any thing that is not of his Institution, under any pretence whatsoever to be intruded upon us.[6]

For the Baptists, worship was to be directed by a command from God, and must be performed in accordance with the specific instructions found in Scripture. The authority of Scripture for the details of practice was supreme. No human idea was permissible or acceptable. They believed and practiced that only God had a right to institute his own worship, and that human innovations, no matter how seemingly beneficial they might be, were still unwarranted, sinful intrusions into that which is the domain of God alone. As the Supreme Being, he only reserved the right to pronounce on what was acceptable in worship, and there were to be no innovations.

At its foundation, the Regulative Principle was not considered negative, but positive. If worship is carried on *coram Deo*, it must reflect that which is appropriate to such a high privilege. The Baptists considered their worship in almost rapturous terms. According to Hanserd Knollys, only antichrist would intrude 'Commandements and Traditions of men upon the Saints and Churches of God', but God-ordained worship brings the church into Christ's 'Guest-chamber, ... Bride-chamber, ... and ... Bed-chamber' where they enjoy 'a more

---

Presbyterian Church of Scotland, 1976 re-issue), 22, 90-91; the Savoy statement in Walker, *The Creeds and Platforms of Congregationalism*, 368-69, 390.

[5]Benjamin Keach, *Preaching from the Types and Metaphors*, 637. This work originally was entitled *Troplologia: A Key to Open Scripture Metaphors, Together with Types of the Old Testament* (1702). Keach's comment here relates the general principle specifically to the observance of the Lord's Supper.

[6]William Kiffin, Robert Steed, George Barrett and Edward Man, *A Serious Answer to A Late Book, Stiled, A Reply to Mr. Robert Steed's Epistle Concerning Singing* (London, Printed in the Year, 1692), 3.

inward and sweet Communion with himself in his holy Administrations'.[7] The simplicity of true worship provided no distractions for the soul's encounter with God.

So pervasive was the importance of the Regulative Principle that Hanserd Knollys maintained

> there ought to be Uniformity among all the Churches of God in every Nation, in every City and in every Village. All that worship God in one place, are to worship him in one way, with one accord and with one shoulder.[8]

So far as he was concerned, the Scriptures taught one form of worship, and that form must characterize the devotions of all of the churches. In this way, 'peace, unity and edification' were promoted, and 'confusion and disorder' were avoided.[9]

This governing principle had profound ramifications for the worship practices of the Particular Baptists. Their primitivism required Scriptural justification for all of the practices, and many of the details of those practices, as they were incorporated into the public devotion of the gathered assembly. From the identity of the day of worship to the administration of the ordinances, careful scrutiny was given to everything facet of corporate devotion.[10]

The Practice of Worship in the Churches

The pervasive influence of the Regulative Principle may be noticed in the various factors contributing to the practice of worship in the churches.

The Day of Worship

English Puritanism is noted for its strict emphasis on Sabbath observance,[11] a strain of which is evident in several Particular Baptist writers from the 1640s onward. Fundamentally, the Lord's Day Sabbath was to be set aside for public and private worship. So closely tied together were these two concepts that the Second London Confession incorporates them into a single chapter entitled 'Of Religious Worship and the Sabbath Day'.[12] The Lord's Day was the pre-

---

[7]Hanserd Knollys, *An Exposition of the first Chapter of the Song of Solomon* (London: W. Godeid, 1656), 16.

[8]Hanserd Knollys, *The Parable of the Kingdom of Heaven Expounded* (London: Benjamin Harris, 1674), 43.

[9]Knollys, *Parable*, 44.

[10]The Regulative Principle was at the heart of the greatest controversy to erupt among them, namely, the propriety of hymn singing. See the discussion below.

[11]M. M. Knappen, *Tudor Puritanism* (Chicago: University of Chicago Press, 1939), 442-50; Packer, *Quest*, 233-243; Davies, *Worship and Theology II*, 240-45.

[12]*A Confession of Faith*, 73. The chapter so designated is Chapter 22.

eminent day on which worship was to be offered up to God. There was little difference between the Baptists and the broader Puritan/Independent/Separatist religious culture on this issue.

In the development of their doctrine of baptism, the Baptists insisted that the New Testament alone was the final basis for their practice. They believed that infant baptism was a remnant of Romanism, unwarranted by the clear teachings of Jesus and the Apostles. No line could be drawn from the practice of circumcision under the Old Covenant to include the children of believers in the initiatory rite of the New Covenant.[13] This type of reasoning brought forth an immediate criticism from Stephen Marshall, a prominent member of the Westminster Assembly.[14] He asserted that the Baptist rejection of infant baptism by insistence on 'an expresse institution or command in the New Testament' similarly enervated the theological basis for an ongoing Sabbath (Lord's Day) observance.[15] Both paedobaptism and Sabbath-keeping were, in Marshall's mind, dependent on theological continuity between the covenants. To reject one would *ipso facto* eliminate the other. John Tombes effectively responded to this objection by pointing out that the two were fundamentally different. Sabbath observance is moral, and thus a universal obligation for humanity. Baptism is of positive institution, and would not be known apart from Apostolic directive. That which is moral is a common duty for all, while that which is merely positive is ceremonial. In this way, the Baptists early in their history maintained the validity of the Lord's Day Sabbath while rejecting paedobaptism.[16]

---

[13]An early example of this type of reasoning may be found in J[ohn] S[pilsbery], *A Treatise Concerning the Lawful Subject of Baptisme.*

[14]For Marshall see *BDBR*, 2:217-19.

[15]Stephen Marshall, *A Sermon of the Baptizing of Infants, Preached in the Abbey-Church at Westminster, at the Morning Lecture, appointed by the Honorable House of Commons* (London: Richard Cotes, 1645), 6. Marshall calls this a 'great mischiefe' implied in Baptist theological reasoning.

[16]John Tombes, *Two Treatises and an Appendix to them Concerning Infant-Baptisme* (London: George Whittington, 1645), 27-31. This material is found in the second 'Treatise', entitled, 'An Examen of the Sermon of Mr. Stephen Marshall, About Infant-Baptisme, in a Letter sent to him'. Though Tombes was not himself part of the separate Baptist churches, he spoke of their position saying, 'For that which is naturall or morall in worship, they [i.e. the Particular Baptists] allow an institution or command in the old Testament as obligatory to Christians, and such doe they conceive a Sabbath to be, as being of the Law of nature, that outward worship being due to God, dayes are due to God to that end, and therefore even in *Paradise*, appointed from the creation; and in all nations, in all ages observed: enough to prove so much to be of the Law of nature, and therefore the fourth Commandment justly put amongst the Morals', 28, emphasis his. Tombes should technically be designated an antipaedobaptist. While he was the major seventeenth-century polemicist for the practice of Believer's Baptism, he also believed in a national church and never severed his relationship to it. See *BDBR*, 3:245-46.

In similar fashion, Hanserd Knollys argued for the perpetuity of Sabbath observance. In 1646, three of his sermons were printed under the title *Christ Exalted*. Rejecting the notion that the positive institutions of the Old covenant were still in force, he nevertheless maintained that Christ the law-giver 'commands his disciples to do the same morall duties' as found in the Law of Moses.[17] When applied to the Sabbath, he is explicit. Arguing that some 'carnall Professors' make loud claims of belief while they are still 'servants of corruption', Knollys describes them:

> They are so far departed from the Faith, which they sometime professed, and seemed to have, 1 Tim. 4.1. that they question whether the Scriptures of truth be the Word of God? Whether Christ be the Son of God? Whether the first day of the Week be the Sabbath of God?[18]

Apparently for Knollys, the matter of the ongoing validity and necessity of Sabbath observance was so clear that he could place the rejection of such a notion on the same level as doubt regarding the divine nature of Scripture or the essence of Christology. In 1688, Knollys licensed his *Exposition of the Whole Book of the Revelation*.[19] His comments on the tenth verse of chapter 1 express the same doctrine he advocated more than forty years earlier. The principle of Sabbath observance continued, though the day was changed by the resurrection of Christ. He spent the final Sabbath of the old era in the tomb, and rose on the first Sabbath of the new era. Knollys says,

> The Lords Day, *properly* so called *here*, was the First Day of the Week, as *Matth.* 28.1.... The Reader may observe, that where in our *English* Translation the LORDS day is called the *First Day of the Week*; it is in the *Greek* Text called the *First of Sabbaths*. This is the Gospel Sabbath that remaineth unto the people of God, from the Day of Christs Resurrection until his second coming.[20]

The first day of the week was the divinely appointed Sabbath for New Testament Christians.

An illustration of the importance of this doctrine is found in the records of the Hexham, County Durham, church. A certain Thomas Rewcastle came to the

---

[17]Hanserd Knollys, *Christ Exalted: A Lost Sinner Sought, and Saved by Christ: Gods People are an Holy People.* (London: Jane Coe, 1646), 23-24.

[18]Knollys, *Christ Exalted*, 34.

[19]Hanserd Knollys, An Exposition of the Whole Book of the Revelation (London: William Marshall, 1689). The license was granted on 12 September 1688.

[20]Knollys, *Exposition of Revelation*, 7, emphasis his. Benjamin Keach, The Breach Repaired in God's Worship: or, Singing Psalms, Hymns, and Spiritual Songs, proved to be an Holy Ordinance of Jesus Christ (London: John Hancock, 1691), 168, expresses the same type of argumentation. That which is moral continues, that which is merely ceremonial and external may be altered. The moral obligation of keeping one day in seven remains, though the day has been changed by divine appointment.

conclusion, based on Romans 14.5, 'that he was not bound in duty from any command or practice, to give a seventh part of time to the worship and service of God, judging it a doctrine not according to godliness'. The church, 'after many tender admonitions' withdrew their fellowship from him.[21] Rejection of the continuing requirement of Sabbath observance was no small thing.

A threat to the observance of the First Day was perceived by the representatives at the 1689 General Assembly. In the series of questions posed at the meeting, the one given the longest response in the *Narrative* is

> Whether it be not the Duty of All Christians, and Churches of Christ, religiously to observe the Lord's Day, or first Day of the Week, in the Worship and Service of God both in publick and private?[22]

The response was affirmative based on eight reasons drawn from the New Testament, summarized as follows: Christ had authority, as Lord of the Sabbath, to change the day of observance, and he did this by rising on the first day of the week. The early church seems to have established a pattern of meeting on this day, and Rev. 1.10 is understood by the most able expositors to refer to this day.

This question was brought before the Assembly not because some were abandoning the necessity of Sabbath observance, but rather because of the presence of Seventh-day sabbatarian churches in London.[23] If the statement that 'there being scarcely one brother, who dissented from the Assembly in the Sentiments of his Mind'[24] during the week of meetings is taken at face value, the Lord's Day Sabbath position advocated in the Confession and specifically reiterated by the Assembly reflected the common convictions of the churches. The first day of the week was the Christian Sabbath, the day of worship.[25]

---

[21]Underhill, *Hexham Records*, 297. The Broadmead, Bristol, Church also enacted discipline for Sabbath breaking. One of their members, Henry Fieldhurst, was placed under admonition when, among other things, he 'upon ye Lord's day, [did] soe publiquely breake the Sabbath'. Hayden, Records of A Church of Christ, 193. When the Maze Pond, London, church was constituted in February 1694, they incorporated this statement into their church covenant: 'We believe that the First day of the Weeke is the Christian Sabbath and ought to be kept in all religious Worship and Servis unto the Lord.' Maze Pond *CMB*, 3.

[22]1689 *Narrative*, 16-17.

[23]MacDonald, 'London Calvinistic Baptists 1689-1727', 34-35.

[24]1689 *Narrative*, 4.

[25]I am aware of only one instance of the advocacy of a non-sabbatarian defense of the Lord's Day among the Particular Baptists, in 1657 at the Abingdon Association. See White, *ARPB*, 176.

The Elements of Worship

Puritan worship was essentially simple in its form.[26] The elements of approach to God must be grounded in Scripture, and must reflect the spirituality of God Himself.[27] In many ways, seventeenth-century Puritan concerns were reactions to their perception of ostentation and man-made intrusion into the public worship in the Church of England parishes.

The Baptists, self-consciously part of the Puritan movement, adopted the current concern for simplicity and rejection of any elements for which Scriptural warrant could not be found. Writing in 1694, Isaac Marlow exemplifies this concern: 'It is the Duty of Christians to withdraw their Communion from all disorderly Persons in False Worship.'[28] Marlow was a strict rigorist, and this work is something of a blast against Benjamin Keach and his introduction of hymn singing into public worship, but it nonetheless exemplifies the concern of these men for purity in worship. If Scriptural warrant could not be produced, a practice must be rejected, and if it is continued, separation is necessary.

C. B. Jewson argues that the worship of the Particular Baptists most likely resembled that of the Independents around them. The leadership of the Norfolk church was nurtured under the tutelage of William Bridge, one of the 'Dissenting Brethren' (Independents) and a member of the committee at the Westminster Assembly responsible for the Directory of Public Worship.[29] What was evident in Norfolk seems to have been true throughout the churches.

While no known 'order of service' documents are available for the confessional Particular Baptist churches, there are indications of the various elements of which worship was composed. The Paul's Alley, Barbican, London church, on the fringes of Particular Baptist circles in London[30] merged in 1695 with the General Baptist church meeting at Turner's Hall. In the forming agreement, they include a note about worship:

---

[26]Packer, *Quest*, 249-51.

[27]Benjamin Keach, quoting an unnamed 'worthy divine' said that 'the Church in her publick Worship is the nearest resemblance of Heaven'. Keach, *The Glory of a True Church*, 67.

[28]Isaac Marlow, *The Purity of Gospel-Communion, or; Grounds and reasons for Separation from Persons of Corrupt Manners, or that hold Erroneous Doctrine in Matters of Faith essential to Salvation; or that are guilty of False Worship, or irregular Administration of Gospel Ordinances* (London: Printed by J. Astwood for the Author, 1694), 15.

[29]C. B. Jewson, *The Baptists in Norfolk* (London: The Carey Kingsgate Press, 1957), 42-44.

[30]This church developed under the ministry of John Gosnold and Thomas Plant, both Calvinists, but kept itself at a distance from the other Calvinistic churches in London. See W. T. Whitley, 'Paul's Alley, Barbican, 1695-1768', *Transactions of the Baptist Historical Society* 4 (1914-15): 47-48.

> The publick Worship in the Congregation on the Lord's Day be thus performed, viz. In the morning about half an hour after nine, some Brother be apointed to begin the Exercise in reading a Psalm, & then to spend some time in Prayer; & after yt to read some other Portion of H. Scripture, till the Minister comes into the Pulpit; and after Preaching & Prayer to conclude wth singing a Psalm. The afternoon exercise to begin abt half an hour after One, & to be carried on & concluded as in the forenoon.[31]

The simplicity of the worship is evident. Scripture reading, prayer, preaching and singing constituted the entire service. This was repeated in the afternoon.

The most detailed expression of Particular Baptist worship is provided by Hanserd Knollys. He described the elements that were to be part of public worship, including prayer, Scripture reading with exposition and interpretation, preaching, baptism, the Lord's Table, and singing.[32] His list is similar to that of Paul's Alley, Barbican, but he provides much more detail.

Public prayer is to be offered extemporaneously,[33] in a known language, by an elder of the church. The people should stand or kneel, only sitting if weakness or illness requires. The men are to have uncovered heads, and the women are to have 'their faces vailed or covered'.[34]

The 'expounding and interpreting' of Scripture is to be done by a 'teacher'. The purpose of this exercise is instruction, and it is considered to be an 'ordinance' to which Christ 'hath promised a Gospel-Blessing'.[35]

Preaching is done by the pastor, who urges the hearers to repent and believe the Gospel, to be holy and to walk according to the Scriptures. He labors 'in the Word and Doctrine to Convert Sinners, edifie Believers, to Convince Gainsayers, and to Comfort, Strengthen and Establish' Christ's disciples.[36]

---

[31]Whitley, 'Paul's Alley, Barbican, 1695-1768', 47.

[32]Hanserd Knollys, *The World that Now is*, 70-80.

[33]Horton Davies cites the open-membership Baptist Vavsor Powell's objections to written prayers: 'Either such Liturgies or Common Prayers are indifferent, or not indifferent; if indifferent, then they are not to be imposed on Christians, but they are to be left to their liberty, as Christians were left by the Apostles; but if be not indifferent, then unless a *Prescript* can be shewed from God (it being in his Worship) it is no less than Will-Worship, forbidden *Col.* 2.23.' Davies, *Worship*, 109, emphasis his. Isaac Marlow condemned 'set-form, prestinted prayers' in no uncertain terms. Marlow, *The Purity of Gospel Communion*, 46-47.

[34]Knollys, *The World that Now is*, 70-71. He says in another place that the woman's veil was required because of the presence of angels in the Christian assemblies (1 Cor. 11.10). Cf. Knollys, *The Parable of the Kingdom of Heaven*, 8. See also *Works of Goodwin*, 1:162. A differing view may be found in *The Works of Richard Sibbes*, ed. A. B. Grosart, vol. 7, *Divine Meditations and Holy Contemplations* (Edinburgh: Banner of Truth, 1982), 191. All of these authors were associated with Katherine Hall, Cambridge in the early seventeenth century.

[35]Knollys, *The World that Now is*, 71. The 'teacher' is most likely a gifted brother. See Benjamin Keach, *Parables: Series Two*, 192.

[36]Knollys, *The World that Now is*, 71-72.

Singing is 'a Gospel-Ordinance' that requires both grace in the heart and melody with the lips. The matter of singing is 'Psalms, Hymns, and Spiritual Songs ... in Meeter and Measure'. While they may be human compositions, he prefers 'those Psalms, Hymns, and Spiritual Songs, which are contained in the holy Scripture'. They may be sung by the congregation as a whole, or by a 'Minister or Member of the Church (if he hath received a Gift of the Spirit to Sing)'.[37]

Baptism requires large amounts of water, and thus cannot be part of the regular worship service of the churches. It is to be performed by appointed administrators, who dip the new believer into the water, drawing each one back out again. Though it could not be done as part of the regular weekly worship of the church, it was nonetheless to be considered an act of worship, and thus was regulated by Scripture.[38]

The Lord's Supper was observed on the first day of the week, according to the apostolic pattern. The 'minister' is to 'consecrate' the bread, break it, and distribute it to the 'communicants' repeating Jesus' words of institution. Similarly, he is to take the cup, consecrate it, and give it to all of the communicants reciting Jesus' words about the cup. Afterwards, the example of Christ and his disciples in singing a hymn is to be followed.[39]

In all of these cases, Knollys seeks to ground the elements of worship in Scripture. He is unwilling to allow any human invention into worship, but desires to incorporate everything commanded in divine revelation. This suits the commitments of the Particular Baptists to the regulative principle.

Perhaps the only unexpected element contained in Knollys' discussion is the permission for solo singing. He bases his argument on 1 Corinthians 14.16, where Paul indicates that some of the Corinthians came to worship with 'a Psalm', 1 Corinthians 14.15 which speaks of 'singing with the spirit' and 'the understanding', and 1 Peter 4.10, 11 where those with gifts are exhorted to minister them to one another 'as good stewards of the manifold grace of God'.[40] Mere natural gifts are insufficient. The ability to sing is considered a spiritual gift, to be used as a steward for the glory of God. The most ardent supporter of singing, Benjamin Keach, was opposed to solos in the church. He was convinced that there was no justification for the practice, and likened it to the performance of a 'Ballad-singer'.[41] It may be that Knollys' position was theoretical and was not actually practiced. In either circumstance, they argued

---

[37]Knollys, *The World that Now is*, 76-80.

[38]Knollys, *The World that Now is*, 72-74. See below for a more detailed discussion of baptism.

[39]Knollys, *The World that Now is*, 74-76.

[40]Knollys, *The World that Now is*, 77-78.

[41]Keach, *The Breach Repaired*, 75, 145. His words are unambiguous: If someone sang a solo in worship Keach would 'charge him with introducing a Practice no where warranted in the Scripture, and so no sign of God's Presence at all, but a meer Innovation in God's Worship, being without Precept or Example', 145.

based on their understanding of Scripture. Worship was to be essentially simple, guided carefully by the injunctions of Scripture.

Preaching: The Word of God is Central

In a primitivist religious environment, Scripture must be at the very center of the life of the participants. This is especially true with regard to preaching. It was the great means by which Christ exercised his prophetic office in the Church. Benjamin Keach said that Christ himself 'may be said to preach ... when his ministers do it in his name, his stead, or by his authority'.[42] Nehemiah Coxe considered the work of preaching to be the eminent 'Work and Business of a Pastor' because 'he is to be the Mouth of God to the People, to deliver his Message from God, and speak to them in his Name'.[43] For the Particular Baptists, preaching the Word of God was an exercise of foundational importance.

The centrality of preaching in Worship may be demonstrated by another quotation from Keach. He said,

> The ordinance of Preaching, or Administration of the Gospel, is a rich Pasture especially when it is preached powerfully by the Influence and Demonstration of the Spirit ... the Work of the Ministry is to open the Scripture ... The Preaching the Gospel, is the feeding of the Soul.[44]

Church members grow by means of preaching the Scriptures. The diligent minister studies hard, speaks plainly and with clarity, is zealous for the Glory of God, the benefit of the souls of his hearers, and can speak about the experiences of the heart.[45] But pre-eminently, he preaches the Word of God.[46]

Hercules Collins advocated a type of preaching based on the collection of observations, or doctrines, from the text of Scripture. He illustrated his method by drawing eight different doctrinal points out of Colossians 1.12.[47] In a

---

[42]Keach, *Parables: Series One*, 122.

[43]Coxe, *Ordination Sermon*, 23.

[44]Cited in Vaughn, 'Benjamin Keach's The Gospel Minister's Maintenance Vindicated', 60. He indicates that the quote is taken from Keach's 1694 book *A Golden Mine*, 131.

[45]Hercules Collins, *The Temple Repair'd: or, An Essay to revive the long-neglected Ordinances of exercising the Spiritual Gift of Prophecy for the Edification of the Churches; and of Ordaining Ministers duly qualified* (London: William and Joseph Marshal, 1702), 23, 28-29, 52-53.

[46]Collins, *Temple*, 26-27.

[47]Collins, *Temple*, 47-49. This book resembles William Perkins' famous *The Art of Prohesying* (Edinburgh: Banner of Truth, 1996). Collins makes reference to Perkins in several places (see pg. 32, 37). Like Perkins' work, Collins' book is in many ways 'more concerned with hermeneutics than homiletics'. R. T. Kendall, 'Preaching in Early Puritanism with special reference to William Perkins's The Arte of Prophesying', in *Preaching and Revival* (London: Westminster Conference, 1984), 23.

slightly different vein, Keach argued that there was no 'Precept or Example' in the Scriptures requiring such a formula, so that preachers 'are left to use what method we think may be ... most profitable for the Edification of the People'.[48]

Knollys' distinction between teaching and preaching is interesting. The reading, expounding and interpreting of Scripture was understood as instruction or teaching 'to know the Will and Mind of God ... revealed for ... Learning and Edification'. It was based on the example of Christ and the Apostles, and was promised a blessing by God.[49] Preaching was a separate act, and involved exhortations to believe, repent, live holy lives and grow in the faith. Knollys relies on Romans 12.6-8, in which a distinction seems to be drawn between 'prophesying', 'teaching', and 'encouraging'. Teaching was essentially noetic, aimed at the mind. Preaching seems to have been, at least in his understanding, casuistic, focused on the conscience and will. This is certainly not to say that preaching by-passed the mind. It is perhaps better to say that it sought to take instruction beyond information to a profound change of personal character. The teacher sought to inform the minds of his hearers, the preacher sought to change their lives. Hercules Collins' method of preaching is not essentially dissimilar. While great emphasis is placed on a proper method of interpreting Scripture, 'proper Uses are to be made upon each Doctrine'.[50] The 'use' was the practical application made to the conscience.[51] The intended goal was changed lives, and this was to be accomplished by the careful and forceful exhortations drawn from the doctrines of Scripture.

In this way, the act of preaching was the high point of public worship. If Christ himself speaks through the mouth of the preacher, the worshiper must give due and careful attention.[52] The church was not merely a religious organization gathered for the purpose of enacting cultic ritual. It was the dwelling place of the living God, and thus involved genuine confrontation between God and each participant.

---

[48]Keach, *The Breach Repaired*, 178-79.

[49]Knollys, *The World that Now is*, 71.

[50]Collins, *Temple Repair'd*, 49.

[51]D. M. Lloyd-Jones says, 'The Puritans were concerned to emphasize that it is only by preaching that holiness can be promoted among the people. In preaching you are taking the Word to them, and applying it to them ....' D. M. Lloyd-Jones, *The Puritans: Their Origins and Successors* (Edinburgh: Banner of Truth, 1987), 381. This quote is from the author's 1977 address to the Westminster Conference entitled 'Preaching'.

[52]Keach says ''Tis Christ's Word we should and ought always to preach, and hear ...we are not tied up by the Lord in Preaching, to do no more than barely read the Scripture, or quote one Scripture after another, (which would be rather Reading than Preaching) but may use other Words to edify the Church, provided they agree with, or are congruous to the Word of Christ, or the Sacred Scripture, (and yet we call that the Word of God which is preached, and so indeed it is). Keach, *The Breach Repaired*, 93-94. This is a high view of preaching, and well illustrates the prominence given to it in worship.

Women in Public Worship

The Baptists considered the Scriptural prohibitions on women speaking in public worship to be in full force. They were not permitted to pray, prophesy, publicly teach, rule, or 'speake ... by way of passing sentence' in doctrinal or discipline cases.[53] But the prohibitions were not absolute. The Abingdon Association determined that a woman might speak in three cases, to apply for membership in a church by giving her profession of faith, to be a witness or participant in discipline cases, and to express repentance if she had been disciplined.[54] It will be noted that none of these cases are related to public worship, but to church business meetings.

In December 1694, the Maze Pond, London, church was troubled by a dispute over the 'duty and Liberty of the Sisters respecting their Silance and Speaking in the church'. After discussion, it was unanimously agreed that the women could not pray, preach, give thanks or exercise any spiritual gift in the church; could not hold church office; and could not engage in debate in the church 'equally as the men have power to doe'. But they were permitted to vote by raising their hands, and speak concerns with regard to a matter for vote upon approval by the church body.[55]

One of the objections leveled against hymn singing was that it of necessity overturned the restriction on women speaking in public worship. Benjamin Keach responded with a lengthy quote from John Cotton who confirmed that a woman was not to teach, but could verbally participate in two ways, by giving an account of her offense as did Sapphira in Acts 5.8, and in singing 'for ''tis evident the Apostle layeth no greater restraint upon Women for silence in the Church, than the Law put upon them before, for so himself speaketh in ... 1 Cor. 14.34'. Since the 'Law' (understood as the Old Testament) permitted women to sing (e.g., Miriam), the apostolic churches must also have permitted the women to sing.[56] In his *An Answer to Mr. Marlow's Appendix*, Keach expands his position. ''Tis a hard case that Women should be debarred to speak in any sense, or any ways to Break Silence in the Church'. If the prohibition is absolute, a woman could not inquire into the well-being of another church member 'when in the Congregation', could not ask 'where the Text is' if she comes in late, could not respond to prayer with a verbal 'Amen', and could not give an account of her Christian experience.[57] The prohibition on speaking enjoins women from 'Ministration of preaching the Gospel, or ministerially, or

---

[53]White, *ARPB*, 55, 184-85.
[54]White, *ARPB*, 185.
[55]Maze Pond *CMB*, 109. This was an anti-singing church, the nucleus of which had separated from Keach's assembly when he introduced singing into worship.
[56]Keach, *The Breach Repaired*, 140-41.
[57]Benjamin Keach, *An Answer to Mr. Marlow's Appendix* (London: John Hancock, 1691), 33.

authoritatively to preach the Word'.[58] It does not hinder other carefully delineated forms of verbal participation.

To summarize, women were not allowed to exercise any kind of authoritative verbal communication in the churches. Some permitted limited participation in church business meetings, and others allowed women to sing with the congregation, speak the amen at the end of prayer, and engage in personal fellowship.[59]

The Ordinances: Baptism and the Lord's Supper

Hanserd Knollys placed Baptism and the Lord's Supper among the elements of worship.[60] This is also how the Second London Confession treats them stating in Chapter 22:5

> The (q) reading of the Scriptures, Preaching, and (r) hearing the word of God, teaching and admonishing one another in Psalms, Hymns and Spiritual songs, singing with grace in our Hearts to (s) the Lord; as also the Administration (t) of Baptism, and (u) the Lords Supper are all parts of Religious worship of *God*, to be performed in obedience to him, with understanding, faith reverence, and godly fear ....
>
> (q) 1 Tim. 4.13.
> (r) 2 Tim. 4.2. Luk. 8.18.
> (s) Col. 3.16. Eph. 5.19.
> (t) Mat. 28,19,20.
> (u) 1 Cor. 11.26.

and again in Chapter 28:1

---

[58]Keach, *Answer to Marlow*, 34. Even this is not an absolute prohibition. Keach cites 'our late Annotators' on 1 Cor. 14.34 who state that 'this Rule must be restrained to ordinary prophesyings, for certainly, if the Spirit of prophecy came upon a woman in the church, she might speak', 36; Cf. Matthew Poole, *A Commentary on the Holy Bible*, vol. 3 (McLean, Va.: MacDonald Publishing, n.d.), 591. Neither Keach nor Poole advocates continuing revelation. They simply use the presence of such activities, *in the apostolic era*, as examples to demonstrate that the prohibitions were not absolute.

[59]Leon McBeth, in his book *A Sourcebook for Baptist Heritage* (Nashville: Broadman Press, 1990), 55-56, asserts that some women did have a speaking ministry, but seriously misrepresents the facts. Based on an excerpt from the Broadmead, Bristol, Records, he argues that 'Baptist deaconesses sometimes exercised a speaking/teaching role as well as a one [*sic*] of healing/nurturing'. In the context of the *Records,* the 'speaking/teaching' role is exercised in private visits to the sick, and does not include teaching *per se*, but rather words of 'support or consolation, to build them up in a spirituall lively faith in Jesus Christ'. Cf. Hayden, *Records of a Church of Christ*, 209. This was not a 'teaching' ministry, nor was it public.

[60]Knollys, *The World that Now is*, 72-76.

Baptism and the Lord's Supper are ordinances of positive, and soveraign institution; appointed by the Lord Jesus the only Law-giver, to be continued in his Church (a) to the end of the world.

(a) Mat. 28.19,20. 1 Cor. 11.26.[61]

They were the two positive ceremonies instituted under the New Covenant, and thus were regarded as part of the worship of the local church.

Baptism

The Confessional statement on baptism in Chapter 29 is very simple and straightforward. It presents the doctrine of these churches in a positive light, without polemical comment. It states:

Of Baptism
1. Baptism is an ordinance of the New Testament, ordained by Jesus Christ, to be unto the party Baptized, a sign of his fellowship with him, in His death, (c) and resurrection; of his being engrafted into him; of (d) remission of sins; and of his (e)giving up unto God through Jesus Christ, to live and walk in newness of Life.

(c) Rom. 6.3,4,5. Col. 2.12. Gal 3.27.
(d) Mar. 1.4. Act. 26.16.[62]
(e) Rom, 6.2,4.

2. Those who do actually professe (f) repentance towards *God*, faith in, and obedience, to our Lord Jesus, are the only proper subjects of this ordinance.

(f) Mar. 16.16; Act. 8.36,37.

3. The outward element to be used in this ordinance (g) is water, wherein the party is to be baptized, in the name of the Father, and of the Son, and of the Holy Spirit.

(g) Mat 28.19,20. with Act. 8.38.

4. Immersion, or dipping of the person (h) in water, is necessary to the due administration of this ordinance.

(h) Mat. 3.16. Joh. 3.23.[63]

Paragraph one asserts that baptism is a 'sign' to the recipient of the blessings of salvation. This is followed by the declaration that only professing believers, those who have experienced the blessings signified, are the 'proper subjects of

---

[61]*A Confession of Faith*, 75, 96, emphasis in original.
[62]This proof text should probably be Acts 22.16.
[63]*A Confession of Faith*, 97-98, emphasis in original.

the ordinance'. The third paragraph affirms that water is necessary for the administration of the ordinance in the triune name of God,[64] and the chapter concludes with the assertion that immersion is the necessary mode of the ordinance.

This simple statement gives no indication of the controversy inherent in the adoption of its teaching. Baptism was the major doctrine that distinguished the Calvinistic Baptists from the Independents around them.[65] From the first Particular Baptist work published in defense of the new practice of Believer's Baptism by immersion in 1643 to the end of the century, books and pamphlets were exchanged on all sides.[66] One[67] of the most influential, and controversial, was published in 1673 by Colonel Henry Danvers,[68] entitled *A Treatise of Baptism*, followed by a second revised and enlarged edition in 1674.[69] This remarkable work of almost 450 pages was something of a *tour de force* for its age, and has been regarded as such since then. William Cathcart wrote of this *Treatise*, it 'was the ablest on the subject published by any Baptist till that time'; while J. M. Cramp said that Danvers' book was 'regarded as the most learned and complete work which at that time had been published on the subject'.[70] Richard Greaves declares that 'it sparked a broad and heated controversy over the nature of baptism . . .' against which 'the paedobaptists

---

[64]While this may seem incredibly obvious, it was a necessary assertion in the light of the Quaker doctrine that Scriptural Baptism did not involve external ceremonies. See Watts, *The Dissenters*, 205-206; Haykin, *Kiffin, Knollys and Keach*, 67-68; Nuttall, *The Holy Spirit*, 100.

[65]A helpful summary of the various positions on baptism in the seventeenth century may be found in E. Brooks Holifield, *The Covenant Sealed: The Development of Puritan Sacramental Theology in Old and New England, 1570-1720* (New Haven: Yale University Press, 1974), 75-108.

[66]The first Particular Baptist work published was J[ohn] S[pilsbery], *A Treatise Concerning the Lawfull Subject of Baptisme* in 1643.

[67]Some portions of this section have been published as James M. Renihan, 'Henry Danvers' *A Treatise of Baptism*: A Study in Seventeenth Century Baptist Historiography', *The Baptist Review of Theology*, 7, no. 1-2 (Spring/Fall 1997): 27-47.

[68]Danvers was pastor of the Houndsditch, London church until he fled to the continent in 1685. His successor, Edward Man, represented the church at the 1689 General Assembly. Richard L. Greaves, *Saints and Rebels: Seven Nonconformists in Stuart England* (Macon, Ga.: Mercer University Press, 1985), 175; 1689 *Narrative*, 22. Danvers and Man are mentioned together in the Petty France *CMB*, 25 (written pagination is incorrectly marked 23).

[69]Henry Danvers, *A Treatise of Baptism: Wherein, that of Believers, and that of Infants, is examined by the Scriptures*, 2d ed., (London: Fran. Smith, 1674).

[70]William Cathcart, *The Baptist Encyclopedia* (Paris, Ark.: Baptist Standard Bearer, 1988; reprint of 1881 edition), s.v. 'D'Anvers, Gov. Henry'; J. M. Cramp, *Baptist History* (Watertown, Wis.: Baptist Heritage Publications, 1987; reprint of 1871 edition), 373.

launched a ferocious assault'.[71] At least 23 books, by 12 different authors addressed the issue within three years.[72]

In the book, Danvers sought to lay out in detail his own understanding of church history, and the place filled in it by Baptists. Additionally, he purposed to demonstrate the validity of the Particular Baptist position by means of exegesis and theology. Danvers' historiography and theology is representative of the views of his contemporaries.[73]

The plan of *A Treatise of Baptism* gives indication of the author's methodology. His table of contents page states, 'The book consists of Two Parts, the first proving Believers; The second disproving Infants Baptism.'[74] Before the body of the work is actually begun, however, there are several important supplementary materials. One is an index, but even more interesting is 'An Abstract of the History of Baptism throughout all Ages since Christ'.[75] In this abstract, Danvers sets up three columns, entitled (1) 'Believers Baptism Instituted and Asserted'; (2) 'Infant Baptism Instituted, Asserted and Imposed'; and (3) 'Infant Baptism Opposed and Witnessed Against'. He then begins with the first century, and moves through the sixteenth, placing in the appropriate column the various witnesses for the different positions. Reference is made to the location throughout the book at which point these diverse writers are discussed. In this way, the reader has at a brief glance a reference for the classifications that Danvers uses throughout his work.

The first part of the book, consisting of seven chapters, is the shorter of the two sections, covering only 88 pages. Danvers presents a positive case for Believer's Baptism by means of exegesis, theology and history. He argues that Christ instituted Baptism as an ordinance for believers, for the purpose of witnessing to several spiritual ends, namely,

> To be a sign of the mysteries of the Gospel; To witness repentance; To evidence present regeneration; To represent the Covenant on man's part; To be a sign of the covenant on God's part; To represent the union betwixt Christ and Believer; [and as the means of] entrance into the visible church.[76]

---

[71]Greaves, *Saints and Rebels*, 169-70.

[72]Greaves, *Saints and Rebels*, 170-71. Greaves provides the names of the books and authors.

[73]His work received the approbation of contemporary Baptists, as some of the most prestigious of London's Baptist leaders, among them Hanserd Knollys, William Kiffin, John Gosnold and Thomas De Laune, came to Danvers' defense when the controversy erupted over his work and he was accused of falsehood. See for example the pamphlet *The Baptists Answer, to Mr. Obed. Wills, His Appeal against Mr. H. Danvers* (London: Francis Smith, 1675), signed by these four men along with David Dyke and Henry Forty.

[74]Danvers, *Treatise*, page unnumbered.

[75]Danvers, *Treatise*. This material covers 5 unnumbered pages, following the index and preceding an advertisement for another of Danvers' books.

[76]Danvers, *Treatise*, 11-25.

Chapter seven of part one is an historical study, moving century by century through the Christian era, for the purpose of demonstrating that Believer's Baptism has an eminent history in the church. The charge of historical novelty had been laid against the English Baptists early on,[77] and Danvers' writing was meant as a counter to that charge. The title of this chapter, though lengthy, gives some indication of his purposes:

> Wherein is an Account of Believers Baptism in a brief History thereof; not only from the Scriptures in the first Century, but from the Humane Authors also, confirming the necessity of Instruction and Profession of Faith before Baptism, in all the Centuries. And that the Children of Christians, as well as Pagans, were not otherwise baptized, whereof you have some famous Instances, especially in the Fourth Century, of several eminent Christians that deferred the Baptizing of their Children till they could give an Account of their Faith. Collected out of several Authors, especially the famous *Magdiburgensian* history.[78]

In this chapter, Danvers seeks to demonstrate that there has been a positive testimony to Believer's Baptism throughout the centuries. He recognizes that the historical argument cannot be given the same weight that would be given to Biblical matters, but appeals to this

> by way of *illustration* only; because they may be of *weight* with *some*, and whereby it may be *manifest*, that ... *Antiquity* itself (which hath been so much *boasted of*) is altogether for *Believers*, and not for *Infants-Baptism*.[79]

This statement gives a clear indication of the author's concern. In his estimation, the argument from antiquity, apparently used to good success by paedobaptists, is specious, and needs correction. For Danvers, antiquity stands as a testimony confirming his own views. Leaning heavily on the *Magdiburgensian* History, he constructs, or perhaps re-constructs, a Baptist reading of early church history, in terms of the subjects, administrators, place, time, manner and ceremonies of baptism. This is followed by quotes from Clement, Ignatius, and other writers. He even states, 'The Ancient *Britains*, who practiced the *Baptizing* of Believers, did by *Evangelists* sent from the *Apostles* themselves, receive the *Gospel* under *Tiberius the Emperor*; as saith *Gildas*, in his book, called *De Victoria Aurelli Ambrosii*.'[80] For the second century, Justin Martyr, Clement of Alexandria, and Walafrid Strabo are cited as authorities testifying that baptism was only to follow faith and repentance, or an understanding of the Gospel. Tertullian, Origen, Eusebius, and Cyril support the argument for the third century, while Athanasius, Hilary, Basil, Gregory

---

[77]Barbone, *Discourse*, 6.

[78]Barbone, *Discourse*, 40.

[79]Barbone, *Discourse*, 45, emphasis his.

[80]Barbone, *Discourse*, 48, emphasis his.

Nazianzen, Ambrose, Arnobius, Jerome and others are noted as supporters in the fourth century. This methodology continues up to the sixteenth century.

It must be stated that Danvers does not necessarily cite these authors as if they were adherents of his own position. He knows that some of them are not. Rather, his concern is to show that they had an understanding of the fact that baptism should follow conversion. Of course, the paedobaptist response would be that some, or many, of Danvers' quotations are to no avail, since no one would dispute that pagans who are converted ought to be baptized upon their profession of faith.[81] The issue centers rather around the children of believers. Danvers argues that these types of statements, when found in paedobaptist writings point up their theological inconsistency. This is an argument which has frequently been used by Baptist authors since Danvers. It asserts that the paedobaptist position must propose two differing qualifications for baptism, one relying on the profession of faith, and the other upon the parental heritage of the subject. He would argue that this conclusion only came as a late imposition into the life of the church, and that it was unknown to the early Christians. He says, 'The Truth is, I do believe *Paedo-Baptism*, how or by whom, I know not, came into the world in the second Century, and in the third and fourth, began to be practiced.'[82] In any case, for Danvers, the earliest records testify in support of Believer's Baptism.

As he progresses through the centuries of the Christian era, Danvers seeks to include testimonies for Believer's Baptism not only from those in the Roman Catholic stream, but also from others outside of it. For example, beginning in the twelfth century, he turns his attention to those whom he calls the 'old Waldenses'.[83] These followers of Peter Bruis and Henricus, according to Danvers, increased rapidly in number in southern France and northern Italy. They were persecuted by the Roman pontiff, but grew so dramatically 'that their Itinerant Preachers (whereof they had many, whom they sent in most Countries) could, in their Travels from *France* to *Milain*, lodge every night at one of their Friends houses'.[84] This group bore a significant testimony for believers baptism, so much so that he actually calls them 'Baptists'.[85]

The second section of the book, beginning on page 89, should perhaps be actually divided into two sections itself, corresponding to the three columns of Danvers' 'Abstract'. The first six chapters of part two seek to demonstrate that

---

[81]Danvers anticipates this objection, and responds by stating that 'their Words and Reasons appear substantial Arguments for the Baptists, ...for is not the Commission it self fully owned, the Order of it, and Practice upon it, viz. That persons ought first to be taught in the Faith, before they are to be baptized into the same....' In Danvers' estimation, the recognition of these facts demands the consistency of accepting the Baptist position, and abandoning the unattested practice of infant baptism. Barbone, *Discourse*, 86.

[82]Barbone, *Discourse*, 64, emphasis his.

[83]Barbone, *Discourse*, 75.

[84]Barbone, *Discourse*.

[85]Barbone, *Discourse*, 79.

the practice of infant baptism has no scriptural warrant, and is an imposition upon the pure ordinances of the gospel. These chapters cover a little more than 130 pages. Chapter seven of part two, however, entitled 'Wherein there is an account of some eminent witness that hath been born against Infants-Baptism from first to last'[86] is itself over 135 pages long. It could easily have become the third part of the work.

The first six chapters of this section cover ground similar to part one, but from a slightly different perspective. Frequently appealing to the same authors, Danvers seeks to establish the fact that many have been highly inconsistent in their practice of infant baptism. He gives evidence of the unusual ceremonies that seemed to have accompanied the introduction of infant baptism, such as the baptism of bells, christening of churches, use of honey and milk, and many others.[87] He also points out the sometimes slanderous reports that were made about those who practice believers baptism, even by such as the well-known Richard Baxter, who recounted that in some cases contemporary Baptists in England had practiced baptism naked.[88] For Danvers, such a slander serves an important polemic purpose. It evidences that at times, even the best of opponents of Believer's Baptism have fallen prey to misrepresentation and innuendo in their accounts of the life and practices of Baptists. As such, it may be that some of the reports put forward with regard to the continental Anabaptists were likewise slanderous and false, unjust accusations intended to discredit their practice without regard to truth. This does raise a serious issue. Is it possible that some groups, about whom little is known except through the reports of their adversaries, could have been misrepresented in church history, and deserve better treatment? Danvers would seem to indicate that this is in fact the case. He is not afraid to identify with some lesser known sects, because he believes that they may well have been abused in the received accounts of their doctrines and practices.

The material presented in these chapters highlights an important issue, present in the writings of many paedobaptist authors, councils and church synods cited by Danvers. He demonstrates that many proponents of infant baptism have admitted that there is little or no scriptural warrant for their position, and that it rests rather on theological, or even traditional arguments. The array of admissions of this fact presented is impressive,[89] and serves Danvers' purposes well. An acquaintance with the details of church history has provided the author with many notable, and potentially embarrassing statements by those who held a position opposite to his own.

As noted above, chapter seven is virtually its own section, as by itself it is longer than either of the other two sections of the book. In this chapter, Danvers

---

[86]Barbone, *Discourse*, 221.

[87]Barbone, *Discourse*, 118.

[88]Barbone, *Discourse*, 119.

[89]Among others cited are Austin, Chrysostom, Bellarmine, the Councils of Trent and Basil, Eck, the Oxford Divines of 1647, and Richard Baxter; an interesting assortment from across a wide spectrum. Barbone, *Discourse*, 132-150.

presents his most sophisticated historical argument, giving much space to a variety of important witnesses for the practice of believers baptism, starting with Tertullian, proceeding to the Donatists and Novatians, the Ancient Britains, the Waldenses, John Wickliffe and the Lollards, and also responding to objections brought against his use of some of these witnesses.

Tertullian, so argues Danvers briefly, was the first to witness against the practice of infant baptism in the third century, indicating that this was when it probably began to be introduced. The second important witnesses against the practice of infant baptism were the Donatists and Novatians. Citing several different sources, Danvers puts these two geographically diverse groups together, and presents their testimony to the practice of Believer's Baptism. Realizing that some will respond that these groups were adjudged to be heretics, he takes up this objection by offering an important and substantial response. In the first place, the label heretic in itself does not necessarily reflect the true status of a particular group. Secondly, he argues that an error on one issue or another should not therefore brand anyone as heretical. He offers 'several gross Errors and Mistakes of Austin himself' as an example of this fact. Thirdly, Danvers states that in his estimation, especially regarding the Novatians, he 'cannot find they were other than a very Holy People'.[90] For these reasons, he judges the testimony of these two groups to be of importance. There is a certain amount of weight in Danvers' reasoning. As noted above, it is possible that those who oppose one sect may to some degree be guilty of misrepresentation of that sect, and thus color the judgments of historians who do not have access to other primary source material. In addition, it is true that some of the best theologians of the church have themselves held to views later considered to be erroneous. One could say that the only reason that the one is considered to be more highly regarded than the other rests upon the history written, or perhaps controlled, by those who hold a similar position. Danvers' third point then, sets up the guide for this. If in fact his investigation has been sound, then it may be that these groups were better than they have been sometimes judged. In reality, only a detailed study of primary source material from the era can lead one to any kind of conclusive opinion. Nevertheless, the point is well taken, and serves as a caution in the study of church history. It must be said, however, that it is also possible to be guilty of revisionism simply for polemical purposes. In Danvers' method of argumentation, an appeal to the ancients is of great value. The more substantial the appeal, the more numerous the witnesses, and the more able that he is to bring these groups into the mainstream of church history, the more successful is his case. From this distance, the issue itself is difficult to judge. But for Danvers' purposes, at least in judging by the responses given to his work,[91] it was a very useful tactic indeed.

The double polemic, based on Scripture and antiquity, characterized the apologetic procedure of the Baptists. Both Hercules Collins and Benjamin

---

[90] Barbone, *Discourse*, 225.
[91] See above, especially footnotes 71, 72, 73.

Keach followed Danvers' example, publishing books using the same method.[92] This approach satisfied both the necessity of grounding practice in Scripture (the regulative principle) and the need to respond to the charge that their practice was an historical novelty.

Baptism was for believers only, but there was no set age at which a person might be qualified for it. Keach says,

> I grant those little Children who do believe in Christ, have an indubitable right to Baptism and to the Lords Supper also, as soon as they are Baptised: But not Infants....
>
> I am subject to think [Timothy] was very young when he did first believe and was Baptised, may be he was a Child; but prove he was Baptised when he was an Infant and I will become a *Pedo Baptist*.[93]

Based on this language, Keach would have allowed believing children into membership, for only church members could come to the Lord's Table. The Petty France, London church received Thomas Harrison into membership in 1679 when he was twelve years old.[94] Believer's Baptism was not the equivalent of adult only baptism.

The actual practice of baptism was simple, though two issues need to be mentioned. The first has to do with the locale of baptism. W. T. Whitley states that a baptistery was built at Horselydown, Southwark, perhaps as early as 1657.[95] He implies that it was used by several churches, but provides no details. Probably more commonly, churches used various bodies of water. The Petty France, London, church seems to have used a tributary of the Thames, and baptized throughout the year. A special note is made in the church book entry for 24 December, 1676:

> Mrs. Hart & Hannah that had bene lately servant to Br. Collins did propound for Baptisme, and were accepted: onely the administration of the ordinance

---

[92]Hercules Collins, *Believers Baptism from Heaven, and of Divine Institution. Infants-Baptism from Earth, and Human Invention* (London: For the author, 1691); Benjamin Keach, *Gold Refin'd; or, Baptism in its Primitive Purity* (London: Printed for the author, 1689); idem, *Believers Baptism, or Love to the antient Britains displayed* (London, n.p., 1705).

[93]Benjamin Keach, *A Counter Antidote to purge out the Malignant Effects of a Late Counterfeit, Prepared by Mr. Gyles Shute, An Unskilful Person in Polemical Cures* (London: H. Bernard, 1694), 16.

[94]Wilson, *The History and Antiquities of Dissenting Churches and Meeting Houses*, 2:187.

[95]W. T. Whitley, *The Baptists of London*, 16. He says that it was derisively called 'the tub of salvation, up Dipping alley'. The Stevington, Bedfordshire, Church used some kind of 'fenced' place for baptism in 1693. See Tibbutt, *Some Early Nonconformist Church Books*, 37.

to them was deferd a while, Because by reason of the extremity of ye present frost, we could not now come at ye water.[96]

In 1701, the Southampton Association debated the question 'Whether there is any ground for a person to dout of ye validity of his baptism because performed in a standing pool and not in a river ...?' They concluded that a baptism in such conditions was valid.[97] The presence of the question indicates the concern of some for precision, thinking that the Scripture examples of river baptisms were binding even in that detail.

The second item of note has to do with the administrators of baptism (and of the Lord's Supper). The First London Confession stated regarding baptism that

> The persons designed by Christ, to dispense this Ordinance, the (1) Scriptures hold forth to be a preaching Disciple, it being no where tyed to a particular Church, Officer, or person extraordinarily sent, the Commission injoyning the administration, being to them under no other consideration, but as considered Disciples.
> 1. Esa. 8.16. Mat. 28.16,17,18,19. John 4.1,2.   Acts 20.7. Mat. 26.26.[98]

Daniel Featly criticized the phrase 'preaching disciple', assuming that it implied that any member of a church could administer baptism.[99] This was not, however, what was intended as Hanserd Knollys wrote in 1645

> We do not affirm, that every common Disciple may Baptize.... Nor do we judge it meet, for any Brother to baptize, or to administer other Ordinances; unlesse he have received such gifts of the Spirit, as fitteth, or inableth him to preach the Gospel. And those guifts being first tried by, and known to the Church, such a Brother is chosen, and appointed thereunto by the Suffrage of the Church.[100]

The 1646 revision of the Confession changed the wording to:

---

[96]Petty France *CMB*, 3. Maze Pond also used the Thames, Maze Pond *CMB*, 139; and Broadmead, Bristol used the river Froome, Hayden, *The Records of a Church of Christ*, 142, 184, 185, 212, 270.

[97]Whitchurch Manuscript, 23, number A6. Early in their history, the Broadmead church asserted that 'ye Ordinance of Baptism must be allwayes so administered or done, *as at first* it was done by ye Apostles ...as to ...ye *Manner how* they did it, which was by Dipping them in Rivers, not sprinkling them'. Hayden, *The Records of a Church of Christ*, 112, emphasis in original.

[98]Lumpkin, *BCF*, 167.

[99]Featly, *The Dippers dipt*, 183. Lumpkin makes this same observation, *BCF*, 167. Featly was not the only one to misunderstand the intention of this article. John Saltmarsh likewise thought that it asserted that any disciple could baptize. See Knollys, *The Shining of a Flaming fire in Zion*, 9.

[100]Knollys, *The Shining of a Flaming fire in Zion*, 9.

> The person designed by Christ to dispense baptism, the Scripture holds forth to be a disciple; it being no where tied to a particular church officer, or person extraordinarily sent the commission enjoining the administration, being given to them as considered disciples, being men able to preach the gospel.[101]

The minimum requirement to be an acceptable administrator of baptism was recognition by the church as a gifted brother. Apparently without exception this was the opinion of the Particular Baptists for the rest of the century. The Abingdon Association affirmed it in 1656,[102] as did the Second London Confession in 1677,[103] Broadmead, Bristol in 1679,[104] Benjamin Keach in 1689,[105] the Southampton Association in 1691,[106] the Bristol (Western) Association in 1693,[107] and the Northern Association in 1701.[108] Baptism was less important than preaching,[109] and therefore those who were approved as preachers could be administrators.[110]

How was the Baptism actually performed? There is little evidence. The woodcut at the front of Daniel Featley's *The Dippers dip't* depicts a face forward motion.[111] Benjamin Keach indicates that there may have been different thoughts current, some advocating a forward motion, other backwards;

---

[101]*The First London Confession of Faith, 1646 Edition*, (Rochester, N.Y.: Backus Books, 1981), 15.

[102]White, *ARPB*, 158. They were asked whether a church could choose any of its male members to administer baptism. In reply they said no, and urged that someone come from 'the next adjacent church' to perform the baptism.

[103]*A Confession of Faith*, 96, (28:2) 'These holy appointments are to be administered by those only, who are qualified and thereunto called according to the commission of Christ.'

[104]Hayden, *The Records of a Church of Christ*, 219.

[105]Benjamin Keach, *Gold Refin'd*, 22.

[106]Whitchurch Manuscript, 16, number A4. This question was specifically related to the Lord's Supper. The answer was the same as given at the Abingdon Association 35 years earlier.

[107]Ivimey, *HEB*, 1:527.

[108]Copson, *Association Life*, 89.

[109]Keach, *Gold Refin'd*, 22.

[110]The Broadmead, Bristol church would only allow men 'sett aparte to ye worke of ye Ministry' to baptize. Gifted brothers who could not meet this further qualification were not proper administrators. Hayden, *The Records of a Church of Christ*, 219. Hercules Collins, held to a higher view of the qualifications necessary to administer the Lord's Supper. Incarcerated in the early 1680s, his church determined to observe the Supper in his absence administered by a gifted brother. Collins was opposed to this, but the church proceeded. After his release, the church reaffirmed this decision. See MacDonald, 'Tensions', 317.

[111]Featley, *The Dippers dipt*, frontispeice. One cannot depend too much on this woodcut, as it depicts men baptizing naked women. It was intended to shock by means of pictorial inuendo.

some for slow motion, holding the baptizand under the water to symbolize burial while others urge swiftness.[112] So far as Keach was concerned, the actual method did not matter, even though these things 'appertain to the Form of the Administration of Christ's Ordinance.... What Ordinance has not lost its Primitive Form under the Apostacy?'[113] All that mattered was that new believers were dipped under the water. Anything else is a 'silly objection'.

Baptism was a vitally important part of the theology of these churches. It was the distinguishing and identifying doctrine. Their practice was driven by their commitment to the Regulative Principle. They saw no warrant for infant baptism in Scripture, but found precept and example for Believer's Baptism. It was their understanding of and adherence to the Word of God that made them Baptists.

The Lord's Supper

E. P. Winter asserts that the Lord's Supper was not a matter of controversy among the seventeenth-century Particular Baptists, and so they did not produce any major works about it.[114] Their doctrine resembles that of the Independents with whom they were companions.[115]

The thirtieth chapter of the Second London Confession describes the Particular Baptists' convictions regarding the Lord's Supper. It was instituted by Christ for 'spiritual nourishment and growth' as a 'bond and pledge of' the communion between Savior and disciple. Rejecting any Romanist understanding of the ceremony, they assert that ministers are to pray, consecrate the elements, break the bread, take the cup and distribute them to the people, participating themselves. There is a real spiritual sense in which the faithful participant receives and feeds on Christ. No one who is ignorant of the

---

[112]Keach, *The Breach Repaired*, 182. It is not clear whether Keach is speaking hypothetically or is providing actual opinions.

[113]Keach, *The Breach Repaired*, 182, 185.

[114]E. P. Winter, 'Calvinist and Zwinglian Views of the Lord's Supper among the Baptists of the Seventeenth Century', *BQ*, 15, no. 7 (July 1954): 325.

[115]Horton Davies says of the Baptists, 'it is probable that their service resembled that of the other Separatists in its simplicity, its fidelity to the account of Dominical institution in I Cor. xi 23 ff, repeating not only the words of delivery but also the manual acts'. Davies, *Worship*, 91. This description exactly fits the procedure (noted above footnote 39) laid out by Knollys. Treatments of the Baptists' position may be found in Winter, 'Calvinist and Zwinglian Views', 323-329; idem, 'The Lord's Supper: Admission and Exclusion among the Baptists of the Seventeenth Century', *BQ* 17, no. 6 (April 1958): 267-281; idem, 'The Administration of the Lord's Supper among Baptists of the Seventeenth Century', *BQ* 18, no. 5 ((January 1960): 196-204; Haykin, *Kiffin, Knollys and Keach*, 77-81. The broader Puritan concept of the Supper is described in Holifield, *The Covenant Sealed*, 109-138.

Gospel should be allowed to partake, and if they do, they bring judgment upon themselves.[116]

The catechism published by the General Assembly under the title *A Brief Instruction in the Principles of Christian Religion* as a supplement to the Confession, contains several questions and answers about the Lord's Supper.[117] Both baptism and the Lord's Supper are said to be 'effectual Means of Salvation', by the 'Blessing of Christ and the working of the Spirit in those that by Faith receive them'.[118] The 102d question is similar in content to paragraph 7 of the Confession's Chapter 30.[119] Worthy participants by faith are made partakers of the body and blood of Christ with all of the attendant spiritual blessings. Question 103 is somewhat unexpected. It asserts that the proper subjects of the ordinance are baptized believers.[120] This answer is consonant with the practices of the majority of closed membership churches, but would seem to contradict those of the few open-membership churches in the Assemblies.[121] In addition, some of the closed-membership churches allowed members of paedobaptist churches to participate in their observance of the Table, but they were roundly criticized as inconsistent by their more strict

---

[116]*A Confession of Faith*, 99-102.

[117]*A Brief Instruction in the Principles of Christian Religion*, 5th ed. (London: Printed in the Year 1695), 19-21. This copy, held by the British Museum, is the earliest known edition of the Catechism. Murdina MacDonald apparently was unaware of its existence when she wrote 'There is no evidence to support McGlothlin's claim the London assembly issued "The Baptist Catechism" about 1694.' MacDonald, 'London Calvinistic Baptists', 68. 'McGlothlin' is William McGlothlin, editor of the 1910 book *Baptist Confessions of Faith*. The *Brief Instruction* is intentionally modeled after the Westminster Shorter Catechism. Cf. *The Confession of Faith; The Larger and Shorter Catechisms*, 313-15.

[118]*A Brief Instruction*, 19. This answer is the same as Question 91 of the Shorter Catechism, except that baptism and Lord's Supper are substituted for 'sacrament'.

[119]Once again the Baptists change 'Sacrament', substituting the phrase 'Ordinance of the New Testament Instituted by Christ'. *A Brief Instruction*, 20. Michael Haykin is probably correct in stating that this change in the Confession (and by implication here) was 'adopted to stress ...Divine Institution'. Haykin, *Kiffin, Knollys and Keach*, 78. This would fit the Baptist insistence on the Regulative Principle.

[120]*A Brief Instruction*, 21.

[121]It is possible that this question and answer are an interpolation into the original document. Throughout the catechism, Scripture proofs are uniformly designated by the assignment of a letter of the alphabet enumerated consecutively. The proofs for question 102 are designated 'e', and the proofs for question 104 pick up with 'f'. But the proofs for question 103 are designated by a '*'. This might point to an addition made to an earlier edition. Other questions with similar Scripture proof designators are 42, 43, 97, and 106. In the case of questions 42, 43 and 97, the markers come after 'z' and before 'a'. Could it be that someone like Benjamin Keach, who has been frequently identified with the Catechism, and who held to a strict closed-membership view of the church, interpolated this statement into the document? In the absence of earlier editions, it is impossible to say with certainty, but such an action would fit the circumstances.

friends.[122] Question 104 describes the spiritual requirements necessary in the recipients of the Supper: self-examination with regard to knowledge, faith, repentance, and obedience.[123] This close adherence to the language of the Westminster Shorter Catechism supports the notion that the Particular Baptist doctrine of the Supper closely resembled that of the paedobaptist dissenters around them.

The Supper was observed on a regular basis, according to the dictates of the church. The Broadmead, Bristol and Devonshire Square, London churches observed it monthly,[124] while the Petty France church followed a three-week pattern until persecution forced them to extend the interval to four weeks.[125] The Broughton, Wiltshire, church purchased 'bread and wine' on a five week cycle, and thus may have celebrated the Supper accordingly.[126] Typically, it was observed on the Lord's Day in the evening according to their understanding of the New Testament pattern,[127] but in March 1680/81, during a period of persecution, the Broadmead church observed it on Monday.[128]

Benjamin Keach provides evidence that there were some differences over the precise form of administration. Some apparently argued for a single loaf, no matter the size of the congregation, broken into pieces after the words of institution. Others (in presumably larger churches) used several loaves. Certain unnamed individuals argued that the wine had to be poured immediately after the loaf is broken, while others insisted that all of the bread and wine had to be consumed. Keach had no time for such picayune 'needless and frivolous Objections'.[129] The spiritual enjoyment of the blessings of salvation was what really mattered.

---

[122]Winter, 'Admission and Exclusion', 272-72. An example of the criticism levied against the 'open communion' churches may be found in Marlow, *Purity*, 37-38.
[123]*A Brief Instruction*, 21.
[124]Davies, *Worship*, 205; Hayden, *The Records of a Church of Christ*, 114, 189; Devonshire Square *CMB*, 34. Broadmead also held a monthly prayer day in conjunction with and just prior to the Supper.
[125]Petty France *CMB*, 21.
[126]Broughton *CB1*, 47, 49, 76, 99. In the 1689 *Narrative*, this church is listed under the name Porton.
[127]Knollys, *World*, 75; Hayden, *The Records of a Church of Christ*, 189. Davies, *Worship*, 205 cites the 1700 'Covenant of the Baptist Church Meeting at Horsleydown' which explicitly enjoins evening observation. Hercules Collins criticizes the Church of England parishes for holding the ordinance at noon, though 'Christ did administer that Ordinance in the Evening'. *Some Reasons for Separation*, 13.
[128]Hayden, *The Records of a Church of Christ*, 240. The pastor, George Fownes, argued that the observance was 'in Scripture tied to no Day, and was first instituted and administered by our Lord on Fryday'. The church was persuaded by his reasoning.
[129]Keach, *The Breach Repaired*, 181.

Laying on Hands

Some Baptists argued for a third ordinance, based on Hebrews 6.2, the laying on of hands. While more characteristic of the General Baptists, several Particular Baptists advocated the practice as well.[130] It involved

> Christ's Ministers laying their hands solemnly upon the Head of the Baptised, with Prayer to Almighty God for an increase of the Graces and Gifts of the Holy Ghost, to inable us to hold fast the Faith which we now visibly own, having entred into the Church by Holy Baptism, and also be helped thereby to maintain a constant War against the World, Flesh, and the Devil.[131]

This act was, according to Collins, an essential part of the life of the church, and requisite for every member of every church. When treating the subject in his *Orthodox Catechism*, he places the series of questions in the section on the ordinances, after the doctrine of baptism and immediately prior to the discussion of the Lord's Supper. For Collins, this was an ordinance of the church.[132] He argued that the churches practiced all of the other 'principles' or 'oracles' of Hebrews 6.1-2 (repentance, faith, baptism, belief in the resurrection and in the judgment), and could not understand why they would eliminate the fourth principle, laying on hands.[133] Benjamin Keach wrote just as strongly about the subject stating,

> If a church want but one essential principle, it is defective, and no complete congregation, according to primitive constitution: if it hath six, as it appears it hath, and wants but one, it is imperfect .... These six principles ... are fundamentals of a gospel church .... True, a church may be materially a true church, and formally true, too, (i.e. they may give themselves up to the Lord, and to one another, as a congregation, to walk together in the fellowship of the gospel) who may not be baptized, nor own laying on of hands; but then they must be considered, not a complete gospel church, but in some things defective, in respect to its constitution and regular gospel form, or as wanting a pillar &c. A house may be a real house, though it may want a principal post it stands on; it may be pretty firm, and may stand though one be missing; however, it is not so safe, to want one principle of the doctrine of Christ.[134]

In spite of these strong words, most of the churches resisted adopting this 'ordinance'. It was rejected by both the Western and Abingdon Associations,

---

[130]Ernest R. Payne, 'Baptists and the Laying on of Hands', *BQ* 15, no. 5 (January 1954): 203-215; Greaves, *Saints and Rebels*, 172; Watts, *The Dissenters*, 206.
[131]Collins, *Orthodox Catechism*, 34.
[132]Collins, *Orthodox Catechism*, 32-38.
[133]Collins, *Orthodox Catechism*, 36, 38.
[134]Keach, *Parables: Series Two*, 32.

arguing that it was an apostolic act related to the granting of extraordinary gifts, and that Hebrews 6.2 could not be used to support the notion that every member of every church should be subject to it.[135] It was not part of the Confession, and played no part in the General Assemblies. Obviously Keach and Collins were able to have fellowship, in this case, with churches practicing a different order.

The subject did occasionally cause friction between churches. In 1693, a member of the Petty France church separated from the church 'on the accot of singing & laying on of hands & went to Mr. Keach'. She was 'declared no member' until such a time as she would make the matter right.[136]

Conclusion

The ordinances were at the very center of the worship of the church. They were even considered to be pillars of the church, part of the foundation of its being. Regulated carefully by Scripture, these practical expressions of worship contributed fundamentally to the nature of devotion. Baptism defined the identity of the church, the Lord's Supper expressed the intimacy of fellowship with God, and for some, the Laying on of Hands completed the proper ordering of the church.

The Great Controversy: Singing Hymns

In the last decade of the seventeenth century, a controversy erupted among the Particular Baptists of London which centered on the application of the regulative principle to a specific aspect of worship. The major issue focused on the propriety of singing hymns in the public worship of the Church. Some advocated the practice, defending its warrant from the Scriptures. Others opposed it as a human invention, and claimed that it degraded worship and dishonored God. The chief proponent of the practice was Benjamin Keach, the prolific author and pastor of the Horselydown, Southwark church. His major protagonist was Isaac Marlow, a wealthy London jeweler and layman. So divisive was the controversy that it shattered the General Assemblies which seemed, at the beginning, to hold out so much promise for good among the churches.[137]

While the General Baptists as a whole rejected singing in worship,[138] some Particular Baptists advocated hymn singing at various times in the seventeenth century. The West Country Association discussed the matter and approved it in 1655,[139] Hanserd Knollys[140] and Hercules Collins[141] endorsed singing in

---

[135]White, *ARPB*, 54, 70-71, 175-76.
[136]Petty France *CMB*, unnumbered page 33.
[137]See MacDonald, 'London Calvinistic Baptists', 32-82.
[138]Nuttall, *The Holy Spirit*, 73. Nuttall notes that in 1689, the General Baptist General Assembly condemned singing as a 'carnal formality'.
[139]White, *ARPB*, 58.

published works, and churches such as Broadmead, Bristol[142] and Wantage[143] incorporated it into their public worship. Nevertheless, the man most responsible for the advocacy of this practice is Benjamin Keach. He had included hymns in some of his published books as early as the mid 1660s, and by 1673 had introduced the practice of hymn singing into his church.[144] Bogue and Bennett summarize the procedure used by Keach:

> The method, employed by Mr. Keach to introduce psalmody into his congregation is worthy of record, as it marks, in the strongest colours, the inveteracy of opposition in some of the flock, and the patience and moderation of their pastor. Being convinced that it was an ordinance of Christ for the edification of his church, he published a treatise on the subject, and also took much pains to enlighten their minds by private conversation. The first step to success, was the permission of the church to sing a hymn at the conclusion of the service, in the celebration of the Lord's supper. After stopping here for six years, leave was obtained to extend the psalmody to days of thanksgiving. At last, after fourteen years perseverance in this method, by a regular act of the church it was in a solemn manner agreed to sing the praises of God in their ordinary worship, every Lord's Day; only five or six members expressed their dissent. "This" says the historian, "if I am not mistaken, was the first baptist church which practiced this holy ordinance".[145]

Keach wrote *The Breach Repaired in God's Worship* in defense of the idea that singing was warranted by Scripture. In that work, he describes the history of the practice in his assembly:

> Hath not the Church sung at breaking of Bread always for 16 or 18 Years last past, and could not, nor would omit it in the time of persecution? ... And

---

[140]Knollys, *The World that Now is*, 76-80. He says, 'Singing is a Gospel-Ordinance'. See also Ian N. Mallard, 'The Hymns of Katherine Sutton' *BQ* 20, no. 1 (January 1963): 22-33.

[141]Hercules Collins, *Orthodox Catechism*, 75-86 (mispaginated '66'). This is entitled 'An Appendix concerning the Ordinance of Singing'.

[142]Hayden, *Records of a Church of Christ*, 133-34, 149, 151, etc.

[143]Stevenson, *Baptist Church, Wantage*, 17; *A Historical Survey of the Baptist Church in Wantage*, 12.

[144]Keach's hymns are described in David W. Music, 'The Hymns of Benjamin Keach: An Introductory Study', *The Hymn* 34 (July 1983): 147-154.

[145]David Bogue and James Bennett, *History of the Dissenters, from the Revolution in 1688, to the year 1808* (London: Printed for the Authors, 1810), 3:341. The unnamed historian is apparently Thomas Crosby, and he was mistaken in his conclusion. Presumably, some of the churches of the West Country Association were singing in 1655, the Wantage church was singing in 1667, and Broadmead by 1671. Strictly speaking, Keach did not introduce 'Psalmody' into worship at his church, but rather the singing of hymns based on parts of Scripture other than the Psalms.

> have we not for this 12 or 14 Years sung in *mixt Assemblies, on Days of Thanksgiving . . .*?
>
> And on that Solemn Day, when the Church would have it put up, to see how the members stood affected by Singing, almost every ones Hand was up for it, or to give Liberty to the Church at such times to sing . Besides, did not the Church agree to sing only after Sermon, and when Prayer was ended?[146]

At first, singing was introduced after the observance of the Lord's Supper, in imitation of Matthew 26.30. This was extended, six years later, to days of Thanksgiving, and finally in 1690 or 1691 the practice was approved by the congregation for inclusion at the end of worship each Lord's Day.

Keach's patient methodology did not prevent all controversy. Apparently, even though the church agreed to sing at the end of the service so that those who were unconvinced in their consciences could leave, there were still some who became disaffected. He states, regarding the day that the meeting to approve singing was held,

> Did any of you, at that time say, if we did proceed to sing at such times, you could not have Communion with us? Which if you had, I perceive the Church, nay every one of us who have born our Burden for many Years, would have born it a little longer?[147]

Evidently, there were some who were yet dissatisfied with the concessions made by the church, and were threatening to, or had already, left the church in disaffection. He describes the issue at hand:

> The matter of Difference that is present between the Church and some few of our dear and beloved Brethren and Sisters, is not about singing it self, nor singing with others, for that has been all along the practice of the Church for many Years ... but only about singing on the Lord's Day.[148]

The situation was made worse by the writings of some outside of the Horselydown fellowship, especially Isaac Marlow. He published several pamphlets about singing, especially seeking to oppose the opinions of Keach. *The Breach Repaired in God's Worship* was a reply to Marlow and his published writings. Keach believed that Marlow was intentionally seeking to foment division in the Horselydown church. In the *Answer to Mr. Marlow's Appendix* he says,

> Whereas Mr. *Marlow* affirms, as if I had brought singing into our Congregation, to the grief and trouble of many of our members; it is false ....
> And though some of our worthy Brethren and Sisters are at present

---

[146]Keach, *The Breach Repaired*, viii-ix, emphasis his.

[147]Keach, *The Breach Repaired*. 'Communion' here refers to membership.

[148]Keach, *The Breach Repaired*, ix-x.

somewhat dissatisfied with it, yet I doubt not but will in a little time see their Mistakes, if such busy Men as he do not in an undue manner blow up Coals of Contention amongst us.

Can any sober Christian think that he hath done well to publish the Private Affairs of a particular Church to the whole World? It seems to some as if he has hopes there will be a Breach in the Church, upon the Account of our Singing the Praises of God, but I hope he will find our worthy Brethren understand themselves better than to go about to impose on the Church or Consciences of their Brethren, or to strive to pull down that which the Church and themselves too, have been a building for so many Years. Can there be a man so left of God as to countenance and Persons to make a Schism in a Congregation, because they cannot forgo a Duty they have so long been satisfied in the practice of, and so the whole Body to submit to the sentiments of a few Persons, as if they had Power over our Faith?[149]

It is probable that Marlow also wrote out of a sense that the Particular Baptist churches were heading towards adopting hymn singing in large numbers. By 1691, Keach states that 'above twenty Baptized Congregations' in England besides his own had adopted the practice.[150] Marlow was obviously unhappy with this new action, and published vituperous pamphlets seeking its discontinuance. According to Keach, Marlow used such 'scurrilous' names as '*Error, Apostacy, Human Tradition, prelimited Forms, mischevious Error, Carnal Forms, Carnal Worship,* &c'.[151] Several other men entered the controversy,[152] and the matter erupted onto the national scene.

The exchange of pamphlets turned into a war, and the matter was brought before the Particular Baptist General Assembly in 1692. On the final day of the Assembly, a committee of seven pastors, appointed to examine the literature, returned a verdict indicating that several of the tracts had descended into name-calling, insinuation and censoriousness. In addition, they called for printed retractions on the part of several of the men involved, and named four books which they requested 'that none of the Members of the Churches do buy, give, or disperse any of these Books ... and that no Person do sell them, or give them to others'.[153] Keach printed a retraction and apology for his statements,[154] as did

---

[149]Keach, *Answer*, 8-9.

[150]Keach, *Answer*, 4.

[151]Keach, *Answer*, 5, emphasis his.

[152]Most notable was the entry of William Kiffin, who sided with the opponents of hymn singing. See Kiffin, Barrett, Steed and Man, *A Serious Answer*.

[153]*1692 Narrative*, 9-13. The seven men appointed to examine the literature were Andrew Gifford (Fryars, Bristol); Henry Austine (Norwich); Edmund White (Evershall); John Scott (Richmond); John Willis (Alcester); and Samuel Buttall (Plymouth).

[154]Benjamin Keach, *To all the Baptized Churches and Faithful Brethren in England and Wales* (privately printed pamphlet dated 27 June 1692).

Kiffin, Barrett, Steed and Man,[155] though they were not satisfied with Keach's efforts.[156]

Though the controversy may seem quaint by modern standards, it was taken very seriously by its participants. Keach defended hymn singing as both a moral and a positive duty. These two types of duty must be carefully distinguished. A moral duty is something required of all men, apart from special revelation. Keach illustrates his point by asserting that 'to fear God, to love God, to pray to God, and divers other Precepts of the same Nature' are moral duties owed by men to God their creator, based solely on 'the Law or Light of God in the Conscience of Men'.[157] Praising God through singing is one of these moral duties. A positive duty is something specifically enjoined in Scripture, and for the Baptists, especially in the New Testament. Keach believed that the activity of singing in worship is based on both the moral obligation that all owe to God, and the positive injunctions of Scripture.

The positive duty receives a longer and more detailed treatment, as it rests upon the Regulative Principle of Worship. Keach argues that the New Testament pattern of worship is dependent on God's commands recorded in Scripture, and so states his first proof in this way: 'Because the Lord (who alone appoints his own Worship) hath commanded and required it at our Hands; and his Command and Precept is the Rule of our Obedience'.[158] He then displays an array of Scripture texts which prescribe singing. For Keach, the testimony of God in Scripture is the most fundamental positive demonstration of duty. Since God himself is the only one who can prescribe the elements of divine worship, and because he does prescribe it in many places, it must be a form of true worship.

Isaac Marlow saw the issue quite differently. In his 1694 book *The Purity of Gospel Communion* Marlow summarizes his three major objections to the practice:

> That we have no Command nor Example, neither under the Law, nor under the Gospel for the Ministers, and all the People to sing with united Voices together in the settled worship of God in his Church. And that his [i.e. Keach's] common way of Singing, is not that Mode of spiritual singing which was used in the Apostles time, nor is it the natural, but an Artificial Mode of Worship: and also that we have not the least ground to conclude, that Christ and his Disciples at or after the Lords Supper did sing the Hymn or Praise, which they gave to God, for those Texts, Math. 26.30. Mark 14.26. and Acts 16.25. are not rightly translated in our last Bibles, which are

---

[155]William Kiffin, George Barrette [sic], Robert Steed, and Edward Man, *To the Baptized Churches, their Elders Ministers and Members* (privately printed pamphlet, n.d.).

[156]Kiffin et.al., *To the Baptized Churches*, 1-4.

[157]Keach, *The Breach Repaired*, 22.

[158]Keach, *The Breach Repaired*, 45-46.

witnessed against by many of our old English Bibles, and many learned Authours.[159]

The first of his objections was based on the fact that public worship was almost always attended by a mixture of believers (or church members) and those who make no profession of faith. To allow the unconverted to participate in singing to God in effect profanes worship, as in some cases it does not proceed from a heart purified by faith. If there was any verbal singing in apostolic worship, it must have been done solo, and was probably charismatic, that is, immediately inspired by the Spirit. Similarly, Marlow argued that certain Scriptures prohibited women from speaking,[160] and thus there could not be an indiscriminate practice permitted in the New Testament. Keach responded by arguing that Marlow effectively re-defined singing, making it have no resemblance to the practice of Scripture. While congregational singing has solid attestation in the New Testament, solo singing has no such warrant. So far as women are concerned, the prohibition on speaking is not absolute, as there are several cases in which it is necessary for a woman to speak in church.[161]

The second objection follows along from this. Marlow could not ignore the presence of passages which seemed to permit singing, and so he interpreted them to refer to a spiritual activity, not a literal activity. When he accused Keach of an 'Artificial Mode of Worship' he was implying that verbal singing introduced an element of human invention into worship, and this could not be pleasing to God. True worship is always spiritual, and so the singing mentioned in the New Testament epistles was 'making melody in the heart' but not with the mouth. Keach responded to Marlow by pointing out that such a line of argument is perilously close to that used by the Quakers.[162]

The third objection rests on Marlow's insistence that the Greek word translated 'singing' is better rendered simply as 'giving thanks' and thus does not include verbal melody. Keach responded by citing the best available

---

[159]Marlow, *Purity*, 54-55. The texts from the Gospels refer to the incident at the conclusion of the Last Supper, while the text in Acts refers to Paul and Silas in the Philippian jail.

[160]Keach quotes Marlow, 'Women ought not to sing in the Church, because not suffered to speak in the Church, and also because singing is teaching', *The Breach Repaired*, 139.

[161]Keach, *The Breach Repaired*, 122, 145, 139-41. The cases in which a woman may speak included giving testimony of her conversion during the process of gaining membership, giving testimony in a case of church discipline, and singing. See above.

[162]Keach, *The Breach Repaired*, 137.

authorities, especially the Baptist commentator on Acts C. M. Du Veil,[163] in demonstration of the fact that 'hymns are songs' and thus involve music.[164]

For both of these men, the purity of worship was central. Neither one dissented from the importance of the Regulative Principal. They argued based on very literal understandings of certain passages of Scripture. Though their conclusions were different, in many ways their presuppositions and methodology were the same. Every element of worship must have divine warrant in order to be included in worship. Whether hymn singing was to be incorporated into worship or not had to be demonstrated from Scripture alone.

According to Crosby, as a result of the controversy 'many of [the churches] from that time *sung the praises of God in their publick assemblies*, who had not used the practice before'.[165] Keach's expression of the Regulative Principle seems to have won the day.

Conclusion

The Particular Baptist churches were deeply concerned with worship in the Puritan tradition, guarded by the regulative Principle. Every aspect of their practice was governed by a careful desire to determine the mind of God as revealed in Scripture, and bring these discoveries to fruition. The day of worship, the simplicity of expression, the focus on preaching and the Word of God, and the observance of the ordinances were at the heart of their ecclesiology. They took their creed seriously, and applied it with great rigor to every activity. It was not enough simply to enact one thing or another. If there was warrant in Scripture for doing the practice in a certain fashion, they would do it that way. They wrestled with the text of the Bible, especially the New Testament, to determine the divine approbation of their deeds.

The emphasis on Moral and Positive duties was at the root of their practices. The observance of one day in seven was considered a moral duty; the precise day of observance was dependent on special revelation and could change according to the will of the Law giver. Baptism was a positive expression of Jesus' command, and had no direct link back to circumcision. The New Covenant community was to include believers alone, and the sign of entry

---

[163]C. M. Du Veil, *A Commentary on the Acts of the Apostles* (London: Hanserd Knollys Society, 1851 reprint), 362. Du Veil was a Jew who converted successively to Catholicism, Anglicanism and then became a Baptist. Cf. W. T. Whitley, 'Charles-Marie de Veil' *BQ* 8, no. 8 (October 1937): 444-46; Ivimey, *HEB*, 2:471-475.

[164]Keach, *The Breach Repaired*, 150-51. He says 'this is the old way of such who ever opposed a Truth, when pinch'd, presently fly out upon the Translators, 'tis *so to be read in the Greek*, &c. whereas all the World knows, that as our translators were able Scholars, so they were very holy and upright Men: Besides, our Annotators, and all Expositors, generally say 'tis truly rendered', 151, emphasis his. In effect, Marlow's argument is simply special pleading.

[165]Crosby, *CHEB*, 3:270-71.

could not be extended beyond them, even to their children. Even in defense of singing, the moral and the positive take on importance.

The precepts of Scripture were central in the worship of these churches. Christianity was a religion of one book, and it deserved careful and prudent attention. It was God's Word, and of necessity had to be obeyed. If God was to be enjoyed as a personal God, that enjoyment would come by means of his stipulations and nothing else. For these churches, that is what God-centered religion was all about.

CHAPTER 6

'So the churches, ... ought to hold communion amongst themselves': Associations of Churches

From[1] their very beginning, the Particular Baptist churches believed in and practiced inter-church communion. They held that the independence of local churches did not mean isolation, and put this belief into practice by means of associations,[2] originally called 'General Meetings'.[3] The First London Confession of 1644 was issued through the cooperative efforts of seven London churches, and the political climate of the 1650s provided opportunities for several regional associations to organize and function.[4] The ebb and flow of persecution and toleration during the uncertain days of the reigns of Charles II and James II tended to drive the churches into survival mode and thus hindered extensive involvement with others.[5] It was not until after the accession of

---

[1]Some portions of this chapter have been published as James M. Renihan, *A Reformed Baptist Perspective on Associations of Churches* (La Mirada, Calif.: Reformed Baptist Publications, 1997).

[2]Scholarly treatments of the history of Baptist Associations are many. See, for example, Slayden A. Yarborough, 'The Origin of Baptist Associations Among the English Particular Baptists', *BHH* 23, no. 2 (April 1988): 14-24; White, 'The Doctrine of the Church', 583 ff.; White, 'The Organization of the Particular Baptists', 216 ff.; Geoffrey F. Nuttall, 'The Baptist Western Association 1653-1658', *Journal of Ecclesiastical History* 11 (1960): 213-218.

[3]White, 'Doctrine of the Church', 585.

[4]The text of the 1644 Confession may be found in Lumpkin, *BCF*, 153-171; the minutes of several regional associations have been transcribed in White, *ARPB*.

[5]Nevertheless, there are examples of the ongoing activity of Associations, even in the darkest days of persecution. For instance, the Petty France church in London records the following in its manuscript church book: 'Mar 24 [1677] Bro: Coxe was appointed to go as a messenger from this church to ye meeting of the messengers of the associated churches to be had at Hempstead the 2d day of the 2d M:1678. Apr: 7th Br. Coxe gave an account of the comfortable issue of the meeting of ye messengers of the Associated Churches, and of their desire that for the future some brethren in the behalf of this & other congregations in ye citye may be as occasion is offered appointed to assist them in their meetings.' On 22 September, Coxe was again appointed to attend an association meeting to be held at Abingdon on 24 September, and on 20 April, 1679, Coxe and his co-elder William Collins were appointed to attend an association meeting to be held that

William and Mary in 1688 that the Baptists (and other Dissenters as well) were truly free to hold public meetings. The leaders of the Particular Baptists in London responded quickly to the new opportunity, and sent out a letter of invitation in which they called for a General Assembly to meet in September 1689. At that meeting, they publicly endorsed what has been variously called the Assembly Confession, or the Second London Confession, or the 1689 Baptist Confession of Faith.

In chapter 26 of that Confession, the theological *rationale* for the practice of associations was expressed in these terms:

> 14. As each *Church*, and all the Members of it are bound to pray (d) continually, for the good and prosperity of all the *Churches* of *Christ*, in all places; and upon all occasions to further it (every one within the bounds of their places, and callings, in the Exercise of their Gifts and Graces) so the *Churches* (when planted by the providence of God so as they may injoy opportunity and advantage for it) ought to hold (e) communion amongst themselves for their peace, increase of love, and mutual edification.
>
> (d) Eph. 6.18. Ps. 122.6.
> (e) Rom. 16.1,2. 3 Joh. 8,9,10.
>
> 15. In cases of difficulties or differences, either in point of Doctrine, or Administration; wherein either the Churches in general are concerned, or any one Church in their peace, union, and edification; or any member or members of any Church are injured, in or by any proceedings in censures not agreeable to truth, and order: it is according to the mind of Christ, that many Churches holding communion together, do by their messengers meet to consider, (f) and give their advice, in or about that matter in difference, to be reported to all the Churches concerned; howbeit these messengers assembled are not entrusted with any Church-power properly so called; or with any jurisdiction over the Churches themselves, to exercise any censures either over any Churches, or Persons: or (g)to impose their determination on the Churches, or Officers.
>
> (f) Act. 15.2,4,6. & 22,23.25.
> (g) 2 Cor. 1.24. 1 Joh. 4.1.[6]

These words are consistent with the doctrine of the Universal church expressed earlier on in the chapter, and with the established practices of the churches over a period of almost fifty years. The task here is to examine certain statements in

---

week in London. Attendance at such meetings is regularly noted in the manuscript. Petty France *CMB*, 7-10. It should be remembered that according to the old reckoning then current, March 24 was the final day of 1677 (though March was considered as the first month of the new year), and so the 2d day of the 2d month 1678 would have been 2 April. See also Dowley, 'A London Congregation during the Great Persecution', 233-239.
[6]*A Confession of Faith*, 92-94. Emphasis in original.

these paragraphs in order to discern how these churches understood and practiced what they confessed in these words.

The catholicity of true churches is acknowledged in the first part of paragraph 14, emphasizing the part that all true churches have in the universal body of Christ. But in the latter section of the paragraph, a realistic assessment of the relations of churches is introduced. There are certain churches that are 'planted by the providence of God' in such a way as to have special responsibilities to one another, described in the phrase, 'they ought to hold communion among themselves'. The Baptists confess that there is an obligation placed on certain churches within geographic proximity to hold communion among themselves. The matter is not one of convenience, but of 'oughtness'.

At this point, an investigation into the meaning of the word 'communion' is essential to an understanding of their ecclesiology. The method will be to investigate its use in contemporary ecclesiological literature, and to flesh out the practice from examples in the church books.

The Meaning of 'Communion' in Chapter 26:14&15

The *Oxford English Dictionary* provides several definitions of the word which seem to have been in use at the end of the seventeenth century. Among them are

> 1. Sharing or holding in common; participation (1382); 2. Fellowship, association in actions or relations; spiritual intercourse (1553); 3. The fellowship or mutual relation between members of the same church, or of bodies which recognize each other as branches of the church Catholic (1386), letter of communion: a certificate of church membership; 4. An organic union of persons united by common religious faith and rites; a church or denomination; the organized body professing one faith (1565).[7]

By examining the Baptists' use of the word 'communion', it will be possible to determine which of these meanings was intended in the Confessional statements.

'Communion' in the Confession of Faith

In the Confession itself, the word appears eleven times in six different chapters: *Of God and of the Holy Trinity* (1 time*); Of Creation* (1 time); *Of the fall of Man, of Sin, and of the Punishment thereof* (1 Time); *Of the Church* (2 times); *Of the Communion of Saints* (4 times); and *Of the Lord's Supper* (2 times). The first three occurrences all relate to personal communion with God. The doctrine of the Trinity is said to be the foundation of all communion with God; the first man and woman were happy in their original communion with God; and by the

---

[7]*The Oxford English Dictionary* 2nd ed., s.v. 'communion'. The numbers in parentheses refer to the earliest attestation dates for these senses of the term.

fall they lost their communion with God. In each of these cases, communion relates to profound personal mutuality. There is a true depth of fellowship and participation. It may be possible to see a reflection of the first two senses of 'communion' above, but on a more profound theological level.[8]

The other occurrences all relate to ecclesiology. Chapter 27 of the Second London Confession, entitled *Of the Communion of Saints*, reads as follows:

> 1. All *Saints* that are united to Jesus Christ their *Head*, by his Spirit, and Faith; although they are not made thereby one person with him, have (a) fellowship in His Graces, sufferings, death, resurrection, and glory; and being united to one another in love, they (b) have communion in each others gifts, and graces; and are obliged to the performance of such duties, publick and private, in an orderly way,(c) as do conduce to their mutual good, both in the inward and outward man.
>
> (a) 1 Joh. 1.3. Joh. 1.16. Phil. 3.10 Rom. 6.5,6.
> (b) Eph. 4.15,16. 1 Cor. 12.7. 3.21,22,23.
> (c) 1 Thes. 5.11.14. Rom. 1.12. 1 Joh. 3.17.18. Gal 6.10.
>
> 2. *Saints* by profession[9] are bound to maintain an holy fellowship and communion in the worship of God, and in performing such other spiritual services, (d) as tend to their mutual edification; as also in relieving each other in (e) outward things according to their several abilities, and necessities; which communion according to the rule of the Gospel, though especially to be exercised by them, in the relations wherein they stand, whether in (f) families, or (g) Churches; yet as God offereth opportunity is to be extended to all the household of faith, even all those who in every place call upon the name of the Lord Jesus; nevertheless their communion one with another as *Saints*, doth not take away or (h) infringe, the title or propriety, which each man hath in his goods and possessions.
>
> (d) Heb. 10.24,25. With ch. 3.12,13.
> (e) Act. 12.29.30.[10]
> (f) Eph. 6.4.
> (g) 1 Cor. 12.14.-27.
> (h) Act. 5.4 Eph. 4.28.[11]

These uses reflect the foundation of communion in the doctrine of the Trinity and Creation. The mutuality of fellowship with Christ is the paradigm for

---

[8]Benjamin Keach extensively discussed this subject in *Parables: Series One*, 420-428. He said, 'true fellowship consisteth in community or communion', p. 422.

[9]The Baptist Confession unexpectedly follows the wording of the Westminster Confession at this point. The Savoy Declaration reads 'All Saints are bound ....' This may be the only place where the Baptists prefer the reading of Westminster over against that of Savoy. Cf. Waldron, *Modern Exposition*, 428.

[10]Since Acts 12 has only 25 verses, this should probably be corrected to read Acts 11.29,30. These verses fit the context of the Confession's statement.

[11]*A Confession of Faith*, 94-95.

church members' communion with each other. As all saints are members of the universal church, they have, in some sense, fellowship with one another in Christ. In the second paragraph, communion is placed in the concrete sphere of the family and of the local church. It evidences itself in worship, spiritual service, and in the necessity of personal relief, but it does not devolve into communism (to use the word anachronistically). It is interesting to note that these obligations are specifically set in formal spheres, namely the family and the church.

The word occurs two times in chapter 30, *Of the Lord's Supper.* The first is found in a description of the institution of the Supper, saying that it is 'to be a bond and pledge of their communion with him, and with each other'. Participation in the Supper exhibits the mutuality of Christ and his people, as well as among themselves. The second is found in the eighth paragraph, stating that 'All ignorant and ungodly persons, as they are unfit to enjoy communion with *Christ*; so are they unworthy of the Lord's Table.' Both of these uses seem to reflect that of the earlier sense of profound personal mutuality. Christ and his people have an intimate bond which is reflected in the observance of the Lord's Table.[12]

In all of these uses of communion, there is a reflection of the theological realities at work in the relationships between God and his people. Communion is an aspect of a concrete relationship, enjoyed or broken, but nevertheless very real. In no case does the word mean simply 'sharing' or 'occasional fellowship'.

When one reads the word in chapter 26, the simple sense of sharing or fellowship again seems inadequate. The practice of inter-church communion among the Particular Baptists was not simply expressions of Christian friendship, but was formal and structured. The ecclesiological and theological climate of the Confession tends to lead one to invest another sense into the meaning of communion as it is used to refer to inter-church relationships. Could 'communion' in paragraphs 14 and 15 of chapter 26 refer to something more like 'an organic union of persons united by common religious faith and rites; ...the organized body professing one faith'[13] as in the dictionary definition?

'Communion' in Ecclesiological Writings

An examination of some contemporary uses of the term sheds light on its use in this part of the Confession. In 1681, Hanserd Knollys, one of the public subscribers to the Confession in 1689, used the word in his book *The World that Now is; and the World that is to Come* in the midst of a discussion of separation from evil in the world. He was seeking to give counsel to those who found themselves in true but defective churches and urged them not to remove

---

[12]*A Confession of Faith*, 99, 102.
[13]*The Oxford English Dictionary*, s.v. 'communion'. According to the diachronic evidence, this sense is well attested in ecclesiological literature since at least 1565.

themselves from membership in their churches, arguing from Christ's dealings with the seven churches in Revelation 2 and 3. He says,

> neither did Christ blame any Believers that were sound in their Judgments, and holy in their Conversations for holding Communion with those Churches.... Therefore I conclude That none of the Ministers nor Members of any true Church of God ought to separate themselves from the Church; nor ought they to forsake the Assembling of themselves with the Church, nor absent themselves from any part of the true Worship of God, nor turn their back of any Gospel-Ordinance of Christ in the Church, because of Offence against any Member or Minister in the Church.[14]

Knollys was speaking to individuals who faced certain difficult situations in local churches, and he urged them to maintain their 'communion' with their churches while there was still a vestige of the truth there. In this case, the term clearly means more than fellowship: it means membership. They must not be quick to remove their membership, but wait to see if perhaps Christ will win the church back to a fully Scriptural position.[15]

---

[14]Knollys, *The World that Now is*, 98.

[15]There is another intriguing matter in Knollys' book which may have some bearing on this issue. In several places, he asserts that there should only be one church in each city or locality, though there may be several congregations or churches which make up this one church. He says, 'The Church at Jerusalem was the first of all those Gospel-Churches ... Which Church was at its first Constitution a particular Congregation of sanctified Believers baptized with Water ... And although the number of the Disciples were multiplied from one hundred and twenty ... to three thousand ... yea to five thousand ... So that the Apostles had their own distinct Companies, Societies, or Congregations in Jerusalem [Act. 4.13,19,23 ....] Yet they all being of one heart, and of one soul, were but one church .... And so were all the particular Congregations in every City denominated and called.... Gospel-Oneness which maketh very much for the Well-Being of a particular Church is threefold: First, That there be but ONE Church in one City; and that all the Congregations of Saints in that City (called Churches) bear but one Name, to wit, the Church of God in that City, as in the Apostles daies, Act. 15.4.22. 1 Cor. 1.2. That so there may be no Schism, Divisions, nor sinful Separations from the Church of God; but that the whole church may be perfectly joyned together in ONE, As a City that is compact together, Psal. 122.3. as an House or Building fitly framed together, Ephes. 2.21,22. and as a Body fitly joyned and compacted by every joynt of supply, Eph. 4.16.' *The World that Now is*, 44-45, 50-51. He goes on to argue that oneness also consists in being of one heart and soul, seeking to love one another, and thirdly that all of the saints must walk by the same rule, submitting to the bishops, pastors, teachers, presbyters, or elders set over them. Further on in the book, he gives lengthy attention to his conviction that the church in each city should choose one of the elders of the churches to have 'Priority, Presidence, and Pre-eminence' over the other elders! He says, 'I mean and intend any one of the Bishops, Pastors, Teachers, Presbyters, or Elders, who are, or shall by the Consent, Approbation and Choice of the rest be appointed, ordained, and set over them as Chief Bishop or Presbyter of the

Another important subscriber to the Confession, William Kiffin, also published a book in 1681, entitled *A Sober Discourse of Right to Church-Communion*.[16] This was a long-overdue response to John Bunyan dealing with the issue of the relationship between baptism and church membership. Bunyan was the leading defender of what has come to be called the Open-membership view of the local church. This position argued that baptism has nothing to do with church membership. The gospel, not baptism, establishes the church, and the insistence on baptism for membership undermines the centrality of the gospel in the church. Kiffin wrote in response to defend the position of the London Baptists who insisted that the Scriptures taught that baptism was essential for orderly membership in the local church.[17] In describing the practice of most of the Dissenting churches, he argues that 'their avowed Principle is, to admit none into Church-Fellowship or Communion, that are Unbaptized'.[18] For Kiffin, Communion implies a formal union.

A similar position may be found in Hercules Collins' 1682 work *Some Reasons for Separation from the Communion of the Church of England*. This brief booklet is an imaginary dialogue between a 'Conformist' (a member of the Church of England) and a 'Nonconformist' (one who has separated from the Church of England). Collins uses this dialogue format to answer the claims of the established church to exclusive loyalty from all of the citizens of the land. The nonconformist leads the conformist through a series of issues relating to true worship, the observance of the ordinances, and liberty of conscience in

---

Church in any City and Villages adjacent, who for Order sake in Gospel-Government, hath Priority, Pre-eminence, and Authority above the rest of the Presbyters or Bishops of the same Church, not alone, nor without them, but when Convened with them, to Act, Rule, Guide, Order and Govern with their Consent, Suffrage and Assistance, according to the Laws of the Lord Jesus Christ, the Constitutions and Commandments, the Practice and Example of his Holy Apostles, Act. 15.2,6,19,22.' *The World that Now is*, 68-69 (see 55-69). This is a high view of inter-church communion!

[16]William Kiffin, *A Sober Discourse of Right to Church-Communion* (London: Geo. Larkin, 1681).

[17]Bunyan's works on the subject were: 'A Confession of My Faith, and Reason of My Practice; or, with whom I can hold Church Fellowship'; 'Difference in Judgment about Water-Baptism no bar to Communion'; and 'Peaceful Principles and True; or, a Brief answer to Mr. D. and Mr. P. about Water-Baptism'. *The Complete Works of John Bunyan*, 2:203-259. 'Mr. D.' is Henry Danvers, and 'Mr. P.' is Thomas Paul. Bunyan's use of 'communion' is important to note. He does not refer primarily to participation at the Lord's Table, but to 'Church Fellowship, or the Communion of Saints'. It came to be identified with the observance of the Lord's Table because, as William Kiffin said, 'it is that Ordinance of Christ wherein the Communion of the Church doth chiefly consist', *Sober Discourse*, 22. Cf. White, 'Open and Closed Membership', 330-334, 341; Harry Poe, 'John Bunyan's Controversy with the Baptists' *BHH* 23, no. 2, (April, 1988): 25-35; Christopher Hill, *A Turbulent, Seditious, and Factious People: John Bunyan and His Church* (Oxford: Oxford University Press, 1988) 292-95.

[18]Kiffin *Sober Discourse*, 2. See also pages 16-17, 29.

order to demonstrate that the Scriptures require believers to come out from the national Church, in spite of its claims to allegiance, whatever the consequences may be. To separate from 'the communion of the Church of England' means formally renouncing its doctrines and practices, and joining with those who follow the Scriptures in truth. It is to deny that membership in the Church is national and based on political law, and to affirm that a true church is

> A society of Persons called out of the World, or their natural worldly State, by the Administration of the Word and Spirit, into the obedience of the Faith of the Knowledge of the Worship of God in Christ, joyned together in a Holy Bond, or by special Agreement for the Exercise of the Communion of Saints and due Observation of all the Ordinances of the Gospel.[19]

Such a definition could not apply to a national church, and so it is incumbent on all true Christians to forsake that 'communion' for one that more closely meets the Scriptural pattern. The 'communion' of the national church is thus not merely fellowship, but formal membership.

In these cases, the use of the term 'communion' seems to carry the third sense of the *Oxford English Dictionary*, 'The fellowship or mutual relation between members of the same church ...certificate of church membership'.[20] A very real and formal relationship is established and maintained. The level of permanency in these connections is of importance in understanding the ecclesiological use of the term in the Confession.

'Communion' as 'Organic Union' in Associational Records

The sense of 'communion' as 'an organic union of persons united by common religious faith and rites ...the organized body professing one faith'[21] may be noticed in the records of the Particular Baptist Associations. As early as 1644, seven churches in London joined together to publish a confession of faith. This act is described in the so-called 'Kiffin Manuscript' as follows:

> Those that ware so minded had comunion togeather were become Seven Churches in London.

> Mr. Green wth Capt Spencer had begun a Congregation in Crutched Fryers, to whom Paul Hobson joyned who was now wth many of that Church one of ye Seven.

---

[19]Collins, *Some Reasons for Separation*, 4. This is a direct quote from John Owen's 'A Brief Instruction in the Worship of God'. Cf. *Works of Owen*, 15:479. The Banner of Truth edition reads 'Holy Band' instead of 'Holy Bond'. The latter seems to fit the context of the statement more precisely.

[20]*The Oxford English Dictionary*, s.v. 'communion'.

[21]*The Oxford English Dictionary*, s.v. 'communion'.

These being much spoken against as unsound in Doctrine as if they ware Armenians, & also against Magistrates &c they joyned togeather in a Confession of their Faith in Fifty two Articles wch gave great satisfaction to many that had been prejudiced.

Thus Subscribed in ye Names of 7 Churches in London.[22]

This early use by the Baptists is interesting. It may imply a formal unity among these churches. Clearly, they desired mutual identification by the issuance of this Confession. In that document, they also hinted at the necessity of associations:

And Although the particular Congregations be distinct and severall Bodies, every one a compact and knit Citie in it selfe; yet are they all to walk by one and the same Rule, and by all meanes convenient to have the counsell and help one of another in all needfull affaires of the Church, as members of one body in the common faith under Christ their onely head.[23]

The theme of oneness in the body of Christ points to a clear desire for visible unity, and will be noted as a Scriptural justification for associations below. The pattern which appears to have been established in London was repeated as churches were planted in other parts of the country.[24] Commenting on the statement in the 1644 Confession, B. R. White said,

The importance of this principle for the first generation of Calvinistic Baptists cannot, I believe, be over-estimated: the duty of fellowship both within individual congregations and between congregations was regarded as of immense importance. In the first generation they no more believed that an individual church should be free to go its own way regardless of other congregations than that an individual believer could be a serious Christian without commitment to a local, visible congregation.[25]

This is undoubtedly true. The practices of these churches were molded from the start by a profound concern for church communion.

---

[22]*TBHS* 1 (1908-1909): 235-36. The entry is followed by the names of the men who subscribed the Confession, among whom are William Kiffin and John Spilsbury. Notably absent from this list is the name of Samuel Richardson.

[23]Lumpkin, *Baptist Confessions*, 168-69.

[24]In 1653, the Abingdon Association sent a letter with this inscription: 'To the church of Christ of which our brethren John Spilsberie and William Kiffin are members and to the rest of the churches in and neere London, agreeing with the said church in principles and constituitions and accordingly holding communion with the same, the churches of Abington, Reading, Henlie, Kensworth and Eversholt send greeting.' White, *ARPB*, 131.

[25]B. R. White, 'The Origins and Convictions of the First Calvinistic Baptists', *BHH* 25, no. 4 (Oct. 1990): 46-47.

In the 1650s, several regional associations were formed, and their records shed light on the matter of inter-church communion. At the second meeting of the Midlands Association on 26 June 1656, an agreement which served as something of a constitution for the Association was adopted. It states:

> The Lord our God having, according to his free and infinite mercy, given us to be in his sonn Jesus Christ and in himself through him and to be baptized into his name and to walke in distinct churches and assemblies of Zion; according to the rule of his word, according to the measure and knowledg of grace which he hath bestowed upon us and given unto us to agree in the same principles ...we do therefore, according to the will of God, clearly apearing in his word, with true thankfullnes unto him for his grace, mutually acknowledg each other to be true churches of Christ, and that it is our duty to hold a close communion each to other as the Lord shall give opportunity and abillity, endeavouring that we may all increase more and more in faith and knowledg and in all purity and holiness to the honour of our God, and it is our resolution, in the strength of Christ, to endeavour thus to doe.[26]

These words approximate and anticipate those of the Second London Confession. They were subscribed by representatives of seven churches, including Warwick, Morton (Moreton-in-Marsh), Alchester (Alcester), Teuxbury (Tewksbury), and Hook Norton, all of which sent representatives to the London General Assembly in 1689. Following the names of the subscribers, an explanation of the implications of this agreement is provided, further defining their understanding of what 'close communion' implies:

> Forasmuch as the churches ... doe mutually acknowledg each other to be true churches of Christ and that it is their duty to hold a clos communion each with other according to the rule of his worde and soe be helpefull each to other as God shall give opertunitie and abillitie and these churches are now desired to consider that they acknowledg each other and are faithfully to hold such communion each with other and to endever to be helpful each to other:
> 1. In giving of advice after searious consultation and deliberation in matters and controversies remaining doubtfull to any perticular church as plainly apeareth in the churches of Jerusalem and Antioch. Acts 15.
> 2. In giving and receiving allsoe in case of poverty and wante of any perticular churches as appeareth in the approved and due acting of the churches of the Gentiles towards the churches of Jerusalem. Ro. 15.26f.
> 3. In sending their gifted brethren to use their giftes for the edification of the churches that need the same: as they shall see it seasonable, as the church at Jerusalem sente Barnabas to Antioch. Acts 11.22.
> 4. In a joynt caring on of any worke of the Lord that is common to the churches as they shall have oppertunty to joyne therein to the glory of God as apeareth in 2 Cor. 8.19.
> 5. In watching over each other and considering each other for good in respect of puritie of doctrine, exercise of love and good conversation: they

---

[26]White, *Origins,* 20.

being all members of the same body of Christ, I. Cor. 12.12 who therefore
ought to have care one of another, I Cor. 12.29 especially considering how
the glory of God is concerned in their standing and holi conversation.[27]

This is immediately followed by the words 'the churches now associated' and
details the issues to be considered by them. This was a formal agreement,
approved by messengers 'authorised and appoynted' by their churches for the
purpose of establishing a formal association. Communion was not merely
fellowship in the gospel, it was mutual recognition, support and commitment.
Over the course of the next few years, other churches sought membership in the
association, including Lemster (Leominster) September, 1657; Gloster
(Gloucester) and Bewdley, both April, 1658.[28] Each of these applications
required formal action on the part of the messengers to the association
meetings.

The Abingdon Association was begun by messengers sent from three
churches in October 1652. These messengers proposed a series of conclusions
justifying their actions, beginning with: 'That perticular churches of Christ
ought to hold a firme communion each with other ....'[29] On 17 March 1653,
messengers from five churches, Abingdon, Henley, Reading, Kensworth and
Eversholt[30] confirmed and subscribed the following:

> The Agreement of certaine churches, viz., of Abington, Reading, Henley,
> Kensworth and Eversholt.
>
> Whereas the Lord hath made it appeare unto us by the holy Scriptures that
> true churches of Christ ought to acknowledge one another to be such and to
> hold a firme communion each with other in point of advice in things
> remaining doubtfull to any particular church or churches as also in giving
> and receiving in case of the want and povertie of any particular church or
> churches and in consulting and consenting (as need shall require and as shall
> be most for the glorie of God) to the joynt carying on of the worke of the
> Lord that is common to the churches. And the same Lord hath made us to
> discerne and minde our agreement in our principles and constitutions and to
> be preswaded (as we hope upon good grounds) of each other's endeavouring
> to walke accordingly. We doe therefore hereby declare that we doe mutually

---

[27]White, *Origins*, 20-21.
[28]White, *Origins*, 33, 37.
[29]White, *ARPB*, 126; see also page 127. The first Scriptural justification for their
practice is of interest. They argued that the relations of individual churches in the body
of Christ are analogous to those of individual Christians in distinct local churches. Just
as every believer is to be a member of the body of Christ (i.e. local church), so also local
churches are to be members of the visible body of Christ: 'in respect of union in Christ
there is a like relation betwixt the particular churches each towards other, as there is
betwixt particular members of one church. For the churches of Christ doe all make up
but one bodye or church in generall under Christ their head, as Eph. 1.22f., Col. 1.24,
Eph. 5.23ff., 1 Cor. 12.13ff.', White, *ARPB*, 126, 128.
[30]Of these founding churches, only Henley was not represented at the 1689 Assembly.

acknowledge each other to be true churches of Christ and doe agree (according to our dutye) to maintaine a strict communion each with other in the particulars aforementioned and, whatsoever else we shall discerne the Word of God to require true churches to hold communion in; and, accordingly, doe engage ourselves in the strength of Christ and through his grace, faithfully to performe each towards other such dutyes of churches so joyning together to the glorie of God.[31]

Once again, 'firme communion' involves formal union and mutual acknowledgment. It is not merely fellowship among churches of like mind. It is formal association, 'joyning together to the glorie of God'.

After entering into this agreement, the associated churches desired to communicate with their friends in London, and at the 4 June 1653 meeting a letter was composed and approved for sending to John Spilsbury and William Kiffin. It said,

The Lord our God having made us lay to heart how the churches of Christ in the apostles' dayes held a firme communion each with other and how necessarie it was for us to endeavour to doe the same, as it becometh particular assemblyes which make up but one Mount Syon, Is. 4.5, that we might endeavour to keep each other pure and to cleare the profession of the Gospell from scandall and to manifest our love to all the saints, and thereby [to mani-] fest ourselves to be true churches of Christ and that we [may] shew ourselves sensible of the need that we have, or may have, of one another and that the worke of God, wherein all the churches are concerned, might be the better caried on by a combination of counsells, prayers and endeavours. Through the assistance of the same God (after many conferences and seeking to the Lord) we solemnly entered into such an association each with other as this enclosed copie of our Agreement doth manifest.[32]

Firm communion necessitates association.

The formality of association is further confirmed by the following note from the eleventh General Meeting, held at Tetsworth on 19-20 June 1655:

At this meeting the churches of Wantage, Watlington, Kingston and Hadnam were received into association by the expresse consent of the churches before associated and did by their messengers subscribe the agreement of the associated churches.[33]

Similar notations are made when Pirton (October 1655), Oxford and Hempsteed (Hemel Hempstead) (March 1656) joined the association.[34] At the

---

[31]White, *ARPB*, 129.

[32]White, *ARPB*, 131. Words in brackets are conjectures supplied by the editor.

[33]White, *ARPB*, 139.

[34]Of these churches, Wantage, Hadnam (Haddenham), Oxford, and Hempsteed (Hemel Hempstead) sent messengers to the 1689 General Assembly.

September 1656 meeting, a letter from the church at North Warmborow was presented and discussed. It spoke of that church's appreciation for 'your love and tendernes towards us and your readiness to receive us into communion and association with you and so under your care'.[35]

When the churches located at the eastern side of the association (Kensworth, Eversholt, Pirton and Hempsteed) requested the formation of a more local association at the October 1657 meeting, an official act of the messengers was required. The matter was sent back to the member churches, and approved at the next meeting held on 30 March 1658. Their communion could not be severed without a mutual agreement, and this was done gladly:

> we, as the messengers of the said respective churches, and by their appointment, doe lovingly and solemnly, as in our Father's presence, committ and commend you ... to be henceforth a distinct association and to receive into association with you in an orderly way any such churches of Christ, true and right in constitution and principles and sutable walking, as shall be readie so to joyne with you.[36]

These facts are of real importance in understanding the sense of 'communion' in chapter 26:14&15 of the Second London Confession. Many of the churches subscribing churches had been part of long-standing regional associations which practiced formal membership and were constituted upon strict lines. There is every reason to believe that the sense intended in the Confession is consonant with these well established practices. It would seem that these terms, when used in paragraphs 14 and 15 of chapter 26, are referring to formal associations rather than to informal or occasional fellowship, or councils called for specific crises.[37] In the associational records, 'communion' means 'an organic union of persons united by common religious faith and rites; ... the organized body professing one faith'.[38]

---

[35]White, *ARPB*, 140, 145, 162.

[36]White, *ARPB*, 181-82.

[37]The Baptists were not alone in using the term in this sense. Independents used it similarly. Philip Nye and Thomas Goodwin spoke of 'an association or communion of churches' in their preface to John Cotton's *The Keys of the Kingdom*, and Cotton himself speaks of a 'holy covenant or communion' between churches. See Larzer Ziff, ed., *John Cotton on the Churches of New England* (Cambridge, Mass.: The Belknap Press, 1968), 75, 158. In the northwest counties, 'The Agreement of the Associated Ministers & Churches of the Counties of Cumberland and Westmoreland' spoke of their desire 'that several churches should hold communion and correspondency together; and to that end we resolve to associate our selves', Walker, *The Creeds and Platforms of Congregationalism*, 454. Walker provides substantial evidence of the willingness of the Independents to enter into formal church unions, idem, *Creeds*, 442. See also Allan Brockett, *Nonconformity in Exeter* (Manchester: University Press, 1962), 8-10 and Yarborough, 'The Origin of Baptist Associations', 18-22.

[38]*The Oxford English Dictionary*, s.v. 'communion'.

'Communion' in the Documents of the General Assemblies

The General Assemblies which met in London from 1689 to 1693 published, or gave approbation to several published works. An examination of the use of the word 'communion' in some of those documents is of relevance to this topic.

In the 1689 *Narrative*, the term is used twice. The first instance occurs in the seven 'rules for our proceeding' adopted at the beginning of the Assembly. It refers to church membership:

> That in those things wherein one Church differs from another Church in their Principles or Practices, in point of Communion, that we cannot, shall not, impose upon any particular Church therein, but leave every church to their own liberty, to walk together as they have received from the Lord.[39]

The issue here is that of open versus closed membership. At the General Assembly, churches of both persuasions were present.[40] It clearly has the sense 'requirements for membership' in each local church.

The other occurrence is in the questions proposed to the Assembly. It was asked

> Q. What is to be done with those Persons that withdraw themselves from the Fellowship of that particular Church of which they are Members, and join themselves to the Communion of the National Church?

> A. To use all due means to reclaim them by Instruction and Admonition; and if not thereby reclaimed, to reject them.[41]

In this case, communion clearly means formal membership.

The term is used once in the 1690 *Narrative*, and sheds much light on the current investigation. At the 1689 meeting, a Fund was established which was intended to provide financial relief for pastors whose churches were unable to give them significant monetary support, and for the education of promising young men for the ministry. Nine men from London churches were appointed as trustees of the Fund, charged with receiving and disbursing the money collected. The 1690 Assembly seems to have spent much of its time considering matters related to the Fund. The *Narrative* records the following entries:

> That Brother *Gregory Page*, Brother *R. Carter*, and Brother *Humphrey Burroughs* be added to the nine Treasurers appointed for the Fund. Resolved also, that any five of the said twelve Brethren may act and do any business.

---

[39]1689 *Narrative*, 10.

[40]The vast majority of churches were closed membership. Broadmead, Bristol is an example of an open membership church.

[41]1689 *Narrative*, 14.

That every particular Congregation contributing towards the Fund, do signify to the Trustees when they send any Sum of Money to them, what particular use they design it for, or how much for one use, and how much for another of the said Sum, and keep a distinct Account of it.

That the particular Cases of those poor Ministers that have not been concluded on by this Assembly, are left to the Trustees of the Fund to act concerning them as in the direction given in the Narrative of the last Assembly.

For the better settling of the Churches, and maintaining the Fund, and amicable Communion one with another;
Resolved,
I. That all the Churches that can, should have their Associations of several Counties together once or more a Year, according as they shall in respect of their distance agree.
II. That of each Association, two Persons should be chosen to visit all the Churches of that Association once in the Year, for the Ends following.
1. Besides preaching to them, to enquire what orderly Officers are amongst them, and press them that are short therein to come up to the Rule, and that Care be taken in each Association to lend all needful Assistance.
2. To enquire what Provision they made for their Minister, whether it be according to their Minister's Necessity and the Churches Ability, that their Ministers may give themselves more to the Work of the Lord.
3. That where any member lie short of their Duty, they endeavour to stir them up to it.
4. Where Churches are that have Ministers that have no need, and will not receive, that they be stirred up to do what they can to the Fund.
5. Those Churches who are able to maintain their own Minister, and can do something to the Fund, be stirred up thereto.
6. That when a Church hath done all they can do to their utmost, and all will not be sufficient, then those Messengers do acquaint their respective Association, and they together do consider what may be needful to be had out of the Fund: and also what Gifted Brethren in each Division are desirous to learn the Tongues, shall be presented to the Association, and if approved, then by them to the Trustees.
7. That no Minister that receives of the Fund should be any of those Messengers, if others can be had.

And in order to the effecting these things:

1. That a Division be made of all the Churches into Associations, and commended to all the Churches good liking.
2. That a Catalogue of all the Ministers that need Supplies out of the Fund, be made by the Trustees against the next General Meeting.
3. That an Account be given what is like to be the Yearly Income of the Fund.
4. That no Messengers be sent to visit Churches out of the Fund's Cost, except in extraordinary Cases.
5. That Seeing the Churches in the Country are at so much Charge in their Associations, and sending of their Messengers to *London*, that the Churches

in *London* would send Messengers into the Country to preach the Gospel, or to plant Churches at their own particular Charge, except in extraordinary cases.

6. That the Churches would speedily associate in their respective Divisions in order to the executing of the aforesaid things.[42]

In this case, 'communion' is extensively defined in terms of the ordering and functioning of associations. The annual meeting at London sought to encourage the on-going work of existing regional associations, and used the management of the Fund as a means by which this might be accomplished. Each local association was encouraged to develop a method by which its constituent churches might be visited annually, both for inquiring into the status of each church's ministry, and to encourage participation in the Fund.

Especially interesting is the sentence 'That where any member lie short of their Duty, they endeavour to stir them up to it.' Does 'member' refer to individual persons in membership in local churches, or does it refer to the churches as 'members' of the associations? While it may be impossible to determine with certainty, it would seem better to understand the word in the latter sense referring to local churches. In the context, the phrase 'to stir them up to it' appears two other times, and in each case refers to a church's participation in the Fund. The concern of the visitation is not that the messengers have bishop-like powers over the churches and members of the churches, but rather that participation in the Fund might be encouraged among the associated churches.

This lengthy section of the 1690 *Narrative* seems to support the idea that 'communion' as described in 26:14-15 of the Second London Confession refers to formal membership in associations.

In the 1691 *Narrative*, churches are specifically called 'members' in several places. Most noteworthy is the following:

> For the preserving of Peace and Concord amongst the Churches of our Association; in a due Tenderness to all the Members in communion with us, the following Questions were proposed, and Answers concluded thereupon as followeth ....[43]

Communion implies membership in the association. There is a significant stylistic parallelism in this statement. The elements of the first clause 'the Churches of our Association' are repeated in the next clause, only in different terms 'the Members in communion with us'. The two phrases are functionally equivalent in the context, and define the nature of the relationship. In this case, association *equals* communion.

The two questions proposed have to do with the hypothetical case of an individual who has been excommunicated from one church, and believing that

---

[42] 1690 *Narrative*, 7-9.

[43] 1691 *Narrative*, 11; see also p. 6.

he has been wronged, desires 'relief' from another church. The assembly ruled that he was entitled to such relief, and then set forth a pattern to be followed in order to attain it. Four times communion is used, and in each case it bears the sense 'membership'.[44]

These instances of the use of the word communion provide important contextual pointers in determining its semantic sense in chapter 26:14&15 of the Second London Confession. In many instances, the word was used with the specific sense of formal membership in the context of associations of churches: 'an organic union of persons united by common religious faith and rites; ... the organized body professing one faith'.[45] It would seem best to understand it in that way in the Confession itself.

Formal Associational Membership in the Manuscript Church Books

If the sense of communion in the paragraphs of chapter 26 under consideration is indeed 'organic union', one might expect that the church books of the participating assemblies would reflect such a meaning in their accounts of the churches' relationships to associations. We now turn to them for confirmation.

Perhaps the most important church book for consideration is that of the Petty France Church in London. As argued above, much circumstantial evidence points to this church and its pastors Nehemiah Coxe and William Collins, as the originators of the Confession. Their practice thus sheds much light on how it was understood. Throughout their manuscript mention is made of sending messengers to associational meetings.[46] In addition to the official designation of men as messengers (most often Coxe or Collins), two other entries shed light on this discussion.

On 28 September 1679, the following was determined:

> The Congregation agreed that the Church walking with Br: Jones should be received into association with them; & that Br: Dyke & Br: Dennis should be desired to acquaint the messengers of the respective congregations herewith at their next meeting which is to be at Hampsteed the 6th day of the next month; forasmuchas those brn: are joyntly agreed upon to represent the state of the churches associated in London, at that meeting.[47]

The entry for 29 February 1679 (1680) states:

> The Congregation agreed to enter into an association with the congregation meeting in Gravel-lane, that our Bro: Collins is pastor of.[48]

---

[44]1691 *Narrative*, 11-12.
[45]*The Oxford English Dictionary*, s.v. 'communion'.
[46]Petty France *CB*, 7, 9, 12, 13, 14, 16, 17, 21, etc.
[47]Petty France *CB*, 12.
[48]Petty France *CB*, 14. Bro: Collins is Hercules Collins, apparently no relation to William Collins, but another leader among the London Particular Baptists.

In both of these cases, formal action on the part of the church was required to enter into 'association'. These acts were not simply friendly relationships for fellowship, but agreements in line with all that has been noted above.

Two other examples, each rejecting proposals to join associations further confirm the point. In 1691, a division took place in Benjamin Keach's Horselydown Church over the issue of hymn singing.[49] Out of that split, a church was constituted in February 1693/94, and is known as the Maze Pond Church. On 20 May 1694, this group discussed whether it should send messengers to an assembly that was to be held in London the next week. The records state:

> A motion being made whether we would send a Messenger or Messengers to the Assembly the next weeke it was agreed in the negative not to send any and further that we did utterly disowne that meeting of the Assembly upon the account of their irregularities, some of which are as follows ....[50]

Among the irregularities was the willingness of the 1691 General Assembly to allow hymn singing churches to maintain 'their communion' in the Assembly. The Maze Pond church was constituted on a rigorist principle, believing that any kind of singing in public worship was a wicked intrusion into God's worship and a sign of apostasy. They would not associate with those who were less rigorous, or with those who refused to separate from the fellowship of hymn singing churches. They could not have communion (association) with compromised churches.[51]

In 1706, the Bagnio/Cripplegate Church[52] refused to participate in the attempted renewal of the London Association. Their records state:

> Some reasons why we did not send Messengers to ye Association yt mett at Joyners Hall ye 25th March last: nor to ye previous meeting at Mr Deerings Coffee House on ye 18 of ye same
> Humbly offered to ye consideration of all those Baptized Churches wch have or can sign the confession of our Faith printed in ye year 1688 and

---

[49]See Chapter 5 on Worship.

[50]Maze Pond *CMB*, 98.

[51]In 1692, the General Assembly decided to separate into two regional meetings during the next year, one to be held in London, and the other in Bristol. While the Bristol Assembly continued for many years, the London Assembly quickly died. The scars from the singing controversy were so deep that no attempt was made to resurrect fellowship among the London churches until most of the protagonists were dead or gone from London. This record from the Maze Pond Church Book gives some indication of the depth of feeling on the issue. See MacDonald, 'London Calvinistic Baptists', 32-83.

[52]Formerly pastored by Hanserd Knollys and Robert Steed successively.

recommended to ye churches by ye Generall Assembly that met at Broken Wharf in London 1689.[53]

Among their reasons for remaining aloof were the presence of a seventh-day Baptist church which the 1689 Assembly had refused to admit, the presence of 'that well known Arminian Church meeting in Barbican', and most importantly,

> Because the solemn owning & ratifying of our so well attested & generall approved Confession of Faith, as transmitted to us in ye full evidence of yt word by our late pastors &c in ye general assembly seems to us as it did also to them a thing absolutely nessesary to ye just & regular constitution of all associations: but ye admitting of the above sd churches into Association renders this altogether impracticable.[54]

They then cite the importance that subscription to Confessions had for the 1644 and 1652 London Association, the 1656 Western Association, the first issuance of the Second London Confession in 1677, and at the 1689 General Assembly. They express fear that the admission of the seventh day church and the Arminian church was a direct attempt to undermine the influence of the Confession in the Associations, and incorporate letters from the Bristol Association and the Bridgenorth, Worcestershire Association in support of their position.[55] For this church, a weakened doctrinal basis barred formal association. They would not join with the revived association simply because it would not maintain the strict theological standard traditionally held among the Particular Baptists.

Conclusion

The weight of this evidence provides strong indication that the final paragraphs of chapter 26 of the Second London Confession advocate formal associationalism in their use of the word 'communion'. From the beginning of the movement in the 1640s the established pattern of inter-church relationships points to this fact. Among the Baptists, and even at times among the Independents, the word was used in a technical sense referring to formal associations.

An examination of these two paragraphs confirms this interpretation. What is held out as the expected practice of the churches (they 'ought to hold communion among themselves') in paragraph 14 is assumed in the resolution of difficulties or differences in paragraph 15. In the latter paragraph, the phrase

---

[53]Bagnio/Cripplegate *CMB*, 26. Broken Wharf was the location of this same church when Knollys' was pastor. They were thus the host church of the 1689 General Assembly.

[54]Bagnio/Cripplegate *CMB*, unnumbered page facing page 27.

[55]Bagnio/Cripplegate *CMB*, 27, unnumbered page facing page 28, 28.

employs a present participle, 'many churches holding communion together' which probably implies an established relationship as over against an occasional convening of messengers.

The Baptists altered the statement of the Savoy Platform, in that they dropped the phrase 'in a Synod or Councel'.[56] This alteration at first may appear to be minor, but in fact takes on significance. Since in some cases the Independent method of holding communion included the occasional convening of synods or councils, and this was not part of the Baptist practice, the deletion of this phrase argues for a peculiarly Baptist understanding of the words 'holding communion'. In their recension of the Savoy material, they recast the statement to reflect the well-established polity already in place. By adopting this language, they confess their commitment to the pattern existing among their churches. The final portion of chapter 26, paragraph 15 must be read carefully. The Baptist polity, expressed in formal organizations, is the basis for the resolution of differences and the giving of advice. The participle 'holding communion' implies a present and established state of communion, and this established state provides the forum at which these issues may find resolution. They did not need to hold occasional 'synods or councels' because they already had in place the means by which to settle matters: association meetings. The churches in association met on a regular schedule according to their custom, and handled these matters at their association meetings. A glance at the printed records of these associations will demonstrate just how well suited the associations were for implementing the polity confessed in this paragraph.[57] Anything less formal simply cannot fit the doctrine or practice of the seventeenth-century confessors.

This established status of 'holding communion together' is the basis for the settling of differences or difficulties. This is how the Particular Baptist associations functioned for almost fifty years. An abundance of material in ecclesiological writings, associational records, documents relating to the General Assemblies and several church books support the notion that they understood their church communion to be formal in nature. When theological circumstances were right, they gladly entered into strict and solemn arrangements. When they were not right, divisions came and churches separated. Both cases illustrate the profound importance of structured and ordered associations in the Particular Baptist ecclesiology of the seventeenth century.

The Functioning of the Particular Baptist Associations

The doctrine of interdependence embedded in these Confessional statements functioned in a variety of ways in the Particular Baptist Associations. In many of them, the purposes of the Association moved in several directions. Primarily,

---

[56]Walker, *The Creeds and Platforms of Congregationalism*, 407; cf. *A Confession of Faith*, 93.
[57]See for example, White, *ARPB*; Copson, *Northern Association*.

they were ordered for the benefits of the member churches, and thus were regional in scope. But there was also an associational mutuality, in which messengers were sent from one General Meeting to another.[58] While these Baptists decried the Episcopalian structure of the National Church, they nevertheless practiced a national catholicity among themselves, and to a much lesser degree, among the other dissenting churches.

How did these associations function? The formality of their mutual recognition provides the basis upon which their actions may be noted. There was structure, mutual expectation and responsibility, and cooperation and activity in supporting the ministries of various local churches.

The structures erected provide insight into their convictions. Several examples are worth noting. The first is from the records of the Western Association meeting in May, 1654. At that gathering a long discussion was held over the propriety of ordaining Thomas Collier to the work that he had already been involved with for almost a decade, namely planting churches in the southwestern counties of England. The records state,

> After some tyme had been spent in way of wayting on the Lord, wee were then exercised in a way of debate conserning the chiefe end of our meeting, namely, the more orderly ordaining of brother Thomas Collyer for the performance of that worke hee hath beene a long tyme exercised in, namely, in gathering and confirming the church.... They briefly and fully, one by one, with much fayth concluded it there duty to procede in a further and more orderly ordaining and appoyntinge our deerly beloved brother Thomas Collier in the name of our Lord Jesus and of his churches who were one in it, to the worke of the ministrey to the worlde and in the churches which was performed by two brethren .... [59]

It is difficult to know exactly what to make of this act. Joseph Ivimey interpreted it thus: 'The office to which Mr. Collier ... had been ordained, was that of a messenger of the churches, exercising a kind of general superintendency over all the associated churches.'[60] Probably, he reads too much into these words.[61] In any case, Collier was the recognized leader of the Western Association, and was ordained by the association. An examination of

---

[58]Benjamin Coxe acted as a liaison between the Midlands Association and the Abingdon Association in the 1650s, his son Nehemiah seems to have done the same for the London and Hertfordshire Associations in 1678, and the Southampton and London Associations cooperated together in 1690-91. See White, *ARPB*, 33, 41; White, 'The Organization of the Particular Baptists', 218; Dowley, 'London Congregation', 235, 239; 'Whitchurch Manuscript', 12, Number A2, and 14-15, Number A3, entitled 'Letter from the Association Meeting in Southampton the 10th Day of the Seventh Month 1690' and 'Letters from the London Association sent to the Association at Southampton A Copy of which was sent to Whitchurch by John Sibley of Southampton Feb. 18th 1691'.
[59]White, *ARPB*, 103.
[60]Ivimey, *HEB*, 4:292.
[61]See White, *ARPB*, 109, note 51.

the circular letters sent out by the association shows that Collier was the most prominent member, even at times signing the letters 'In the name, and by the appointment of the whole, Thomas Collier'. In a personal letter written in 1657 and addressed to 'the churches of Christ in the county of Somerset and the counties near adjacent' he says, 'I have found my heart somewhat enlarged in that care God and his people have laid upon me and reposed in me, though unfit for such a work as this is', and at the end of the same letter, he sounds apostolic:

> amongst the rest of Zion's sons, I can say, I trust through grace that you are in my heart to live and die with you and, if you stand fast, I live. I have written these things unto you, not as one that hath dominion over your faith but as a poor helper of your joy, that if by any means I might fulfill my ministry and give account with joy in faithfulness to the Lord and your souls have I written this.[62]

Whatever he was, it was not simply a pastor of a specific local church. He was in some sense part of an associational structure approved and even ordained by the Association.

Thirty years later, a different type of structure was employed by the General Assembly. After the period of persecution, it was generally recognized that serious deficiencies existed in many of the churches. The first generation of ministers was almost gone from the scene (only William Kiffin, Hanserd Knollys and Henry Forty remained from the signers of the First Confession), several other important leaders had died during the years of persecution, and in some churches, a reluctance to give financial support to their pastors had taken hold. It was these problems, among others, that led to the call for a General Assembly issued in July of 1689. In the letter sent out to call for the Assembly, the London pastors state,

> the great neglect of the present ministry is one thing, together with that general unconcernedness there generally seems to be, of giving fit and proper encouragement for the raising up an able and honourable ministry for the time to come; with many other things which, we hope, we are not left wholly in the dark about, which we find we are not in a capacity to prevent and cure (as instruments in the hand of God, and his blessing attending our christian endeavours) unless we can obtain a general meeting here in London.... [63]

This letter argues that there are several pressing issues, especially the lack of pastoral support and the need for pastoral training, which could only be remedied by a 'general meeting'. The Assembly, when convened, took several concrete steps to address the problems and implement solutions. They endorsed the anonymous publication of *The Gospel Minister's Maintenance Vindicated*

---

[62]White, *ARPB*, 88, 92.
[63]Ivimey, *HEB*, 1:478-480.

(written by Benjamin Keach), a lengthy appeal to the churches to take up their responsibility to provide financial support for their pastors.[64]

In addition, they erected a means to attempt to deal with this problem, as well as that of the provision of ministerial education. They established a fund, to be administered by a committee of nine men from different London Churches. These men were authorized to solicit, receive and distribute financial contributions from the member churches for the support of poor pastors and young men desiring to train for the ministry. The churches were strongly urged to participate in this fund.[65] In the *Narratives*, one notices that much of the discussion at the Assemblies was taken up with organizing and promoting the fund. At the 1690 Assembly, they modified the working of the fund, and expanded the board of trustees to 12 (although 5 was a quorum).[66] The *Narrative* from that year stated that preachers were sent out at the expense of the fund, and were well received in Essex and Suffolk, so much so that 'divers were baptized, and two Churches are like to be gathered'.[67] The 1691 *Narrative* is mostly taken up with matters relating to the fund, especially exhortations to churches to give liberally,[68] and the 1692 *Narrative* similarly continues the emphasis on the importance of the fund.[69] Cooperative effort was considered a primary function of the General Assemblies.

This is the logical expression of their doctrine of church communion. To use the words of paragraph 15 of chapter 26 in the Confession, this was a case of 'difficulty' in 'administration' in which 'the churches in general [were] concerned', and since they held communion together, they decided on a course of action, and reported it to the churches. The future well-being of their cause was at stake, and they developed extensive means in an attempt to resolve the difficulty.

The procedural details of the meetings themselves are seldom explicitly stated in the extant records. They were convened by messengers appointed by the churches for the specific gatherings.[70] When the London elders called for the first General Assembly, they requested 'that you would be pleased to appoint two of your brethren—one of the ministry, and one principal brother of your congregation with him—as your messengers'.[71] The 1689 *Narrative* records the names of 155 individuals in its account of the churches that

---

[64]1689 *Narrative*, 18.

[65]1689 *Narrative*, 10-12.

[66]1690 *Narrative*, 7.

[67]1690 *Narrative*, 5. See also MacDonald, 'London Calvinistic Baptists', 42.

[68]1691 *Narrative*, 4-11.

[69]1692 *Narrative*, 4-5, 7-8.

[70]See above for information on the messengers sent to Association meetings by the Petty France church. For a discussion of the various uses of the word 'messenger' among both the General and Particular Baptists, see J. F. V. Nicholson, 'The Office of "Messenger" amongst the British Baptists in the Seventeenth and Eighteenth Centuries', *BQ* 17, no. 5 (1957-58): 206-225.

[71]Ivimey, *HEB* 1:479.

attended or communicated with the Assembly. Of those 155, 46 are listed with the title 'pastor', 28 as 'minister', 5 as 'preacher', 4 as 'messenger', and 72 are blank.[72] 'Minister' is in some cases equivalent to 'pastor',[73] though in others it seems to be more akin to 'gifted brother'.[74] Since 'pastor', 'minister', and 'preacher' all refer to men authorized for public ministry, at least 79 of the men present had been 'approved and called'[75] by the churches for preaching and teaching. The majority of the other 76 attendees were probably laymen.[76] This makes the mixture at the initial General Assembly to be almost exactly what the London Elders had asked for in their letter.[77]

Business was conducted according to the priorities of each association gathering. The Hampshire Association records state that a 'moderator' or 'mouth of the assembly' was chosen to preside in their meetings.[78] It may be assumed that this was the case in the other gatherings as well. The 1694 Bristol, or Western, Association meeting included a 'sermon suitable to the occasion'.[79]

---

[72]1689 *Narrative*, 19-25.

[73]For example, Robert Keate of Wantage is listed as minister, but he was clearly pastor of this church at this time. The Wantage Church Book indicates that he was installed as 'Minister and Pastor' apparently in 1648. He continued in this position until at least 1696, when John Tull was called to be his assistant. Tull succeeded him in the pastorate. Wantage Baptist Church Minute Book, 1760-1824, Wantage Baptist Church, 1. The first section of the book is a summary of the church's history prior to the beginning date of composition.

[74]For the Plymouth church, Samuel Buttall is listed as 'minister' while Robert Holdenby is listed as 'pastor'. Holdenby was called as pastor in August of 1688, but was quickly discontent and requested dismission from his office. The church refused, only to grant his second petition on 4 June 1690. Three months later, Samuel Buttall was called to be pastor of the church. Thus, in 1689, his title 'minister' did not refer to the pastoral office. Henry M. Nicholson, compiler, *Authentic Records Relating to the Christian Church, now meeting in George Street and Mutley Chapels, Plymouth, 1640 to 1870* (London: Elliot Stock, n.d.) 56; Plymouth (George St.) *CMB*, 25-26.

[75]This is the phrase from chapter 26:11 of the Confession referring to 'Gifted Brothers'.

[76]Crosby says, 'I cannot but observe ... the prudent conduct of the ministers of the English Baptists, who, in all their publick administrations, either in general assemblies, or particular associations, have always required two or more judicious gentlemen of the laity, from each church, chosen by the congregation, to assemble with them, to aid and assist in all their debates and determinations'. Crosby, *CHEB*, 3:295-96. While he overstated the number of laymen requested, the point is well taken.

[77]This does not mean that every church sent one minister and one 'principal brother'. Many sent only one representative, while some of the London churches sent as many as four.

[78]Whitchurch Manuscript, 19, number A5; 23 number A6.

[79]J. G. Fuller, *A Brief History of the Western Association* (Bristol: I. Hemmons, 1843) 22. According to Fuller, this is 'the first instance recorded, of preaching constituting any part of the Association services'. The minutes of the 1693 Bristol Association request that one of the London messengers preach at the 1694 Bristol meeting, but there were no London representatives at that meeting. Ivimey, *HEB* I:529, 534-35. One might expect

This may have become a standard part of the Bristol Association's proceedings, as several of the following meetings incorporated sermons.[80]

The local Association meetings seem to have lasted from one to three days.[81] The venues included the grounds of an estate,[82] farms,[83] and a coffee house.[84] In all likelihood, they also met in the place where the host church worshipped. The Abingdon Association met at Tetsworth from 1652 until at least 1661. According to B. R. White, there was no church in the vicinity. This location was probably chosen for its central location near Oxford on the London road. It may be that the association met at an inn.[85] The national Assemblies in London were hosted by Hanserd Knollys' Broken Wharf congregation.[86]

The General Assemblies met for eight days. In the 1689 *Narrative*, seven rules were agreed upon for the proceedings. They disavowed any kind of 'superiority', 'superintendency', 'authority', or 'power' over any churches,[87] and refused to allow differences over open and closed membership to divide them. In the case of offenses between churches or individuals, they would not allow discussion until 'the rule Christ hath given'[88] was applied and both parties consented to have the issue discussed. No decisions would be binding on any churches until they themselves gave consent, that all decisions be supported by Scripture, that the report of the meeting would be published, that the only messengers allowed to sit in the assembly would be those 'recommended by a Letter from the Church', and that speakers would only be allowed by general consent.[89] No mention is made of an individual moderator, or of any sermons preached during the week.

> The first day of the Assembly was spent in humbling ourselves before the Lord, and to seek of him a right way to direct into the best Means and

---

that preaching was common at these meetings, but the extant minutes do not mention it. The Whitchurch Manuscript notes that Richard Chalk was chosen to preach at the October 1701 meeting of the Hampshire Association. Whitchurch Manuscript, 26, number A6.

[80]Fuller, *Western Association*, 23.

[81]White, *ARPB*, *passim*; Whitchurch Papers, *passim*; Copson, *Northern England*, *passim*.

[82]Ernest Payne, *The Baptists of Berkshire Through Three Centuries* (London: The Carey Kingsgate Press, 1951) 150-52.

[83]Copson, *Northern England*, 33.

[84]Whitchurch Manuscript, 86, number C17.

[85]White, *ARPB*, 207.

[86]See above, footnote 53.

[87]This is in contrast to the General Baptists who practiced a more heavily centralized structure. See Nicholson, 'The Office of Messenger', 212-13.

[88]Presumably, this refers to the process of settling offenses found in Matt. 18.15-17.

[89]1689 *Narrative*, 10.

Method to repair our Breaches, and to recover our selves into our former Order, Beauty, and Glory.[90]

The second day was spent in organizing and determining the by-laws of the Assembly, and in reading letters from the churches. Beginning on the third day, proposals and recommendations began to be made. A fast day was called in all the churches, to be observed on 10 October. They unanimously adopted the 1677 Confession of Faith, and urged all the members of each church to familiarize themselves with its contents. Similarly, they declared their 'Approbation' of the anonymously published book *The Gospel Minister's Maintenance Vindicated* and urged that every church obtain a copy.[91]

The fund was proposed and approved and a standing committee of nine trustees from London churches was appointed, charged with soliciting and distributing the receipts. The Assembly debated a series of theological questions, all of the business had been accomplished, and they dismissed, with the intention of reconvening the next June.[92] The 1690, 1691 and 1692 meetings seem to have followed the same pattern. Their *Narratives* are less detailed, but give no indication of any changes in procedure.

The primary order of business in the local associations was the discussion of questions proposed by the messengers from the member churches.[93] Both doctrinal and practical in nature, they range across the whole spectrum of theology and practice. Among the theological issues discussed were matters such as the presence of Scriptural rules for the proper ordering of a church,[94] the relative nearness of the coming of Christ,[95] the validity of a baptism 'performed in a standing pool and not a river',[96] the nature of God's covenant,[97] sanctification and good works,[98] eternal justification,[99] and the abiding validity of the Lord's Day Sabbath.[100]

More commonly, the questions proposed and answered were practical in nature. They addressed issues relating to church membership,[101] the

---

[90]1689 *Narrative*, 9.

[91]1689 *Narrative*, 7, 18.

[92]1689 *Narrative*, 10-18.

[93]The General Assemblies also incorporated questions and answers into their deliberations.

[94]Copson, *Northern Association*, 82.

[95]Copson, *Northern Association*, 86.

[96]Whitchurch Manuscript, 23, number A6. The baptism was judged valid.

[97]Copson, *Northern Association*, 94.

[98]Copson, *Northern Association*, 93-94.

[99]1689 *Narrative*, 14; Copson, *Northern Association*, 91.

[100]1689 *Narrative*, 16.

[101]Whitchurch Manuscript, 19, number A5, 24-25, number A6; Copson, *Northern Association*, 82-83 and *passim*; 1689 *Narrative*, 14.

ordinances,[102] discipline,[103] marriage,[104] inter-church relationships,[105] ministerial activity,[106] relations with paedobaptist churches and ministers,[107] and a host of other subjects.[108] The answers to these questions were offered as 'advice'[109] to the churches, and were not considered binding until the churches had given consent. The Confession clearly stated that the messengers when assembled

> are not intrusted with any church-power properly so called; or with any jurisdiction over the churches themselves, to exercise any censures either over any churches or persons; or to impose their determination on the churches or officers.[110]

A vigorous doctrine and practice of interdependence did not undermine a similarly vigorous doctrine of independence. The conclusions of messengers could not have binding authority over local churches. Only they could determine for themselves what course of action should be followed.

In the Confessional statement, holding communion provided the means for the giving of advice in 'matter[s] of difference' in the churches. Several examples are extant. In 1696, a dispute arose in the Bromsgrove, Worcestershire church between the pastor, John Eckells, and the people of the church consisting of charges of disorderliness against Eckells and his family.[111] The contention dragged on for 4 years. In 1697, the church sought the help of the association, and sent a long letter explaining the circumstances. The association responded with an equally long and detailed letter specifically addressing the problems and sorting out the sins of the various individuals concerned. They called for repentance and asked all of the churches in the association to observe a day of prayer and fasting. Eckells and a group of

---

[102]Copson, *Northern Association*, 89; Whitchurch Manuscript, 20, number A5; 1689 *Narrative*, 18.

[103]Copson, *Northern Association*, 88; Whitchurch Manuscript, 19-20, number A5; Whitley, *Baptists of Northwest England*, 77-78.

[104]Copson, *Northern Association*, 93; 1689 *Narrative*, 13.

[105]Copson, *Northern Association*, 83; 1691 *Narrative*, 11-12; Whitchurch Manuscript, 21, number A5.

[106]Copson, *Northern Association*, 84, 89; Whitchurch Manuscript, 14, number A3; Ivimey, *HEB*, 1:527.

[107]Copson, *Northern Association*, 86, 93; 1689 *Narrative*, 13.

[108]The extant Association records are replete with discussions of a wide variety of topics.

[109]1689 *Narrative*, 10; 1690 *Narrative*, 7; Whitchurch Manuscript, 11, number A2.

[110]*A Confession of Faith*, 93-94.

[111]Bromsgrove *Church Book*, 69-107 (134-170). The double pagination is in the original. It is difficult to determine the exact nature of the incidents precipitating the dispute. When it was finally resolved it was decided that 'all papers should be burnt to ashes or obliterated' 106 (169), and this seems to have been applied to the Church book as there are many gaps in the transcript.

supporters denounced the majority and claimed to be the church in Bromsgrove. Appeal was made to the association a second time, wherein it was ruled that the original church continued to be the church. In 1699, a third appeal to the association was made because Eckells had refused to heed the advice given earlier, and had sought help from a 'higher court',[112] the elders in London. From all appearances, the London elders made a judgment based solely on Eckells' testimony and asserted that the church members had severely wronged their pastor. Benjamin Keach wrote a letter vindicating Eckells and charging the church with schism.[113] The association responded in no uncertain terms:

> 'Tis our opinion, that Mr. Eckells and those who went out with him departed from ye Church of Christ and do lie under ye guilt of schisms. Whatsoever our London Elders may judge, we humbly conceive that we had a proper call to examine this matter, receiving appeals from ye Church respecting that difference, with ye cases and circumstances upon evidence, we herein have a greater advantage to find out ye breach, than our London Brethren have or possibly can, they having heard but one side.[114]

In 1700, the matter was finally settled when both parties acknowledged wrong and decided to exist as two distinct churches with 'no more disputing on either side'.[115]

In this case, the local association claimed a right to rule on the matter of schism after appeal had been received by the aggrieved church. They addressed the specific issues involved, urged a course of action to take, and protested when others became involved.

Another attempt at settling a church division is contained in the minutes of the Hampshire Association. In 1701, a separation took place in the Broughton church. Both parties were present at the 22 April meeting of the association, at which time each had opportunity to express their concerns, and were 'examined face to face' with a 'full enguairie into all yt could be produced on either side'.[116] The disputants left the room, and the assembly reduced the issues to the main points, determined a course of action, and called the dissenting parties back in order to give their advice. They ruled that the church should strive to show 'meekness, gravity and love' to the dissidents, that those who separated should 'mistrust their own case, and endevor as much as in them lieth after a reunion', and that both parties should meet together for fasting, prayer and humbling themselves, seeking to 'live together in love as Xns'.[117]

---

[112]Bromsgrove *CB*, 99 (160).

[113]Bromsgrove *CB*, 100 (161).

[114]Bromsgrove *CB*, 103 (166).

[115]Bromsgrove *CB*, 106 (169).

[116]Whitchurch Manuscript, 24, number A6.

[117]Whitchurch Manuscript, 24-25.

The most famous attempt at resolving difficulties was at the 1692 General
Assembly. Benjamin Keach's introduction of hymn singing into worship at his
Horsely-down church precipitated a pamphlet war over the propriety of the
matter. The paper debate was acrimonious, and the controversy was brought
before the General Assembly. Seven men were chosen to 'examine and
determine' the matter, and the parties on both sides of the debate agreed to
submit to their judgments. It was concluded that three books contained
offensive remarks, errors and 'unbrotherly censures', and four books were
condemned with the pronouncement 'that none of the Members of the Churches
do buy, give or disperse any of the Books ... and that no person do sell them or
give them to others'. Richard Adams was appointed to collect copies of the
offending books and to dispose of them.[118] After the Assembly, Keach
published a recantation, as did William Kiffin, George Barrett, Robert Steed
and Edward Man.[119] The attempt did not bring about the desired result, and the
work of the London Assembly was effectively destroyed.[120] Communion could
not exist in an atmosphere of mistrust and recrimination.

The 1692 Assembly had determined that there were inconveniences attached
to the annual meeting in London, and so provided for two meetings in the years
ahead, one in the metropolis, and the other in Bristol. Although the London
Assembly ended after a feeble meeting in 1693, the Bristol Association carried
on throughout the eighteenth century.

Conclusion

Associationalism was a vital element in the Particular Baptist ecclesiology.
Independency did not imply isolation, but rather required mutual
encouragement, edification and cooperation. Whether local and regional or
national, the churches subscribing the Confession entered into associational
relationships with fellow churches. These unions were always careful to
maintain and respect the rights of their local churches, but they did not view
autonomy and independency as antagonistic to cooperation across a wide
spectrum of activities. Men were appointed to visit churches in order to help
them establish a settled ministry, others to solicit, receive and distribute funds
in the name of the General Assembly, and others to go out into dark places and
plant churches. They sought to work together for ministerial education and
increased support for under-funded pastors. They gave advice on a wide
spectrum of questions, and attempted the settling of disputes. In so many ways,
these associations were active and alive. Fellowship in itself was a good thing,
but prayer and friendship did not satisfy the level of 'communion' required

---

[118]1692 *Narrative*, 9-13.

[119]Benjamin Keach, *To all the Baptized Churches*; William Kiffin, George Barrette,
Robert Steed and Edward Man, *To The Baptized Churches, Their Elders, Ministers and
Members*. While both pamphlets acknowledge faults, they still engage in self-
justification.

[120]MacDonald, 'London Calvinistic Baptists', 69.

from the body of Christ. Mutual recognition, principled cooperation and financial support were important components of true communion. These Baptists were 'an organic union of persons united by common religious faith and rites; ... the organized body professing one faith'.[121]

---

[121] *The Oxford English Dictionary*, s.v. 'communion'.

Bibliography

Primary Sources

Ames, William. *The Marrow of Theology*. Translated by John Dykstra Eusden. Durham, N.C.: The Labyrinth Press, 1983.

The Anabaptists Catechisme: With All their Practices, Meetings and Exercises. London: Printed for R. A., 1645.

An Apologeticall Narration, Humbly Submitted to the Honourable Houses of Parliament. London: Robert Dawlman, 1643.

Bagnio/Cripplegate Church Minute Book 1695-1723. The Angus Library, Regent's Park College, Oxford.

Bampton Church Book 1690-1825. The Angus Library, Regent's Park College, Oxford.

Barebone, P[raise God]. *A Discourse Tending to Prove that the Baptisme In, or Under the Defection of Antichrist to be the Ordinance of Jesus Christ.* London: R. Oulton and G. Dexter, 1642.

[—] *A Reply to the Frivolous and Impertinent Answer of R. B. to the Discourse of P. B.* London: n.p., 1643.

Barrow, R[obert]. *A Briefe Answer to A Discourse Lately Written by one P. B. to Prove Baptisme under the Defection of AntiChrist, to be the Ordinance of Jesus Christ.* London: n.p., 1642.

— *A Briefe Answer to R. H. His Booke, Entitled, The True Guide &c.* London: Printed for Giles Calvert, 1646.

Bastwick, John. *Independency Not God's Ordinance.* London: John Macock, 1645.

Baxter, Richard. *Richard Baxter's Review of the State of Christian Infants.* London: Nevil Simons, 1674.

Baylie, Robert. *A Dissuasive from the Errors of the Time.* London: Samuel Gellibrand, 1645.

Bourton on the Water, Accounts of Building First Church with List of Subscribers 1701. The Angus Library, Regent's Park College, Oxford.

Bridlington Church Book. Public Record Office Microfilm R64-3019, Public Record Office, London.

A Brief Instruction in the Principles of Christian Religion. The Fifth Edition. London: n.p., 1695.

Bromsgrove Baptist Church, *Church Record Book Volume One 1670-1715.* Peter Wortley, Transcriber. Typescript. London: The Baptist Historical Society, 1974.

Broughton Baptist Church Manuscript Collection. The Angus Library, Regent's Park College, Oxford.

Broughton Church Book 1 1657-1684. The Angus Library, Regent's Park College, Oxford.

Broughton Church Book 2 1699-1730. The Angus Library, Regent's Park College, Oxford.

Bunyan, John. *The Works of the Eminent Servant of Christ, John Bunyan.* 2 vols. Philadelphia: J. W. Bradley, 1860.

Cary, Philip. *A Solemn Call Unto all that would be owned as Christ's Faithful Witnesses, speedily, and seriously, to attend unto the Primitive Purity of the Gospel Doctrine and Worship: Or, a Discourse concerning Baptism.* London: John Harris, 1690.

Chandler, Samuel, and William Leigh. *A Dialogue Between a Paedo-Baptist, and an Anti-Paedo-Baptist.* London: A. Chandler, 1699.

The Church Book of Bunyan Meeting 1650-1821. London: J. M. Dent and Sons, 1928 facsimile reprint.

Clark, John. *Ill Newes from New-England: or A Narrative of New-Englands Persecution.* London: Henry Hills, 1652.

Coleman, Henry. *Actual Justification Rightly Stated. Containing A True Narrative of A Sad Schism made in a Church of Christ, at Kilby in Leicester-Shire.* London: B. Harris, 1696.

Colyer [Collier], Thomas. *A brief Discovery of the Corruption of the Ministrie of the Church of England.* London: Giles Calvert, n.d.

— *The Body of Divinity, Or, a Confession of Faith, being the substance of Christianity.* London: Nath. Crouch, 1674.

— *A Confession of Faith, Published on Special Occasion.* London: Francis Smith, 1678.

— *A Compendious Discourse.* London: Tho. Fabian, 1682.

Collins, Hercules. *An Orthodox Catechism: Being the Sum of Christian Religion, Contained in the Law and Gospel.* London: n.p., 1680.

— *Some Reasons for Separation From the Communion of the Church of England.* London: John How, 1682.

— *Counsel for the Living, Occasioned from the Dead.* London: George Larkin, 1684.

— *Voice from the Prison, or, Meditations on Revelations 3.11.* London: George Larkin, 1684.

— *Mountains of Brass: Or, A Discourse upon the Decrees of God.* London: John Harris, 1690.

— *Believers Baptism From Heaven, and of Divine Institution. Infants Baptism from Earth, and Human Invention.* London: J. Hancock, 1691.

— *The Sandy Foundation of Infant Baptism Shaken.* London: Printed for the Author, 1695.

— *The Scribe Instructed unto the Kingdom of Heaven.* London: By the author, 1696.

— *The Temple Repair'd.* London: William and Joseph Marshall, 1702.

A Confession of Faith of Seven Congregations or Churches of Christ in London, Which Are Commonly (But Unjustly) Called Anabaptists. The Second Edition Corrected and Enlarged. London: Matth. Simmons, 1646; Rochester, N.Y.: Backus Book Publishers, 1981 reprint.

A Confession of Faith. Put Forth by the Elders and Brethren Of many Congregations of Christians (Baptized upon Profession of their Faith) in London and the Country. London: n.p., 1677.

The Confession of Faith, of those Churches which are commonly (though falsly) called Anabaptists. London: Matthew Simmons, 1644; in William Lumpkin, *Baptist Confessions of Faith*, rev. ed. Valley Forge: Judson Press, 1969.

Copson, Stephen, ed. *Association Life of the Particular Baptists of Northern England, 1699-1732.* London: The Baptist Historical Society, 1991.

Cox, Marion, transcriber. A Collection of Manuscript Letters Relating to the Calvinistic Baptist Church at Whitchurch. The Angus Library, Regent's Park College, Oxford.

Coxe, Benjamin, Hanserd Knollys, and William Kiffin. *A Declaration Concerning the Publike Dispute Which Should have been in the Publicke Meeting-House of Aldermanbury, the 3d, of this instant Moneth of December; Concerning Infants-Baptism.* London: n.p., 1645.

Coxe, Nehemiah. *Vindiciae Veritatis, or A Confutation of the Heresies and Gross Errours Asserted by Thomas Collier.* London: Nath. Ponder, 1677.

— *A Discourse of the Covenants That God made with Men before the Law.* London: J. D., 1681.

— *A Sermon Preached at the Ordination of an Elder and Deacons in a Baptized Congregation in London.* London: Tho. Fabian, 1681.

Danvers, Henry. *A Treatise of Baptism: Wherein, That of Believers, and that of Infants, is examined by the Scriptures.* London: Fran. Smith, 1674.

— *Innocency and Truth Vindicated: Or A Short Reply to Mr. Will's Answer to a Late treatise of Baptisme.* London: Francis Smith, 1675.

— *A Rejoynder to Mr. Wills his Vindiciae.* London: Francis Smith, 1675.

— *A Second Reply in Defence of the Treatise of Baptism.* London: Frances Smith, 1675.

— *A Third Reply; Or a Short return to Mr. Baxter's brief Answer to my Second Reply.* N.p.: n.p., 1676.

"Debate on Infant Baptism, 1643." *Transactions of the Baptist Historical Society* 1 (1908-1909): 237-245.

D[e Laune], T[homas]. *The Image of the Beast.* N.p.: n.p., 1684.

Devonshire Square Church Book 1664-1727. The Guildhall Library, London.

Devonshire Square Ledger Book. The Guildhall Library, London.

Devonshire Square Members Book. The Guildhall Library, London.

[Doe, Charles]. *The Reason Why, Not Infant Sprinkling, But Believers Baptism.* London: n.p., 1694.

Du Veil, C. M. *A Commentary on the Acts of the Apostles.* London: The Hanserd Knollys Society, 1851 reprint.

Erbery, William. *The Testimony of William Erbery, Left upon Record for the Saints of the Succeeding Ages*. London: Calvert, 1658.

Featley, Daniel. *The Dippers dipt, or, The Anabaptists Duck'd and Plung'd over Head and Eares, at a Disputation in Southwark*. 6th ed. London: Richard Cotes, 1651.

Flavel, John. *Vindiciae Legis et Foederis: or, A Reply to Mr. Philip Cary's Solemn Call*. In *The Works of John Flavel*, vol. 6. Edinburgh: The Banner of Truth Trust, 1982.

Freeman, C. E. "A Luton Baptist Minute Book, 1707-1806," *Publications of the Bedfordshire Historical Record Society* 25 (1947): 138-159.

George, Timothy and Denise, ed. *Baptist Confessions, Covenants and Catechisms*. Nashville: Broadman Press, 1996.

Goodwin, Thomas. *The Works of Thomas Goodwin, D.D.* Edited by Thomas Smith. 12 Vols. Edinburgh, James Nichol, 1866; reprint, Eureka, Calif.: Tanski Publications, 1996.

Gosnold, John. *Of the Doctrine of Baptisms, or, A Discourse of the Baptism of Water and of the Spirit*. London: J. S., 1657.

Hayden, Roger, ed. *The Records of a Church of Christ in Bristol, 1640-1687*. Bristol: The Bristol Record Society, 1974.

Henley in Arden Church Book Minutes 1803-1885, Warwickshire County Record Office Microfilm MI197. The Warwickshire County Record Office, Warwick.

Howard, K. W. H., ed. *The Axminster Ecclesiastica 1660-1698*. Ossett, West Yorkshire: Gospel Tidings Publications, 1976.

Ivimey, Joseph, ed. *The Life of Mr. William Kiffin*. London: For the Author, 1833.

Jacob, Henry. *An Attestation of Many Divines*. Norwood, N.J.: Walter J. Johnson, 1975 facsimile reprint.

Jessey, H[enry]. *A Catechism for Babes, or, Little Ones*. London: Henry Hills, 1652.

Keach, Benjamin. *Gold Refin'd; or, Baptism in its Primitive Purity*. London: Nathaniel Crouch, 1689.

[—] *The Gospel Minister's Maintenance Vindicated*. London: John Harris, 1689.

— *An Answer to Mr. Marlow's Appendix*. London: John Hancock, 1691.

— *The Breach Repaired in God's Worship: or, Singing of Psalms, Hymns, and Spiritual Songs, proved to be an Holy Ordinance of jesus Christ. With an Answer to all Objections. As Also An Examination of Mr. Isaac Marlow's two Papers, one called A Discourse Against Singing, &c. the other An Appendix. Wherein his Arguments and Cavils are detected and refuted.* London: For the author, 1691.

[—] *Pedo-Baptism disproved; being an Answer to two printed Papers sent forth by some gentlemen Called The Athenian Mercury*. London: John Harris, 1691.

— *To all the Baptized Churches and faithful Brethren in England and Wales, Christian Salutations.* London: n.p., 1692.

— *A Counter Antidote to Purge out the Malignant Effects of a late Counterfeit, Prepared by Mr. Gyles Shute, An Unskilful Person in Polemical Cures.* London: H. Bernard, 1694.

— *The Glory of a True Church, And its Discipline display'd.* London: n.p., 1697.

— *The Display of Glorious Grace: Or, The Covenant of Peace Opened.* London: S. Bridge, 1698.

— *Spiritual Songs: Being the Marrow of Scripture in Songs of Praise to Almighty God.* London: John Marshall, 1700.

— *The Travels of True Godliness.* 4th ed. London: E. Tracy, 1700.

— *Preaching from the Types and Metaphors of the Bible.* (Reprint of the 1855 edition of the original 1683 edition entitled *Troposchematologia*). Grand Rapids: Kregel, 1972.

— *An Exposition of the Parables: Series One.* (Reprint of the 1861 edition of the original 1701 edition entitled *Gospel Mysteries Unveil'd, or Exposition of all the Parables*). Grand Rapids: Kregel, 1991.

— *An Exposition of the Parables: Series Two.* (Reprint of the 1861 edition of the original 1701 edition entitled *Gospel Mysteries Unveil'd, or Exposition of all the Parables*). Grand Rapids: Kregel, 1991.

Kiffin, William. *Certaine Observations upon Hosea the Second the 7 & 8 Verses.* London: William Larner, 1642.

— *A Sober Discourse of Right to Church-Communion.* London: Geo. Larkin, 1681.

Kiffin, William, George Barrett, Robert Steed and Edward Man. *A Serious Answer to a Late Book, Stiled, A Reply to Mr. Robert Stedd's Epistle concerning Singing.* London: n.p., 1692.

Kiffin, William, George Barrett, Robert Steed and Edward Man. *To the Baptized Churches, Their Elders, Ministers, and Members.* London: n.p., n.d.

Knollys, Hanserd. *A Moderate Answer unto Dr. Bastwicks Book, Called, Independency not God's Ordinance.* London: Jane Coe, 1645.

— *Christ Exalted: A Lost Sinner Sought, and Saved by Christ: God's People are an Holy people.* London: Jane Coe, 1646.

— *The Shining of a Flaming fire in Zion. Or, A clear Answer unto 13 Exceptions against the Grounds of New Baptism.* London: Jane Coe, 1646.

— *An Exposition of the first Chapter of the Song of Solomon.* London: W. Godeid, 1656.

— *Apocalyptical Mysteries, Touching the Two Witnesses, the Seven Vials, and the Two Kingdoms, to wit, of Christ, and of Antichrist, Expounded.* London: n.p., 1667.

— *The Parable of the Kingdom of Heaven Expounded.* London: Benjamin Harris, 1674.

— *Mystical Babylon Unvailed.* N.p.: n.p., 1679.

— *The World that Now is; and the World that is to Come: Or the First and Second Coming of Jesus Christ.* London: Tho. Snowden, 1681.

— *An Exposition of the Whole Book of the Revelation. Wherein the Visions and Prophecies of Christ are opened and Expounded.* London: William Marshall, 1688.

— *The Life and Death of That Old Disciple of Jesus Christ, and Eminent Minister of the Gospel, Mr. Hanserd Knollys, Who Dyed in the Ninety Third year of his Age. Written with his own Hand to the year 1672 and continued in general, in an epistle by Mr. William Kiffin.* London: John Harris, 1692.

Knollys, Hanserd, William Kiffin, Daniel Dyke, John Gosnold, Henry Forty and Thomas De Laune. *The Baptists Answer to Mr. Obed. Wills, His Appeal against Mr. Danvers.* London: Francis Smith, 1675.

Lumpkin, William. *Baptist Confessions of Faith.* Rev. ed. Valley Forge, Penn.: Judson Press, 1969.

Mabbatt, John. *A Briefe or Generall reply unto Mr. Knuttons Answers unto the VII Questions, About the Controversie betwen [sic] the Church of England, and The Separatist and Anabaptist Briefly discussed.* N.p.: n.p., 1645.

Marlow, Isaac. *The Purity of Gospel Communion, or, Grounds and Reasons for Separation from Persons of Corrupt Manners, or that hold Erroneous Doctrine in Matters of Faith essential to Salvation; or that are guilty of False Worship, or irregular Administration of Gospel Ordinances.* London: J. Astwood, 1694.

Maze Pond Church Book 1691-1708. The Angus Library, Regent's Park College, Oxford.

Mitchel, William. "Jachin and Boaz," *Transactions of the Baptist Historical Society* 3 (1912-1913): 66-88, 154-175.

A Narrative of the Proceedings of the General Assembly of Divers Pastors, Messengers and Ministring-Brethren of the Baptized Churches, met together in London, from Septemb. 3. To 12. 1689, from divers parts of England and Wales: Owning the Doctrine of Personal Election, and Final Perseverance. London: n.p., 1689.

A Narrative of the Proceedings of the General Assembly of the Elders and Messengers of the Baptized Churches sent from divers parts of England and Wales, which began in London the 9th of June, and ended the 16th of the same, 1690. London: n.p., 1690.

A Narrative of the Proceedings of the General Assembly of the Elders and Messengers of the Baptized Churches sent from divers parts of England and Wales, which began in London the 2d of June, and ended the 8th of the same, 1691. London: n.p., 1691.

A Narrative of the Proceedings of the General Assembly, Consisting of Elders, Ministers and Messengers, met together in London, from several Parts of England and Wales, on the 17th Day of the 3d Month, 1692, and continued unto the 24th of the same. London: n.p., 1692.

Orme, William, ed. *Remarkable Passages in the Life of William Kiffin.* London: Burton and Smith, 1823.

Owen, John. *The Works of John Owen.* Edited by William H. Gould. 16 Vols. Edinburgh: The Banner of Truth Trust, 1965.

Patient, Thomas. *The Doctrine of Baptisms, and the Distinction of the Covenants.* London: Henry Hills, 1654.

[Paul, Thomas.] *Some Serious Reflections on that Part of Mr. Bunion's Confession of Faith Touching Church Communion with Unbaptized Persons.* London: Francis Smith, 1673.

Perkins, William. *The Art of Prophesying.* Edinburgh: The Banner of Truth Trust, 1996.

Petty France Church Book 1675-1727. The Guildhall Library, London.

Piggott, John. *Eleven Sermons Preach'd upon Special Occasions, by the Late Reverend Mr. John Piggott, Minister of the Gospel.* London: John Darby, 1714.

Plymouth (George St.). Church Manuscript Copy Extracts from Church Book 1648-1776. The Angus Library, Regent's Park College, Oxford.

Poole, Matthew. *A Commentary on the Holy Bible.* 3 vols. McLean, Va.: MacDonald, n.d.

A Proposall Humbly Offered, For the Farming of Liberty of Conscience. N.p., 1662.

Records & Letters Relative to the Baptist Church at Hexham From Oct 1651 to July 1680. Followed by records of the Church at Hamsterly in the County of Durham (rebound in One Volume at the Request and Expense of Richd. Pengilly, Newcastle, 1832). The Angus Library, Regent's Park College, Oxford.

Records of the Jacob-Lathorp-Jessey Church 1616-1641. Transactions of the Baptist Historical Society 1 (1908-1909): 203-45.

Robinson, H. Wheeler. "Baptist Church Discipline 1689-1699." *The Baptist Quarterly* 1 (1922): 112-128; 179-185.

Saltmarsh, John. *The Smoke in the Temple.* London: Ruth Raworth, 1642.

Sibbes, Richard. *The Works of Richard Sibbes.* Edited by A. B. Grossart. Vol. 7, *Divine Meditations and Holy Contemplations.* Edinburgh: The Banner of Truth Trust, 1982.

Spilsberie, John. *A Treatise Concerning the Lawfull Subject of Baptisme.* London: Printed in the Yeare, 1643.

— *God's Ordinance, the Saints Priviledge.* London: M. Simmons, 1646.

— *A Treatise Concerning the Lawfull Subject of Baptism.* 2d ed., corrected and enlarged. London: Henry Hills, 1652.

Tibbutt, H. G., ed. *Some Early Nonconformist Church Books.* Bedford: The Bedfordshire Historical Record Society, 1972.

Tombes, John. *Fermentum Pharisaeorum, or, The Leaven of Pharisaicall Wil-Worship.* London: Richard Cotes, 1643.

— *Two Treatises and an Appendix to them Concerning Infant-Baptisme.* London: George Whittington, 1645.

— *An Addition to the Apology for the Two Treatises concerning Infant-Baptisme Published December 15, 1645.* London: Hen. Hills, 1652.

— *Praecursor: or A Forerunner To a large Review of the Dispute concerning Infant Baptism*. London: H. Hills, 1652.

— *Felo de Se. or, Mr. Richard Baxters Self-destroying*. London: Henry Hills, 1659.

Tottlebank Church Book 1669-1854. The Angus Library, Regent's Park College, Oxford.

Underhill, E. B., ed. *The Records of a Church of Christ, Meeting in Broadmead, Bristol. 1640-1687*. London: The Hanserd Knollys Society, 1847.

— *Records of the Churches of Christ, Gathered at Fenstanton, Warboys, and Hexham, 1644-1720*. London: The Hanserd Knollys Society, 1854.

Walker, Williston, ed. *The Creeds and Platforms of Congregationalism*. New York: The Pilgrim Press, 1991.

Wantage Baptist Church Church Book 1760-1824. Wantage Baptist Church, Wantage, Oxfordshire.

Warwick Baptist Church Church Book 1698-1760. The Warwickshire County Record Office, Warwick.

White, B. R., ed. *Association Records of the Particular Baptists of England, Wales and Ireland to 1660*. 3 vols. Consecutive pagination. London: The Baptist Historical Society, 1971-74.

Whitley, W. T., ed. *The Church Books of Ford or Cuddington and Amersham in the County of Bucks*. London: The Kingsgate Press, 1912.

Willcox, Thomas. *Honey out of the Rock*. Pensacola, Fla.: Chapel Library, n.d.

Wills, Obed. *Infant-baptism Asserted and Vindicated by Scripture and Antiquity*. London: Jonathan Robinson, 1674.

— *Vindiciae Vindiciarum; or, A Vindication of a late Treatise, entitled, Infant-Baptism Asserted and Vindicated by Scripture and Antiquity*. London: Jonathan Robinson, 1675.

Ziff, Larzer, ed. *John Cotton on the Churches of New England*. Cambridge, Mass.: Belknap Press, 1968.

Secondary Sources

Arber, Edward. *The Term Catalogues, 1668-1709 A.D.* 3 Vols. London: By the author, 73 Shepherd's Bush Road, West Kensington, 1903.

Armitage, Thomas. *A History of the Baptists*. 2 vols. New York: Bryan, Taylor & Co., 1890; reprint, Watertown, Wis.: Baptist Heritage Press, 1988.

Bassett, William. *History of the Baptist Church assembling at Arnsby, in the County of Leicester*. London: B. L. Green, 1856.

Belcher, Richard, and Anthony Mattia. *A Discussion of the Seventeenth Century Particular Baptist Confessions of Faith*. Southbridge, Mass.: Crown Publications, 1990.

Bogue, David, and James Bennett. *History of the Dissenters, from the Revolution in 1688, to the Year 1808*. 4 vols. London: Printed for the Authors, 1810.

Brachlow, Stephen. *The Communion of the Saints: Radical Puritan and Separatist Ecclesiology, 1570-1625*. Oxford: Oxford University Press, 1988.

Brockett, Allan. *Nonconformity in Exeter 1650-1875*. Manchester: Manchester University Press, 1962.

Brown, Raymond. *The English Baptists of the 18th Century*. London: The Baptist Historical Society, 1986.

Buffard, Frank. *Kent and Sussex Baptist Associations*. Rushden, Northamptonshire: Stanley L. Hunt, n.d. [1963].

Burrage, Champlin. *Early English Dissenters in the Light of Recent Research*. 2 Vols. New York: Russell & Russell, 1967.

Bush, L. Russ, and Tom J. Nettles. *Baptists and the Bible*. Chicago: Moody Press, 1980.

Caffyn, John. *Sussex Believers: Baptist Marriage in the 17th and 18th Centuries*. Worthing, West Sussex: Churchman Publishing, 1988.

Cathcart, William. *The Baptist Encyclopedia*. Philadelphia: Louis Everts, 1881; reprint, Paris, Ark.: The Baptist Standard Bearer, 1988.

Champion, L. G. "The Social Status of some Eighteenth Century Baptist Ministers." *The Baptist Quarterly* 25 (Jan. 1973): 10-14.

Cramp, J. M. *Baptist History: From the Foundation of the Christian Church to the Present Time*. London: Elliot Stock, 1871; reprint, Watertown, Wis.: Baptist Heritage Press, 1987.

Crosby, Thomas. *The History of the English Baptists, From the Reformation to the Beginning of the Reign of King George I*. 4 vols. London: For the Editor, 1738; reprint in 2 vols., Lafayette, Tenn.: Church History Research & Archives, 1979.

Culross, James. *Hanserd Knollys*. London: Alexander and Shepeard, 1895.

Cunningham, William. "The Reformers and the Regulative Principle." Chap. in *The Reformation of the Church*. Edited by Iain Murray. London: The Banner of Truth Trust, 1965.

Davies, Horton. *The Worship of the English Puritans*. Westminster: Dacre Press, 1948.

— *Worship and Theology in England: From Cranmer to Baxter and Fox, 1534-1690*. Grand Rapids: Eerdmans, 1996.

— *Worship and Theology in England: From Watts and Wesley to Martineau, 1690-1900*. Grand Rapids: Eerdmans, 1996.

Dexter, H. M. *The Congregationalism of the Last Three Hundred Years*. New York: Harper & Brothers, 1880.

Dickson, Donald R. "The Complexities of Biblical Typology in the Seventeenth Century." *Renaissance and Reformation* n.s. 3 (1987): 253-272.

Dix, Kenneth. *Baptists in Fellowship, 1630-1660*. Dunstable, Bedfordshire: The Strict Baptist Historical Society Bulletin No. 16, 1989.

Douglas, David. *History of the Baptist Churches in the North of England, from 1648 to 1845*. London: Houlston and Stoneman, 1846.

Dowley, T. E. "Baptists and Discipline in the 17th Century." *The Baptist Quarterly* 24, no. 4 (Oct. 1971): 157-166.

— "A London Congregation during the Great Persecution: Petty France particular Baptist Church, 1641-1688." *The Baptist Quarterly* 27, no. 5, (Jan. 1978): 233-239.

Duncan, Pope A. *Hanserd Knollys: Seventeenth Century Baptist.* Nashville: Broadman Press, 1965.

Engehausen, Frank. "Luther und die Wunderzeichen: Eine englische Übersetzung der Adventspostille im Jahr 1661." *Archive für Reformationsgeschichte* 84 (1993): 276-288.

Estep, William R. "Anabaptists and the Rise of the English Baptists," *The Quarterly Review* 28, no. 4 (Oct. 1968): 43-53; 29, no. 1 (Jan. 1969): 50-62.

— *The Anabaptist Story.* Rev. ed. Grand Rapids: Eerdmans, 1975.

Farrer, A. J. D. "The Relation between English Baptists and the Anabaptists of the Continent." *The Baptist Quarterly* 2 (1924): 30-36

Foreman, H. "Baptist Provision for Ministerial Education in the 18th Century." *The Baptist Quarterly* 27 (Oct. 1978): 358-369.

Fuller, J. G. *A Brief History of the Western Association.* Bristol: I. Hemmons, 1843.

Garrett, Jr., James Leo. "Restitution and Dissent Among Early English Baptists: Part 1." *Baptist History and Heritage* 12 (Oct. 1977): 198-210.

Goadby, J. J. *Bye-Paths in Baptist History.* London: Elliot Stock, 1871; reprint, Watertown, Wis.: Baptist Heritage Publications, 1987.

George, Timothy, and David S. Dockery, ed. *Baptist Theologians.* Nashville: Broadman Press, 1990.

Greaves, Richard L. "The Ordination Controversy and the Spirit of Reform in Puritan England." *Journal of Ecclesiastical History* 21, no. 3 (July 1970): 225-241.

— "The Tangled Careers of Two Stuart Radicals: Henry and Robert Danvers," *The Baptist Quarterly* 29 (January 1981): 32-43.

— *Saints and Rebels: Seven Nonconformists in Stuart England.* Macon, Ga.: Mercer University Press, 1985.

Greaves, Richard L., and Robert Zaller, *Biographical Dictionary of British Radicals in the Seventeenth Century.* Brighton, Sussex: The Harvester Press, 1982.

Gritz, Paul. "Samuel Richardson and the Religious and Political Controversies Confronting the London Particular Baptists, 1643-1658." Ph.D. diss., Southwestern Baptist Theological Seminary, 1987.

Goodwin, W. T. "Warwick Baptist Church." *The Baptist Quarterly* 16, no. 2 (April 1955): 58-66.

Haller, William. *The Rise of Puritanism.* New York: Columbia University Press, 1938.

Hayden, Roger. *English Baptist History and Heritage.* Didcot, Oxon.: The Baptist Union of Great Britain, 1990.

Haykin, Michael A. G. "Hanserd Knollys (ca. 1599-1691) on the Gifts of the Spirit." *Westminster Theological Journal* 54 (1992): 99-113.

— *Kiffin, Knollys and Keach: Rediscovering our English Baptist Heritage.* Leeds: Reformation Today Trust, 1996.

Hetherington, William M. *History of the Westminster Assembly of Divines.* Edmonton: Still Waters Revival Books, 1993.

Hill, Christopher. *The Experience of Defeat: Milton and Some Contemporaries.* New York: Elisabeth Sifton Books—Viking, 1984.

— *A Turbulent, Seditious and Factious People: John Bunyan and His Church.* Oxford: Oxford University Press, 1988.

— *Change and Continuity in 17th-Century England.* Rev. ed. New Haven: Yale University Press, 1991.

A Historical Survey of the Baptist Church in Wantage. Newbury: G. W. Simpson & Son, 1949.

Holifield, E. Brooks. *The Covenant Sealed: The Development of Puritan Sacramental Theology in Old and New England, 1570-1720.* New Haven: Yale University Press, 1974.

Hudson, Winthrop. "Baptists were not Anabaptists." *The Chronicle* 16 (1953): 171-179.

— "Who were the Baptists?" *The Baptist Quarterly* 16 (July, 1956): 303-312.

Ivimey, Joseph. *A History of the English Baptists.* 4 vols. London: B. J. Holdsworth, 1811-1830.

Jewson, C. B. *The Baptists in Norfolk.* London: The Carey Kingsgate Press, 1957.

John, Mansell, ed. *Welsh Baptist Studies.* Llandysul: The South Wales Baptist College, 1976.

Jones, Hywel. Review of *Kiffin, Knollys and Keach: Rediscovering our English Baptist Heritage,* by Michael A. G. Haykin. In *The Banner of Truth* 401 (Feb. 1997): 32.

Kendall, R. T. "Preaching in Early Puritanism with special reference to William Perkin's The Arte of Prophesying." In *Preaching and Revival.* London: The Westminster Conference, 1984.

Kevan, Ernest F. *London's Oldest Baptist Church.* London: The Kingsgate Press, n.d. [1933].

King, Henry Melville. *Rev. John Myles and the Founding of the First Baptist Church in Massachusetts.* Providence: Preston & Rounds, 1905.

Knappen, M. M. *Tudor Puritanism.* Chicago: The University of Chicago Press, 1939.

Leonard, Bill J. *Dictionary of Baptists in America.* Downers Gorve, Ill.: InterVarsity Press, 1994.

Lewendon, W. J. *Notes on Newbury Baptists.* Newbury: G. W. Simpson & Son, 1940.

Lewis, Evan R. *History of the Bethesda Baptist Church, Barnoldswick.* Cwmavon: Ll. Griffiths, 1893.

Lloyd-Jones, D. M. *The Puritans: Their Origins and Successors.* Edinburgh: The Banner of Truth Trust, 1987.

MacDonald, Murdina. "London Calvinistic Baptists 1689-1727: Tensions Within a Dissenting Community Under Toleration." D.Phil. Thesis, Regent's Park College, Oxford University, 1982.

Mallard, Ian. "The Hymns of Katherine Sutton." *The Baptist Quarterly* 20, no. 1 (January 1963): 22-33.

Martin, Hugh. "The Baptist Contribution to Early English Hymnody." *The Baptist Quarterly* 19, no. 5 (Jan. 1962): 195-208.

Matthews, A. G. *Calamy Revised.* Oxford: The Clarendon Press, 1934.

McBeth, H. Leon. *The Baptist Heritage.* Nashville: Broadman Press, 1987.

— *A Sourcebook for Baptist Heritage.* Nashville: Broadman Press, 1990.

McGlothlin, W. J. "The Sources of the First Calvinistic Baptist Confession of Faith." *Review and Expositor* 13, no. 4, (Oct. 1916): 502-505.

McGoldrick, James Edward. *Baptist Successionism: A Crucial Question in Baptist History.* ATLA Monograph Series, No. 32. Metuchen, N.J.: The American Theological Library Association and The Scarecrow Press, 1994.

McGregor, J. F., and Barry Reay. *Radical Religion in the English Revolution.* Oxford: Oxford University Press, 1984.

McKibbins, Thomas. R. "Our Baptist Heritage in Worship." *Review and Expositor* 80 (1983): 53-69.

The Mennonite Encyclopedia. Hillsboro, Kan.: Mennonite Brethren Publishing House, 1955. S.v. "Collegiants," by N. van der Zijpp.

Mosteller, James D. "Baptists and Anabaptists." *The Chronicle* 20 (1957): 3-27.

Muller, Richard A. *Dictionary of Latin and Greek Theological Terms.* Grand Rapids: Baker Book House, 1985.

Murray, Iain. *The Puritan Hope.* Edinburgh: The Banner of Truth Trust, 1971.

Music, David W. "The Hymns of Benjamin Keach: An Introductory Study." *The Hymn* 34 (July 1983): 147-154.

Naylor, Peter. *Picking up a Pin for the Lord: English Particular Baptists from 1688 to the Early Nineteenth Century.* London: Grace Publications Trust, 1992.

Neal, Daniel. *The History of the Puritans.* 3 Vols. Minneapolis, Minn.: Klock & Klock Christian Publishers, 1979.

Nelson, Stanley A. "Reflecting on Baptist Origins: The London Confession of Faith of 1644." *Baptist Heritage and History* 29 (April 1994): 33-46.

Nettles, Thomas J. *By His Grace and For His Glory.* Grand Rapids: Baker Book House, 1986.

Nicholson, Henry M., compiler. *Authentic Records Relating to the Christian Church, now meeting in George Street and Mutley Chaples, Plymouth. 1640 to 1870.* London: Elliot Stock, n.d.

Nicholson, J. F. V. "The Office of 'Messenger' amongst the British Baptists in the Seventeenth and Eighteenth Centuries." *The Baptist Quarterly* 17 (1957-1958): 206-225.

Nuttall, Geoffrey F. *Visible Saints: The Congregational Way 1640-1660.* Oxford: Basil Blackwell, 1957.

— "The Baptist Western Association 1653-1658." *Journal of Ecclesiastical History* 11 (1960): 213-218.

— "Henry Danvers, His Wife and the 'Heavenly Line'," *The Baptist Quarterly* 29 (January 1982): 217-219.

— *The Holy Spirit in Puritan Faith and Experience*. Chicago: The University of Chicago Press, 1992.

Oliver, Robert. *From John Spilsbury to Ernest Kevan: The Literary Contribution of London's Oldest Baptist Church*. London: Grace Publications Trust, 1985.

— "Baptist Confession Making, 1644 and 1689." Unpublished paper delivered to the Strict Baptist Historical Society, March, 1989.

Overend, Frederick. *History of the Ebenezer Baptist Church, Bacup*. London: The Kingsgate Press, 1912.

The Oxford English Dictionary. Second Edition, Oxford: Oxford University Press.

Packer, James I. *A Quest for Godliness*. Wheaton, Ill.: Crossway Books, 1990.

Parkes, Joan. *Travel in England in the Seventeenth Century*. Westport, Conn.: Greenwood Press, 1970.

Patterson, W. Morgan. "The Development of the Baptist Successionist Formula." *Foundations* 5 (Oct. 1962): 331-345.

Payne, Ernest A. *The Baptists of Berkshire Through Three Centuries*. London: The Carey Kingsgate Press, 1951.

— "Baptists and the Laying on of Hands." *The Baptist Quarterly* 15, no. 5 (January 1954): 203-215.

— "Who were the Baptists?" *The Baptist Quarterly* 16 (Oct. 1956): 339-342.

— "Thomas Tillam." *The Baptist Quarterly* 17, no. 2, (April 1957): 61-66.

Poe, Harry. John Bunyan's Controversy with the Baptists." *Baptist History and Heritage* 23, no. 2 (April 1988): 25-35.

Poh Boon Sing. *The Keys of the Kingdom: A Study on the Biblical Form of Church Government*. Kuala Lumpur, Malaysia: Good News Enterprises, 1995.

Pollard, A. W., and G. R. Redgrave. *A Short-Title Catalogue of Books Printed in England, Scotland, & Ireland and of English Books Printed Abroad 1475-1640*. 2d ed., revised and enlarged. 2 vols. London: The Biographical Society, 1986.

Porter, Roy. *English Society in the Eighteenth Century*. Rev. ed. New York: Penguin Books, 1990.

Ramsey, Carroll C., and Willard A., ed. *The American Baptist Heritage in Wales*. Gallatin, Tenn.: Church History Research and Archives, 1976.

Rawlinson, Leslie. "Worship in Liturgy and Form." Chap. in *Anglican and Puritan Thinking*. London: The Westminster Conference, 1977.

Renihan, James M. "An Examination of the Possible Influence of Menno Simons' *Foundation Book* upon the Particular Baptist Confession of 1644." *American Baptist Quarterly* 15, no. 3 (Sept. 1996): 190-207.

— "Henry Danvers' *A Treatise of Baptism*: A Study in Seventeenth Century Baptist Historiography." *The Baptist Review of Theology*, 7, no. 1 (Spring 1997): 27-47.

— *A Reformed Baptist Perspective on Associations of Churches*. La Mirada, Calif.: Reformed Baptist Publications, 1997.

Richardson, Paul A. "Baptist Contributions to Hymnody and Hymnology." *Review and Expositor* 87 (1990): 59-72.

Ryken, Leland. *Worldly Saints: The Puritans as They Really Were*. Grand Rapids: Academie Books, 1986.

Sellers, Ian. "Edwardians, Anabaptists and the Problems of Origins." *The Baptist Quarterly* 29 (July 1981): 97-112.

Shakespeare, J. H. *Baptist and Congregational Pioneers*. London: National Council of Evangelical Free Churches, 1906.

Sparkes, I. G. *Introducing Faringdon Baptist Church: 1657-1957*. London: Advance Publicity Service, 1957.

Spufford, Margaret. *Contrasting Communities: English Villagers in the Sixteenth and Seventeenth Centuries*. Cambridge: Cambridge University Press, 1974.

Spurr, John. *The Restoration Church of England*. New Haven: Yale University Press, 1991.

Starr, Edward C. *A Baptist Bibliography*. 25 Vols. Rochester: American Baptist Historical Society, 1952-76.

Stassen, Glen H. "Anabaptist Influence in the Origin of the Particular Baptists." *The Mennonite Quarterly Review* 36, no. 4, (Oct. 1962): 322-348.

Stephen, Leslie, ed. *Dictionary of National Biography*. New York: MacMillan and Co., 1888.

[Stevenson, G.] *Baptist Church, Wantage. Its Rise and Progress 1649-1899*. Oxford: Stead & Brayne, 1899.

Stone, Lawrence. "Social Mobility in England, 1500-1700." In *17th Century England: A Changing Culture* vol. 2, Modern Studies. Totowa, N.J.: Barnes and Noble, 1980.

Stuart, James. *Beechen Grove Baptist Church, Watford. Memorials of Two Hundred Yeares and More*. London: The Kingsgate Press, 1907.

Thompson, Roger. *Women in Stuart England and America*. London: Routledge & Kegan Paul, 1974.

Tolmie, Murray. *The Triumph of the Saints: The Separate Churches of London 1616-1649*. Cambridge: Cambridge University Press, 1977.

Torbet, Robert G. *A History of the Baptists*. 3rd ed. Valley Forge, Penn.: Judson Press, 1982.

Tucker, Arthur. "Porton Baptist Church, 1655-85." *Transactions of the Baptist Historical Society* 1 (1908-1909): 56-61.

Underwood, A. C. *A History of the English Baptists*. London: The Baptist Union Publication Dept. (Kingsgate Press), 1947

Underwood, T. L. *Primitivism, Radicalism, and the Lamb's War: The Baptist-Quaker Conflict in Seventeenth-Century England*. Oxford Studies in Historical Theology. New York: Oxford University Press, 1997.

Vaughn, J. Barry. "Benjamin Keach's *The Gospel Minister's Maintenance Vindicated* and the Status of Ministers among Seventeenth-Century Baptists." *The Baptist Review of Theology* 3, no. 1 (Spring 1993): 53-60.

Waldron, Samuel E. *A Modern Exposition of the 1689 Baptist Confession of Faith*. Darlington, County Durham: Evangelical Press, 1989.

Walker, Michael J. "The Doctrines of Church and Baptism, with Special Reference to the Status of Infants, in Baptist Theology of the Seventeenth Century." M.Th. Thesis, King's College, University of London, 1963.

— "The Relation to Church, Baptism and Gospel in Seventeenth Century Baptist Theology." *The Baptist Quarterly* 21 (1966): 242-262.

Watts, Michael. *The Dissenters: From the Reformation to the French Revolution*. Oxford: Clarendon Press, 1978.

Westin, Gunnar. "Who were the Baptists?" *The Baptist Quarterly* 17 (Sept. 1957): 55-60.

White, B. R. "The Organization of the Particular Baptists, 1644-1660." *Journal of Ecclesiastical History* 17, no. 2, (Oct. 1966): 209-226.

— "Who Really Wrote the Kiffin Manuscript?" *Baptist History and Heritage* 1 (Oct. 1966): 3-10, 14.

— "Baptist Beginnings and the Kiffin Manuscript," *Baptist History and Heritage* 2 (Jan. 1967): 29-34.

— "William Kiffin—Baptist Pioneer and Citizen of London." *Baptist History and Heritage* 2 (July 1967): 91-103, 126.

— "The Baptists of Reading 1652-1715." *The Baptist Quarterly* 22, no. 5 (Jan. 1968): 249-270.

— "The Doctrine of the Church in the Particular Baptist Confession of 1644." *Journal of Theological Studies* n.s., 19, no. 2, (Oct. 1968): 570-590.

— *The English Separatist Tradition: From the Marian Martyrs to the Pilgrim Fathers*. Oxford: Oxford University Press, 1971.

— "Thomas Collier and Gangraena Edwards." *The Baptist Quarterly* 24, no. 3 (July 1971): 99-110.

— "Open and Closed membership among the English and Welsh Baptists." *The Baptist Quarterly* 24, no. 7 (July 1972): 330-34, 341.

— "Baptists in Barnstaple, Devon 1650-1652." *The Baptist Quarterly* 24, no. 8 (Oct. 1972): 385-388.

— "Baptist Beginnings in Watford." *The Baptist Quarterly* 26, no. 5 (Jan. 1976): 205-208.

— *Hanserd Knollys and Radical Dissent in the 17th Century*. London: Dr. William's Trust, 1977.

— *The English Baptists of the 17th Century*. London: The Baptist Historical Society, 1983.

— "The Origins and Convictions of the First Calvinistic Baptists." *Baptist History and Heritage* 25, no. 4 (Oct. 1990): 39-47.

Whitley, W. T. "The Baptist Interest under George I." *Transactions of the Baptist Historical Society* 2 (1910-1911): 95-109.

— *Baptists of Northwest England, 1649-1913*. London: The Kingsgate Press, 1913.

— "Paul's Alley, Barbican, 1695-1768." *Transactions of the Baptist Historical Society* 4 (1914-1915): 46-54.
— "Loughwood and Honiton, 1650-1800." *Transactions of the Baptist Historical Society* 4 (1914-1915): 129-144.
— "Benjamin Cox." *Transactions of the Baptist Historical Society* 6 (1918-1919): 50-59.
— *A Baptist Bibliography.* 2 Vols. London: 1916-1922.
— "London Churches in 1682." *The Baptist Quarterly* 1 (1922): 82-87.
— "London Preaching about 1674." *The Baptist Quarterly* 1 (1922): 233-235.
— "Continental Anabaptists and Early English Baptists." *The Baptist Quarterly* 2 (1924): 24-30.
— *The Baptists of London 1612-1928.* London: The Kingsgate Press, n.d.
— *A History of British Baptists.* Rev. ed. London: n.p., 1932.
— "Charles-Marie de Veil." *The Baptist Quarterly* 8, no. 8 (Oct. 1937): 444-446.
Whitsitt, William H. *A Question in Baptist History.* Louisville, Ken.: Charles Dearing, 1896.
Wilson, John F. "A Glimpse of Syon's Glory." *Church History* 31, no. 1 (March 1962): 66-73.
Wilson, Walter. *The History and Antiquities of Dissenting Churches and Meeting Houses, in London, Westminster, and Southwark.* 4 vols. London: For the Author, 1808-1814.
Wing, Donald. *Short-Title Catalogue of Books Printed in England, Scotland, Ireland, Wales, and British America and of English Books Printed in Other Countries 1641-1700.* 2d ed., revised and enlarged. 3 Vols. New York: The Index Committee of the Modern Language Association of America, 1972.
Winnard, E. *The History of the Baptist Church, Barnoldswick, 1500-1916, in the Light of Passing Events of that Period.* N.p.: n.p., n.d.
Winter, E. P. "Calvinist and Zwinglian Views of the Lord's Supper among the Baptists of the Seventeenth Century." *The Baptist Quarterly* 15, no. 7 (July 1954): 323-329.
— "The Lord's Supper: Admission and Exclusion among the Baptists of the Seventeenth Century." *The Baptist Quarterly* 17, no. 6 (April 1958): 267-281.
— "The Administration of the Lord's Supper among Baptists of the Seventeenth Century." *The Baptist Quarterly* 18, no. 5 (January 1960): 196-204.
Wrigley, E. A. and R. S. Schofield, *The Population History of England, 1541-1871.* Cambridge, Mass.: Harvard University Press, 1981.
Yarborough, Slayden A. "The Origin of Baptist Associations Among the English Particular Baptists." *Baptist History and Heritage* 23, no. 2 (April 1988): 14-24.
Yeovil Baptist Church. *Celebration of the 250th Anniversary.* Yeovil: Yeovil Baptist Church., 1938.

General Index

Studies in Baptist History and Thought

(All titles uniform with this volume)
Dates in bold are of projected publication
Volumes in this series are not always published in sequence

David Bebbington and Anthony R. Cross (eds)
Global Baptist History
(SBHT vol. 14)
This book brings together studies from the Second International Conference on Baptist Studies which explore different facets of Baptist life and work especially during the twentieth century.
2006 / 1-84227-214-4 / approx. 350pp

David Bebbington (ed.)
The Gospel in the World
International Baptist Studies
(SBHT vol. 1)
This volume of essays from the First International Conference on Baptist Studies deals with a range of subjects spanning Britain, North America, Europe, Asia and the Antipodes. Topics include studies on religious tolerance, the communion controversy and the development of the international Baptist community, and concludes with two important essays on the future of Baptist life that pay special attention to the United States.
2002 / 1-84227-118-0 / xiv + 362pp

John H.Y. Briggs (ed.)
Pulpit and People
Studies in Eighteenth-Century English Baptist Life and Thought
(SBHT vol. 28)
The eighteenth century was a crucial time in Baptist history. The denomination had its roots in seventeenth-century English Puritanism and Separatism and the persecution of the Stuart kings with only a limited measure of freedom after 1689. Worse, however, was to follow for with toleration came doctrinal conflict, a move away from central Christian understandings and a loss of evangelistic urgency. Both spiritual and numerical decline ensued, to the extent that the denomination was virtually reborn as rather belatedly it came to benefit from the Evangelical Revival which brought new life to both Arminian and Calvinistic Baptists. The papers in this volume study a denomination in transition, and relate to theology, their views of the church and its mission, Baptist spirituality, and engagements with radical politics.
2007 / 1-84227-403-1 / approx. 350pp

Damian Brot
Church of the Baptized or Church of Believers?
A Contribution to the Dialogue between the Catholic Church and the Free
Churches with Special Reference to Baptists
(SBHT vol. 26)

The dialogue between the Catholic Church and the Free Churches in Europe has hardly taken place. This book pleads for a commencement of such a conversation. It offers, among other things, an introduction to the American and the international dialogues between Baptists and the Catholic Church and strives to allow these conversations to become fruitful in the European context as well.

2006 / 1-84227-334-5 / approx. 364pp

Dennis Bustin
Paradox and Perseverence
Hanserd Knollys, Particular Baptist Pioneer in Seventeenth-Century England
(SBHT vol. 23)

The seventeenth century was a significant period in English history during which the people of England experienced unprecedented change and tumult in all spheres of life. At the same time, the importance of order and the traditional institutions of society were being reinforced. Hanserd Knollys, born during this pivotal period, personified in his life the ambiguity, tension and paradox of it, openly seeking change while at the same time cautiously embracing order. As a founder and leader of the Particular Baptists in London and despite persecution and personal hardship, he played a pivotal role in helping shape their identity externally in society and, internally, as they moved toward becoming more formalised by the end of the century.

2006 / 1-84227-259-4 / approx. 324pp

Anthony R. Cross
Baptism and the Baptists
Theology and Practice in Twentieth-Century Britain
(SBHT vol. 3)

At a time of renewed interest in baptism, *Baptism and the Baptists* is a detailed study of twentieth-century baptismal theology and practice and the factors which have influenced its development.

2000 / 0-85364-959-6 / xx + 530pp

Anthony R. Cross and Philip E. Thompson (eds)
Baptist Sacramentalism
(SBHT vol. 5)
This collection of essays includes biblical, historical and theological studies in the theology of the sacraments from a Baptist perspective. Subjects explored include the physical side of being spiritual, baptism, the Lord's supper, the church, ordination, preaching, worship, religious liberty and the issue of disestablishment.

2003 / 1-84227-119-9 / xvi + 278pp

Anthony R. Cross and Philip E. Thompson (eds)
Baptist Sacramentalism 2
(SBHT vol. 25)
This second collection of essays exploring various dimensions of sacramental theology from a Baptist perspective includes biblical, historical and theological studies from scholars from around the world.

2006 / 1-84227-325-6 / approx. 350pp

Paul S. Fiddes
Tracks and Traces
Baptist Identity in Church and Theology
(SBHT vol. 13)
This is a comprehensive, yet unusual, book on the faith and life of Baptist Christians. It explores the understanding of the church, ministry, sacraments and mission from a thoroughly theological perspective. In a series of interlinked essays, the author relates Baptist identity consistently to a theology of covenant and to participation in the triune communion of God.

2003 / 1-84227-120-2 / xvi + 304pp

Stanley K. Fowler
More Than a Symbol
The British Baptist Recovery of Baptismal Sacramentalism
(SBHT vol. 2)
Fowler surveys the entire scope of British Baptist literature from the seventeenth-century pioneers onwards. He shows that in the twentieth century leading British Baptist pastors and theologians recovered an understanding of baptism that connected experience with soteriology and that in doing so they were recovering what many of their forebears had taught.

2002 / 1-84227-052-4 / xvi + 276pp

Steven R. Harmon
Towards Baptist Catholicity
Essays on Tradition and the Baptist Vision
(SBHT vol. 27)

This series of essays contends that the reconstruction of the Baptist vision in the wake of modernity's dissolution requires a retrieval of the ancient ecumenical tradition that forms Christian identity through rehearsal and practice. Themes explored include catholic identity as an emerging trend in Baptist theology, tradition as a theological category in Baptist perspective, Baptist confessions and the patristic tradition, worship as a principal bearer of tradition, and the role of Baptist higher education in shaping the Christian vision.

2006 / 1-84227-362-0 / approx. 210pp

Michael A.G. Haykin (ed.)
'At the Pure Fountain of Thy Word'
Andrew Fuller as an Apologist
(SBHT vol. 6)

One of the greatest Baptist theologians of the eighteenth and early nineteenth centuries, Andrew Fuller has not had justice done to him. There is little doubt that Fuller's theology lay behind the revitalization of the Baptists in the late eighteenth century and the first few decades of the nineteenth. This collection of essays fills a much needed gap by examining a major area of Fuller's thought, his work as an apologist.

2004 / 1-84227-171-7 / xxii + 276pp

Michael A.G. Haykin
Studies in Calvinistic Baptist Spirituality
(SBHT vol. 15)

In a day when spirituality is in vogue and Christian communities are looking for guidance in this whole area, there is wisdom in looking to the past to find untapped wells. The Calvinistic Baptists, heirs of the rich ecclesial experience in the Puritan era of the seventeenth century, but, by the end of the eighteenth century, also passionately engaged in the catholicity of the Evangelical Revivals, are such a well. This collection of essays, covering such things as the Lord's Supper, friendship and hymnody, seeks to draw out the spiritual riches of this community for reflection and imitation in the present day.

2006 / 1-84227-149-0 / approx. 350pp

Brian Haymes, Anthony R. Cross and Ruth Gouldbourne
On Being the Church
Revisioning Baptist Identity
(SBHT vol. 21)

The aim of the book is to re-examine Baptist theology and practice in the light of the contemporary biblical, theological, ecumenical and missiological context drawing on historical and contemporary writings and issues. It is not a study in denominationalism but rather seeks to revision historical insights from the believers' church tradition for the sake of Baptists and other Christians in the context of the modern–postmodern context.

2006 / 1-84227-121-0 / approx. 350pp

Ken R. Manley
From Woolloomooloo to 'Eternity': A History of Australian Baptists
Volume 1: Growing an Australian Church (1831–1914)
Volume 2: A National Church in a Global Community (1914–2005)
(SBHT vols 16.1 and 16.2)

From their beginnings in Australia in 1831 with the first baptisms in Woolloomoolloo Bay in 1832, this pioneering study describes the quest of Baptists in the different colonies (states) to discover their identity as Australians and Baptists. Although institutional developments are analyzed and the roles of significant individuals traced, the major focus is on the social and theological dimensions of the Baptist movement.

2 vol. set 2006 / 1-84227-405-8 / approx. 900pp

Ken R. Manley
'Redeeming Love Proclaim'
John Rippon and the Baptists
(SBHT vol. 12)

A leading exponent of the new moderate Calvinism which brought new life to many Baptists, John Rippon (1751–1836) helped unite the Baptists at this significant time. His many writings expressed the denomination's growing maturity and mutual awareness of Baptists in Britain and America, and exerted a long-lasting influence on Baptist worship and devotion. In his various activities, Rippon helped conserve the heritage of Old Dissent and promoted the evangelicalism of the New Dissent

2004 / 1-84227-193-8 / xviii + 340pp

Peter J. Morden
Offering Christ to the World
Andrew Fuller and the Revival of English Particular Baptist Life
(SBHT vol. 8)
Andrew Fuller (1754–1815) was one of the foremost English Baptist ministers of his day. His career as an Evangelical Baptist pastor, theologian, apologist and missionary statesman coincided with the profound revitalization of the Particular Baptist denomination to which he belonged. This study examines the key aspects of the life and thought of this hugely significant figure, and gives insights into the revival in which he played such a central part.
2003 / 1-84227-141-5 / xx + 202pp

Peter Naylor
Calvinism, Communion and the Baptists
A Study of English Calvinistic Baptists from the Late 1600s to the Early 1800s
(SBHT vol. 7)
Dr Naylor argues that the traditional link between 'high-Calvinism' and 'restricted communion' is in need of revision. He examines Baptist communion controversies from the late 1600s to the early 1800s and also the theologies of John Gill and Andrew Fuller.
2003 / 1-84227-142-3 / xx + 266pp

Ian M. Randall, Toivo Pilli and Anthony R. Cross (eds)
Baptist Identities
International Studies from the Seventeenth to the Twentieth Centuries
(SBHT vol. 19)
These papers represent the contributions of scholars from various parts of the world as they consider the factors that have contributed to Baptist distinctiveness in different countries and at different times. The volume includes specific case studies as well as broader examinations of Baptist life in a particular country or region. Together they represent an outstanding resource for understanding Baptist identities.
2005 / 1-84227-215-2 / approx. 350pp

James M. Renihan
Edification and Beauty
The Practical Ecclesiology of the English Particular Baptists, 1675–1705
(SBHT vol. 17)
Edification and Beauty describes the practices of the Particular Baptist churches
at the end of the seventeenth century in terms of three concentric circles: at the
centre is the ecclesiological material in the Second London Confession, which is
then fleshed out in the various published writings of the men associated with
these churches, and, finally, expressed in the church books of the era.
2005 / 1-84227-251-9 / approx. 230pp

Frank Rinaldi
'The Tribe of Dan'
A Study of the New Connexion of General Baptists 1770–1891
(SBHT vol. 10)
'The Tribe of Dan' is a thematic study which explores the theology,
organizational structure, evangelistic strategy, ministry and leadership of the
New Connexion of General Baptists as it experienced the process of
institutionalization in the transition from a revival movement to an established
denomination.
2006 / 1-84227-143-1 / approx. 350pp

Peter Shepherd
The Making of a Modern Denomination
John Howard Shakespeare and the English Baptists 1898–1924
(SBHT vol. 4)
John Howard Shakespeare introduced revolutionary change to the Baptist
denomination. The Baptist Union was transformed into a strong central
institution and Baptist ministers were brought under its control. Further,
Shakespeare's pursuit of church unity reveals him as one of the pioneering
ecumenists of the twentieth century.
2001 / 1-84227-046-X / xviii + 220pp

Karen Smith
The Community and the Believers
A Study of Calvinistic Baptist Spirituality in Some Towns and Villages of
Hampshire and the Borders of Wiltshire, c.1730–1830
(SBHT vol. 22)
The period from 1730 to 1830 was one of transition for Calvinistic Baptists. Confronted by the enthusiasm of the Evangelical Revival, congregations within the denomination as a whole were challenged to find a way to take account of the revival experience. This study examines the life and devotion of Calvinistic Baptists in Hampshire and Wiltshire during this period. Among this group of Baptists was the hymn writer, Anne Steele.
2005 / 1-84227-326-4 / approx. 280pp

Martin Sutherland
Dissenters in a 'Free Land'
Baptist Thought in New Zealand 1850–2000
(SBHT vol. 24)
Baptists in New Zealand were forced to recast their identity. Conventions of communication and association, state and ecumenical relations, even historical divisions and controversies had to be revised in the face of new topographies and constraints. As Baptists formed themselves in a fluid society they drew heavily on both international movements and local dynamics. This book traces the development of ideas which shaped institutions and styles in sometimes surprising ways.
2006 / 1-84227-327-2 / approx. 230pp

Brian Talbot
The Search for a Common Identity
The Origins of the Baptist Union of Scotland 1800–1870
(SBHT vol. 9)
In the period 1800 to 1827 there were three streams of Baptists in Scotland: Scotch, Haldaneite and 'English' Baptist. A strong commitment to home evangelization brought these three bodies closer together, leading to a merger of their home missionary societies in 1827. However, the first three attempts to form a union of churches failed, but by the 1860s a common understanding of their corporate identity was attained leading to the establishment of the Baptist Union of Scotland.
2003 / 1-84227-123-7 / xviii + 402pp

Philip E. Thompson
The Freedom of God
Towards Baptist Theology in Pneumatological Perspective
(SBHT vol. 20)
This study contends that the range of theological commitments of the early Baptists are best understood in relation to their distinctive emphasis on the freedom of God. Thompson traces how this was recast anthropocentrically, leading to an emphasis upon human freedom from the nineteenth century onwards. He seeks to recover the dynamism of the early vision via a pneumatologically-oriented ecclesiology defining the church in terms of the memory of God.
2006 / 1-84227-125-3 / approx. 350pp

Philip E. Thompson and Anthony R. Cross (eds)
Recycling the Past or Researching History?
Studies in Baptist Historiography and Myths
(SBHT vol. 11)
In this volume an international group of Baptist scholars examine and re-examine areas of Baptist life and thought about which little is known or the received wisdom is in need of revision. Historiographical studies include the date Oxford Baptists joined the Abingdon Association, the death of the Fifth Monarchist John Pendarves, eighteenth-century Calvinistic Baptists and the political realm, confessional identity and denominational institutions, Baptist community, ecclesiology, the priesthood of all believers, soteriology, Baptist spirituality, Strict and Reformed Baptists, the role of women among British Baptists, while various 'myths' challenged include the nature of high-Calvinism in eighteenth-century England, baptismal anti-sacramentalism, episcopacy, and Baptists and change.
2005 / 1-84227-122-9 / approx. 330pp

Linda Wilson
Marianne Farningham
A Plain Working Woman
(SBHT vol. 18)
Marianne Farningham, of College Street Baptist Chapel, Northampton, was a household name in evangelical circles in the later nineteenth century. For over fifty years she produced comment, poetry, biography and fiction for the popular Christian press. This investigation uses her writings to explore the beliefs and behaviour of evangelical Nonconformists, including Baptists, during these years.
2006 / 1-84227-124-5 / approx. 250pp

Other Paternoster titles
relating to Baptist history and thought

George R. Beasley-Murray
Baptism in the New Testament
(Paternoster Digital Library)

This is a welcome reprint of a classic text on baptism originally published in 1962 by one of the leading Baptist New Testament scholars of the twentieth century. Dr Beasley-Murray's comprehensive study begins by investigating the antecedents of Christian baptism. It then surveys the foundation of Christian baptism in the Gospels, its emergence in the Acts of the Apostles and development in the apostolic writings. Following a section relating baptism to New Testament doctrine, a substantial discussion of the origin and significance of infant baptism leads to a briefer consideration of baptismal reform and ecumenism.

2005 / 1-84227-300-0 / x + 422pp

Paul Beasley-Murray
Fearless for Truth
A Personal Portrait of the Life of George Beasley-Murray

Without a doubt George Beasley-Murray was one of the greatest Baptists of the twentieth century. A long-standing Principal of Spurgeon's College, he wrote more than twenty books and made significant contributions in the study of areas as diverse as baptism and eschatology, as well as writing highly respected commentaries on the Book of Revelation and John's Gospel.

2002 / 1-84227-134-2 / xii + 244pp

David Bebbington
Holiness in Nineteenth-Century England
(Studies in Christian History and Thought)

David Bebbington stresses the relationship of movements of spirituality to changes in their cultural setting, especially the legacies of the Enlightenment and Romanticism. He shows that these broad shifts in ideological mood had a profound effect on the ways in which piety was conceptualized and practised. Holiness was intimately bound up with the spirit of the age.

2000 / 0-85364-981-2 / viii + 98pp

Clyde Binfield
Victorian Nonconformity in Eastern England 1840–1885
(Studies in Evangelical History and Thought)
Studies of Victorian religion and society often concentrate on cities, suburbs, and industrialisation. This study provides a contrast. Victorian Eastern England—Essex, Suffolk, Norfolk, Cambridgeshire, and Huntingdonshire—was rural, traditional, relatively unchanging. That is nonetheless a caricature which discounts the industry in Norwich and Ipswich (as well as in Haverhill, Stowmarket and Leiston) and ignores the impact of London on Essex, of railways throughout the region, and of an ancient but changing university (Cambridge) on the county town which housed it. It also entirely ignores the political implications of such changes in a region noted for the variety of its religious Dissent since the seventeenth century. This book explores Victorian Eastern England and its Nonconformity. It brings to a wider readership a pioneering thesis which has made a major contribution to a fresh evolution of English religion and society.
2006 / 1-84227-216-0 / approx. 274pp

Edward W. Burrows
'To Me To Live Is Christ'
A Biography of Peter H. Barber
This book is about a remarkably gifted and energetic man of God. Peter H. Barber was born into a Brethren family in Edinburgh in 1930. In his youth he joined Charlotte Baptist Chapel and followed the call into Baptist ministry. For eighteen years he was the pioneer minister of the new congregation in the New Town of East Kilbride, which planted two further congregations. At the age of thirty-nine he served as Centenary President of the Baptist Union of Scotland and then exercised an influential ministry for over seven years in the well-known Upton Vale Baptist Church, Torquay. From 1980 until his death in 1994 he was General Secretary of the Baptist Union of Scotland. Through his work for the European Baptist Federation and the Baptist World Alliance he became a world Baptist statesman. He was President of the EBF during the upheaval that followed the collapse of Communism.
2005 / 1-84227-324-8 / xxii + 236pp

Christopher J. Clement
Religious Radicalism in England 1535–1565
(Rutherford Studies in Historical Theology)
In this valuable study Christopher Clement draws our attention to a varied assemblage of people who sought Christian faithfulness in the underworld of mid-Tudor England. Sympathetically and yet critically he assess their place in the history of English Protestantism, and by attentive listening he gives them a voice.
1997 / 0-946068-44-5 / xxii + 426pp   July 2005

Anthony R. Cross (ed.)
Ecumenism and History
Studies in Honour of John H.Y. Briggs
(Studies in Christian History and Thought)
This collection of essays examines the inter-relationships between the two fields in which Professor Briggs has contributed so much: history—particularly Baptist and Nonconformist—and the ecumenical movement. With contributions from colleagues and former research students from Britain, Europe and North America, *Ecumenism and History* provides wide-ranging studies in important aspects of Christian history, theology and ecumenical studies.
2002 / 1-84227-135-0 / xx + 362pp

Keith E. Eitel
Paradigm Wars
The Southern Baptist International Mission Board
Faces the Third Millennium
(Regnum Studies in Mission)
The International Mission Board of the Southern Baptist Convention is the largest denominational mission agency in North America. This volume chronicles the historic and contemporary forces that led to the IMB's recent extensive reorganization, providing the most comprehensive case study to date of a historic mission agency restructuring to continue its mission purpose into the twenty-first century more effectively.
2000 / 1-870345-12-6 / x + 140pp

Ruth Gouldbourne
The Flesh and the Feminine
Gender and Theology in the Writings of Caspar Schwenckfeld
(Studies in Christian History and Thought)
Caspar Schwenckfeld and his movement exemplify one of the radical communities of the sixteenth century. Challenging theological and liturgical norms, they also found themselves challenging social and particularly gender assumptions. In this book, the issues of the relationship between radical theology and the understanding of gender are considered.
2005 / 1-84227-048-6 / approx. 304pp

David Hilborn
The Words of our Lips
Language-Use in Free Church Worship
(Paternoster Theological Monographs)
Studies of liturgical language have tended to focus on the written canons of Roman Catholic and Anglican communities. By contrast, David Hilborn analyses the more extemporary approach of English Nonconformity. Drawing on recent developments in linguistic pragmatics, he explores similarities and differences between 'fixed' and 'free' worship, and argues for the interdependence of each.

2006 / 0-85364-977-4

Stephen R. Holmes
Listening to the Past
The Place of Tradition in Theology
Beginning with the question 'Why can't we just read the Bible?' Stephen Holmes considers the place of tradition in theology, showing how the doctrine of creation leads to an account of historical location and creaturely limitations as essential aspects of our existence. For we cannot claim unmediated access to the Scriptures without acknowledging the place of tradition: theology is an irreducibly communal task. *Listening to the Past* is a sustained attempt to show what listening to tradition involves, and how it can be used to aid theological work today.

2002 / 1-84227-155-5 / xiv + 168pp

Mark Hopkins
Nonconformity's Romantic Generation
Evangelical and Liberal Theologies in Victorian England
(Studies in Evangelical History and Thought)
A study of the theological development of key leaders of the Baptist and Congregational denominations at their period of greatest influence, including C.H. Spurgeon and R.W. Dale, and of the controversies in which those among them who embraced and rejected the liberal transformation of their evangelical heritage opposed each other.

2004 / 1-84227-150-4 / xvi + 284pp

Galen K. Johnson
Prisoner of Conscience
John Bunyan on Self, Community and Christian Faith
(Studies in Christian History and Thought)
This is an interdisciplinary study of John Bunyan's understanding of conscience across his autobiographical, theological and fictional writings, investigating whether conscience always deserves fidelity, and how Bunyan's view of conscience affects his relationship both to modern Western individualism and historic Christianity.
2003 / 1-84227- 151-2 / xvi + 236pp

R.T. Kendall
Calvin and English Calvinism to 1649
(Studies in Christian History and Thought)
The author's thesis is that those who formed the Westminster Confession of Faith, which is regarded as Calvinism, in fact departed from John Calvin on two points: (1) the extent of the atonement and (2) the ground of assurance of salvation.
1997 / 0-85364-827-1 / xii + 264pp

Timothy Larsen
Friends of Religious Equality
Nonconformist Politics in Mid-Victorian England
During the middle decades of the nineteenth century the English Nonconformist community developed a coherent political philosophy of its own, of which a central tenet was the principle of religious equality (in contrast to the stereotype of Evangelical Dissenters). The Dissenting community fought for the civil rights of Roman Catholics, non-Christians and even atheists, on an issue of principle which had its flowering in the enthusiastic and undivided support which Nonconformity gave to the campaign for Jewish emancipation. This reissued study examines the political efforts and ideas of English Nonconformists during the period, covering the whole range of national issues raised, from state education to the Crimean War. It offers a case study of a theologically conservative group defending religious pluralism in the civic sphere, showing that the concept of religious equality was a grand vision at the centre of the political philosophy of the Dissenters.
2007 / 1-84227-402-3 / x + 300pp

Donald M. Lewis
Lighten Their Darkness
The Evangelical Mission to Working-Class London, 1828–1860
(Studies in Evangelical History and Thought)
This is a comprehensive and compelling study of the Church and the complexities of nineteenth-century London. Challenging our understanding of the culture in working London at this time, Lewis presents a well-structured and illustrated work that contributes substantially to the study of evangelicalism and mission in nineteenth-century Britain.
2001 / 1-84227-074-5 / xviii + 372pp

Stanley E. Porter and Anthony R. Cross (eds)
Semper Reformandum
Studies in Honour of Clark H. Pinnock
Clark Pinnock has clearly been one of the most important evangelical theologians of the last forty years in North America. Always provocative, especially in the wide range of opinions he has held and considered, Pinnock, himself a Baptist, has recently retired after twenty-five years of teaching at McMaster Divinity College. His colleagues and associates honour him in this volume by responding to his important theological work which has dealt with the essential topics of evangelical theology. These include Christian apologetics, biblical inspiration, the Holy Spirit and, perhaps most importantly in recent years, openness theology.
2003 / 1-84227-206-3 / xiv + 414pp

Meic Pearse
The Great Restoration
The Religious Radicals of the 16th and 17th Centuries
Pearse charts the rise and progress of continental Anabaptism – both evangelical and heretical – through the sixteenth century. He then follows the story of those English people who became impatient with Puritanism and separated – first from the Church of England and then from one another – to form the antecedents of later Congregationalists, Baptists and Quakers.
1998 / 0-85364-800-X / xii + 320pp

Charles Price and Ian M. Randall
Transforming Keswick
Transforming Keswick is a thorough, readable and detailed history of the convention. It will be of interest to those who know and love Keswick, those who are only just discovering it, and serious scholars eager to learn more about the history of God's dealings with his people.
2000 / 1-85078-350-0 / 288pp

Jim Purves
The Triune God and the Charismatic Movement
A Critical Appraisal from a Scottish Perspective
(Paternoster Theological Monographs)
All emotion and no theology? Or a fundamental challenge to reappraise and realign our trinitarian theology in the light of Christian experience? This study of charismatic renewal as it found expression within Scotland at the end of the twentieth century evaluates the use of Patristic, Reformed and contemporary models (including those of the Baptist Union of Scotland) of the Trinity in explaining the workings of the Holy Spirit.
2004 / 1-84227-321-3 / xxiv + 246pp

Ian M. Randall
Evangelical Experiences
A Study in the Spirituality of English Evangelicalism 1918–1939
(Studies in Evangelical History and Thought)
This book makes a detailed historical examination of evangelical spirituality between the First and Second World Wars. It shows how patterns of devotion led to tensions and divisions. In a wide-ranging study, Anglican, Wesleyan, Reformed and Pentecostal-charismatic spiritualities are analysed.
1999 / 0-85364-919-7 / xii + 310pp

Ian M. Randall
One Body in Christ
The History and Significance of the Evangelical Alliance
In 1846 the Evangelical Alliance was founded with the aim of bringing together evangelicals for common action. This book uses material not previously utilized to examine the history and significance of the Evangelical Alliance, a movement which has remained a powerful force for unity. At a time when evangelicals are growing world-wide, this book offers insights into the past which are relevant to contemporary issues.
2001 / 1-84227-089-3 / xii + 394pp

Ian M. Randall
Spirituality and Social Change
The Contribution of F.B. Meyer (1847–1929)
(Studies in Evangelical History and Thought)
This is a fresh appraisal of F.B. Meyer (1847–1929), a leading Free Church minister. Having been deeply affected by holiness spirituality, Meyer became the Keswick Convention's foremost international speaker. He combined spirituality with effective evangelism and socio-political activity. This study shows Meyer's significant contribution to spiritual renewal and social change.
2003 / 1-84227-195-4 / xx + 184pp

Geoffrey Robson
Dark Satanic Mills?
Religion and Irreligion in Birmingham and the Black Country
(Studies in Evangelical History and Thought)
This book analyses and interprets the nature and extent of popular Christian belief and practice in Birmingham and the Black Country during the first half of the nineteenth century, with particular reference to the impact of cholera epidemics and evangelism on church extension programmes.
2002 / 1-84227-102-4 / xiv + 294pp

Alan P.F. Sell
Enlightenment, Ecumenism, Evangel
Theological Themes and Thinkers 1550–2000
(Studies in Christian History and Thought)
This book consists of papers in which such interlocking topics as the Enlightenment, the problem of authority, the development of doctrine, spirituality, ecumenism, theological method and the heart of the gospel are discussed. Issues of significance to the church at large are explored with special reference to writers from the Reformed and Dissenting traditions.
2005 / 1-84227330-2 / xviii + 422pp

Alan P.F. Sell
Hinterland Theology
Some Reformed and Dissenting Adjustments
(Studies in Christian History and Thought)
Many books have been written on theology's 'giants' and significant trends, but what of those lesser-known writers who adjusted to them? In this book some hinterland theologians of the British Reformed and Dissenting traditions, who followed in the wake of toleration, the Evangelical Revival, the rise of modern biblical criticism and Karl Barth, are allowed to have their say. They include Thomas Ridgley, Ralph Wardlaw, T.V. Tymms and N.H.G. Robinson.
2006 / 1-84227-331-0

July 2005

Alan P.F. Sell and Anthony R. Cross (eds)
Protestant Nonconformity in the Twentieth Century
(Studies in Christian History and Thought)
In this collection of essays scholars representative of a number of Nonconformist traditions reflect thematically on Nonconformists' life and witness during the twentieth century. Among the subjects reviewed are biblical studies, theology, worship, evangelism and spirituality, and ecumenism. Over and above its immediate interest, this collection provides a marker to future scholars and others wishing to know how some of their forebears assessed Nonconformity's contribution to a variety of fields during the century leading up to Christianity's third millennium.

2003 / 1-84227-221-7 / x + 398pp

Mark Smith
Religion in Industrial Society
Oldham and Saddleworth 1740–1865
(Studies in Christian History and Thought)
This book analyses the way British churches sought to meet the challenge of industrialization and urbanization during the period 1740–1865. Working from a case-study of Oldham and Saddleworth, Mark Smith challenges the received view that the Anglican Church in the eighteenth century was characterized by complacency and inertia, and reveals Anglicanism's vigorous and creative response to the new conditions. He reassesses the significance of the centrally directed church reforms of the mid-nineteenth century, and emphasizes the importance of local energy and enthusiasm. Charting the growth of denominational pluralism in Oldham and Saddleworth, Dr Smith compares the strengths and weaknesses of the various Anglican and Nonconformist approaches to promoting church growth. He also demonstrates the extent to which all the churches participated in a common culture shaped by the influence of evangelicalism, and shows that active co-operation between the churches rather than denominational conflict dominated. This revised and updated edition of Dr Smith's challenging and original study makes an important contribution both to the social history of religion and to urban studies.

2006 / 1-84227-335-3 / approx. 300pp

July 2005

David M. Thompson
Baptism, Church and Society in Britain from the Evangelical Revival to
Baptism, Eucharist and Ministry
The theology and practice of baptism have not received the attention they deserve. How important is faith? What does baptismal regeneration mean? Is baptism a bond of unity between Christians? This book discusses the theology of baptism and popular belief and practice in England and Wales from the Evangelical Revival to the publication of the World Council of Churches' consensus statement on *Baptism, Eucharist and Ministry* (1982).
2005 / 1-84227-393-0 / approx. 224pp

Martin Sutherland
Peace, Toleration and Decay
The Ecclesiology of Later Stuart Dissent
(Studies in Christian History and Thought)
This fresh analysis brings to light the complexity and fragility of the later Stuart Nonconformist consensus. Recent findings on wider seventeenth-century thought are incorporated into a new picture of the dynamics of Dissent and the roots of evangelicalism.
2003 / 1-84227-152-0 / xxii + 216pp

Haddon Willmer
Evangelicalism 1785–1835: An Essay (1962) and Reflections (2004)
(Studies in Evangelical History and Thought)
Awarded the Hulsean Prize in the University of Cambridge in 1962, this interpretation of a classic period of English Evangelicalism, by a young church historian, is now supplemented by reflections on Evangelicalism from the vantage point of a retired Professor of Theology.
2006 / 1-84227-219-5

Linda Wilson
Constrained by Zeal
Female Spirituality amongst Nonconformists 1825–1875
(Studies in Evangelical History and Thought)
Constrained by Zeal investigates the neglected area of Nonconformist female spirituality. Against the background of separate spheres, it analyses the experience of women from four denominations, and argues that the churches provided a 'third sphere' in which they could find opportunities for participation.
2000 / 0-85364-972-3 / xvi + 294pp

Nigel G. Wright
Disavowing Constantine
Mission, Church and the Social Order in the Theologies of
John Howard Yoder and Jürgen Moltmann
(Paternoster Theological Monographs)
This book is a timely restatement of a radical theology of church and state in the
Anabaptist and Baptist tradition. Dr Wright constructs his argument in dialogue
and debate with Yoder and Moltmann, major contributors to a free church
perspective.

2000 / 0-85364-978-2 / xvi + 252pp

Nigel G. Wright
Free Church, Free State
The Positive Baptist Vision
Free Church, Free State is a textbook on baptist ways of being church and a
proposal for the future of baptist churches in an ecumenical context. Nigel
Wright argues that both baptist (small 'b') and catholic (small 'c') church
traditions should seek to enrich and support each other as valid expressions of
the body of Christ without sacrificing what they hold dear. Written for pastors,
church planters, evangelists and preachers, Nigel Wright offers frameworks of
thought for baptists and non-baptists in their journey together following Christ.

2005 / 1-84227-353-1 / xxviii + 292

Nigel G. Wright
New Baptists, New Agenda
New Baptists, New Agenda is a timely contribution to the growing debate about
the health, shape and future of the Baptists. It considers the steady changes that
have taken place among Baptists in the last decade – changes of mood, style,
practice and structure – and encourages us to align these current movements and
questions with God's upward and future call. He contends that the true church
has yet to come: the church that currently exists is an anticipation of the joyful
gathering of all who have been called by the Spirit through Christ to the Father.

2002 / 1-84227-157-1 / x + 162pp

www.ingramcontent.com/pod-product-compliance
Lightning Source LLC
Chambersburg PA
CBHW060333100426
42812CB00003B/978